LASAGNA GARDENING
WITH HERBS

Also by Patricia Lanza:

Lasagna Gardening

Lasagna Gardening for Small Spaces

LASAGNA GARDENING
WITH HERBS

Enjoy Fresh Flavor, Fragrance, and Beauty *with*

NO DIGGING,

NO TILLING,

NO WEEDING,

NO KIDDING!

Patricia Lanza

RODALE

© 2004 by Patricia Lanza
Illustrations © 2004 by Elayne Sears

Cover designed by Christina Gaugler
Interior designed by Patricia Field

We're always happy to hear from you. For questions or comments concerning the editorial content of this book, please write to:
Rodale Book Readers' Service
33 East Minor Street
Emmaus, PA 18098
Look for other Rodale books wherever books are sold. Or call us at (800) 848-4735.

For more information about Rodale magazines and books, visit us at
www.organicgardening.com

Library of Congress Cataloging-in-Publication Data

Lanza, Patricia.
    Lasagna gardening with herbs : enjoy fresh flavor, fragrance, and beauty with no digging, no tilling, no weeding, no kidding! / Patricia Lanza.
        p.   cm.
    Includes bibliographical references and index.
    ISBN 0–87596–897–X paperback
    1. Herb gardening.   2. Organic gardening.   I. Title.
SB351.H5L27   2004
635'.7—dc22   2003025308

Distributed in the book trade by St. Martin's Press

2   4   6   8   10   9   7   5   3   1   paperback

To Judith Patricia Lanza Bakunas, my beautiful, talented, and loving daughter whose life was a blessing to me and a joy to others, whose last year of life was a hard-earned gift, and whose death left a deep void

Contents

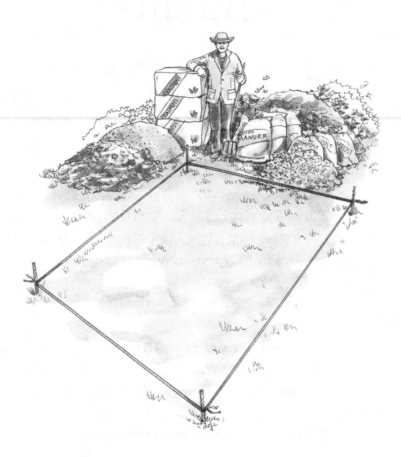

Renewing Your Spirit

In a world gone slightly askew, it is the common daily activities that can bring everything back into balance and provide comfort and security. People find comfort in many things and in many ways. For some, it's a pot of soup or the smell of homemade bread. Others may make a cup of tea and call family and friends. Many turn to familiar music, and others head to church to seek comfort.

I rely on all of those things to restore and renew my spirit. Just coming home at the end of the day makes me feel good. When I'm stressed and overworked, I come home, put on soothing music, grab a good book, and snuggle under a favorite quilt. In the long run, it's all about being among my things—photos of family and friends, favorite mementos, and the special ambience I've created in my home.

I most certainly get stressed and I'm grossly overworked, but it's my own fault. I like working, and if I don't have enough stress, I seem to create some! My large family, overfull work calendar, and book projects keep me dancing as fast as I can.

If we're going to be together for the next 270 pages, you should know a few things about me. I'm pretty calm, I never meditate, and I rarely go barefoot. I'm often described as an obsessive gardener, a workaholic, and one who generally disregards the rules. I like doing things my way but will often compromise to get the job done (if it's the right thing to do). And I see the humorous side in most things (I had seven children, you know!).

When you're able to find me, it will most often be in the garden. Gardening of any kind is what helps me get in tune with the earth and helps refuel my spirit. Of all the different kinds of gardens I've made, herb gardens are my favorite. I enjoy the history and diversity of herb plants, and the edible kitchen herbs and flowers I grow bring excitement to the foods I prepare. Herbs enhance many aspects of my life.

Being in the garden can be a great stress reliever, but I know that it's hard to find time to get out to the garden with today's busy schedules. Traditional gardening techniques are intimidating because of all that work of lifting sod and tilling the soil, so I knew there had to be an easier way. I may not be your grandmother's kind of gardener but I think my way of gardening could have lightened the load for many gardeners in the past.

My smart, easy-layering method called lasagna gardening will help you make a garden in no time. If you're like me, you'll find comfort in your herb garden as you nourish and tend to your herb plants and admire the results of your efforts. After harvesting those first sprigs of herbs for cooking, I know you'll feel good, too!

My lasagna garden method returns some of the earth's bounty back to the garden where it enhances the soil. As I collect kitchen and garden wastes and layer them on the site of a new or old garden, I feel good about this process that lets me compost right on a garden bed. Lasagna gardening saves work, time, energy, and money. There's less weeding and no back-breaking sod removal or double digging, and most of the lasagna ingredients can be found in your own backyard. Best of all, lasagna gardening makes a difference environmentally. Each time I place a layer of garden waste on one of my gardens, I am feeding the earth and saving room in the landfill.

I've always given Mother Nature credit for creating the basis for lasagna gardening. However, I am quick to point out that even though Mother Nature and I have a lot in common, I've learned that it doesn't take years to create great soil for gardening. It takes just minutes with the right tools—wet newspapers, grass clippings, chopped leaves, and a variety of other readily available organic materials.

CHAPTER 1

The old-fashioned gardening methods of the past—and all the hard work they required—have almost nothing to do with lasagna gardening. Trust me! It doesn't matter what's underneath the ground: rocks, clay, or shale. It doesn't even matter what's on top of the ground: grass, weeds, or groundcovers. Lasagna gardening will help you create the best garden ever. This earth-friendly, organic layering method is a recipe from Mother Nature and Mama Lanza for easy gardening.

Lasagna Gardening Basics

Following the Traditional Path

It is completely natural to learn how to do things by watching our parents or grandparents do them. Like many people of my generation, that's how I learned to garden—by watching my grandmother. Her routine, undoubtedly learned by watching her own elders, went like this:

With spring came preparations for the vegetable garden; seed was ordered and plants started from seeds saved from last year's garden. As soon as the ground thawed, my grandmother harnessed the mule, walked him to the garden where the plow lay, and hitched him to the plow. She threw the reins over her shoulders and guided the mule and plow up and down the garden, turning over the sod. Next came the harrowing and, finally, row making. All this was done before she planted a single seed.

As a child I wasn't aware that what my grandmother was doing was way too hard. It would be many years before I would think of her and realize that she had worked harder than many men.

I never had to lift that plow, although I would later find one with the wooden handles still intact and lift it just to see if I could do it. I never had to hitch a mule and guide the plow up and down the garden. I never had to do most of the hard work my grandmother did, but even what I did do was way too hard.

What I did do was hire a man to plow and prepare the garden for planting. I gardened as my grandmother had: I made rows, planted seeds and plants, then I hoed weeds for the rest of the summer. I fretted over dry soil and worked even harder to keep my garden alive.

Later I hired a man to till the garden instead of one to plow it. And even later, we bought our own rotary tiller. I could never use it because when I tried, it got away from me and scared me nearly to death. After that I resigned myself to having to rely on someone else to handle the annual garden preparation chores.

Growing as a Gardener

Early in my marriage I was a stay-at-home mom. My husband was in the U.S. Navy, and his base of operations was subject to change every 2 or 3 years. When orders came, we packed and moved. Our marriage and his career started in Jacksonville, Florida. Jacksonville is a Navy town, and we received five sets of orders, to different squadrons, and never left there.

From the time my fifth child was born, I was in the garden most of my free time. (What am I saying? Mothers have no free time!) For training, I had only memories of how my grandmother had gardened, so

I worked very hard for some small results during the first years. Regardless, over the years I got better at gardening. It was a way I could be creative, keep to the household budget, and put fresh vegetables on the table for my family.

By marrying someone from the Northeast and from an Italian family, I expanded my cooking experience and my palate. My husband introduced me to southern Italian cuisine. That's not a play on my southern origins and his Italian ancestry, but reflects the traditional foods of southern Italy and Sicily. I grew accustomed to the flavors of basil, oregano, garlic, and flat-leaf parsley. When we married, my food experiences were limited to the foods and flavors I had known while growing up—sage was the only herb I was familiar with. I had never tasted pizza, lasagna, or tomato sauce cooked with pork, beef, and veal and simmered for hours. It wasn't long before I wanted to grow fresh herbs to use in the foods I prepared for my growing family.

I first planted basil from seed. It was easy to grow in Florida, and with the long growing season, I had plenty of fresh basil for most of the year. When the true leaves of those first plants were ready to harvest, I experienced the heady fragrance only basil gives and knew I was hooked on that smell and flavor for life.

Soon I added oregano, parsley, and sage to the basil in my garden. With just four culinary herbs, I learned about annuals (basil), biennials (parsley), and perennials (sage and oregano). It was not only a new phase in my education as a gardener but also the beginning of a lifelong interest in herbs.

HERBAL HINT

*Peat moss doesn't have to be wet when applying it in
1- to 2-inch layers, but it can be very dusty. If you do apply it
dry, wear safety goggles or glasses to protect your eyes;
you may also want to wear a simple paper dust mask to keep
the dust out of your nose and mouth.*

Lanza's Tomato and Herb Sauce

1	cup olive oil	1	cup fresh basil, chopped
8	cloves fresh garlic, crushed	1	cup Italian parsley, chopped
3	large onions, diced	4	bay leaves
1	#10 can whole tomatoes	¼	cup fresh oregano, chopped
1	#10 can crushed tomatoes		Salt and pepper
1	#10 can tomato puree		

In a large stockpot combine olive oil, garlic, and onions. Cook over medium heat until onions are tender. Add the can of whole tomatoes, crushing the tomatoes as you add them to the pot, the can of crushed tomatoes, and the tomato puree. Stir all ingredients until blended and continue cooking on medium heat. Add basil, parsley, bay leaves, and oregano. Add salt and pepper to taste, but start with about 2 tablespoons salt and 2 teaspoons pepper. Turn heat to medium-low and continue cooking, stirring frequently, for about 1 hour. Using the crusts of good Italian bread, dip and taste to determine when the sauce is done.

Lanza's Tomato, Herb, and 3-Meat Sauce

Using the recipe above, start with a stockpot that's bigger by about one-third. Purchase ½ pound each of meaty country pork ribs, meaty beef soup bones, and veal neck bones. Add half the olive oil to the pot and turn heat to medium high. Add all the meat and bones to the pot and brown in the oil, turning until all sides are brown. Continue with remaining ingredients, as above.

An Ongoing Herbal Education

More sets of orders followed, with more moves, new gardens, and two more children. By this time I was a serious gardener and making considerable contributions to the larder with fresh herbs and vegetables. In the long, hot growing season of Florida—and later Georgia and Tennessee—I was amazed by what I could grow. Basil grew into hedges, and we had to buy a ladder to reach the tomatoes. Even then, I planted sage out by the laundry room, mostly for the fragrance that reminded me of my grandmother.

In Lake Helen, Florida, I planted my first big herb garden. We had moved to a big old house with about an acre surrounding the house where I could garden. Even better, the porch wrapped around the house on three sides, and I could fill it with containers of herbs and annuals.

As my husband's job took us from base to base, I expanded my herb gardens even as I downsized my vegetable gardens. I found herbs easier to plant and care for. They needed less space and could even be grown in containers, making them easy to take to our next home.

It became a common thing to carry the pots of herbs to the family boat and stash them under the bow for a ride to their new home. One thing we could depend on was a set of orders sending us to a new duty station. Our last set of orders before my husband's retirement came, and we prepared to make the move from Albany, Georgia, to Eatontown, New Jersey.

We moved one last time, from New Jersey to New York, and with that move became innkeepers. We made the move with my husband driving the truck (loaded with plants) and pulling the boat (loaded with plants), followed by me driving the car with two of our girls.

The inn had 7 acres for me to garden, and it seemed the new gardens called to me to wade right in. However, as much as the gardens needed me, I was also needed in the rest of the inn: registering and caring for overnight guests, cooking and serving, and even tending bar and making pizza.

The more successful the inn, the less time I had to spend in my gardens. There were many times when I needed to get away to be able to continue living and working with the public. In fall I walked the adjacent wooded properties. I also welcomed winter when business was slow and I had time to myself. It was on one of those walks that I discovered how to make Nature's layering process work for me. It was during winter when I dreamed of having the time to devote to gardening again.

From Traditional Gardening to Lasagna Gardening

After all those years and all those traditional gardens, I was just about ready to give up on gardening. I didn't want to, but it was simply too labor-intensive: lifting the sod, turning the soil, removing rocks and adding amendments, raking and raking and raking some more. By the time I was finished preparing a garden, I was usually too tired to plant and too stressed to remember why I was in the garden in the first place.

Lasagna-style layers seemed like the perfect solution: I could satisfy my desire to garden without hours of backbreaking labor and without the need for power equipment of any sort. I began gathering materials—peat moss, leaves, hay, and manure—and layering them into a garden bed. It was the beginning of a whole new and easy way of gardening for me.

Mother Nature Doesn't Own a Tiller

After gardening in the traditional way for many years, I knew I needed to make a change, but I didn't quite "get it" until I took a walk in the woods one bright, sunny day and got inspired by Mother Nature. While walking in the woods surrounding the inn, I stopped long enough to really look around me. What I discovered was how Mother Nature renews the earth in layers: by dropping layers of leaves, twigs, bark, and even whole trees to the forest floor to naturally decompose and, in time, become humus. Into this inch of humus, seeds fall, germinate, and grow into wildflowers, shrubs, and more trees.

I had been too busy to notice what had been there all the time. Mother Nature creates the best growing conditions from the top down. Mother Nature doesn't own a tiller. She doesn't turn the earth with a spade. For mil-lions of years, the earth has renewed itself without any help from man (or woman).

Even though this is the way it has been since the world began, it only became clear to me that day. I knew I could emulate Mother Nature and, by layering what was readily avail-able to me in the form of organic yard waste, make wonderful gardens without the tradi-tional work of moving soil around.

Mother Nature's recipe for layered soil im-provement is very slow. It can take years for leaves, twigs, and trees to decompose to form just 1 inch of humus. My lasagna gardens would grow great soil quickly because I would collect layering materials and bring them to the garden site. This was the beginning of lasagna gardening. With the layering concept firmly planted in my mind, everything became much easier.

LASAGNA . . . WITH WEEDS

Unfortunately, the idea wasn't complete because I had not bargained on the ability of weeds to make their way through the now-rich soil to become mon-ster weeds. My first attempt at natural layered gardening wasn't the success I had expected. It took another revelation to uncover the missing component.

My gardens were rich and full of worms because I had used grass clip-pings, peat moss, leaves, hay, and manure to make my layers. Weeds grew at an alarming rate in the enriched soil, and so did my vegetables, herbs, and flowers. The problem was I had no time or energy to weed. My plants and seeds had also grown, but I couldn't find the good stuff among the bad stuff.

> ### HERBAL HINT
>
> *When mowing grass, mow in one direction to create a windrow of chopped material that is easy to pick up by flipping it onto a dragging cloth to haul to the garden. Or, if you don't mind stopping to empty the bag, catch your clippings as you mow and empty the bag someplace near where you plan to build a lasagna bed.*

A NEWS FLASH

In what seemed like an unrelated incident, I found the missing information I needed to complete the lasagna gardening picture. Each week I bundled the week's newspapers, tied the bundles, and placed them on the curb for pickup and recycling.

After placing my newspaper bundle on the lawn next to the curb before leaving on vacation, I returned three weeks later to find it had rained. The paper was thoroughly wet and the recycling workers wouldn't take it. When I picked up the bundle, I found the grass beneath it had disappeared, earthworms were in view, and so were the tunnels they had made. The idea was complete as I imagined a layer of newspaper on top of the sod, covered with layers of organic material.

My First Lasagna Herb Garden

When I made my first real lasagna herb garden, I spent considerable time thinking about it: the location, the design, the size, and where I would find enough material to install it. I picked the area, then I walked the area, sat by the area, and climbed the fire escape to the second floor of the inn to get a different view.

I thought about it during the winter, the next spring, and most of the following summer. By the time I was ready to begin the installation, I had spent so much time thinking I had to hurry to get it done before the ground was frozen.

First I got help measuring and laying out the design. Because it was a big square with many straight lines, all the measurements needed to be accurate. I traded dinner and drinks for a surveyor's time and expertise. We measured the outline, the first beds, the inside path, the inside beds, more paths, and

finally the center bed and surrounding paths. Long gutter nails and plastic survey tape marked the layout for the beds and pathways.

The site was perfect for growing herbs—it had full sun and level ground and was close to water. There was room around the garden for benches, and small flowering trees, already planted on the perimeter, provided respite from the sun. The trees were close enough so visitors could sit in the shade and enjoy the garden. Water from the inn was just 50 feet away.

HERBAL HINT

When adding fresh manure to your garden, cover it with a layer of wet newspaper. If there are grass or weed seeds in the manure, this will help keep them from sprouting in your garden.

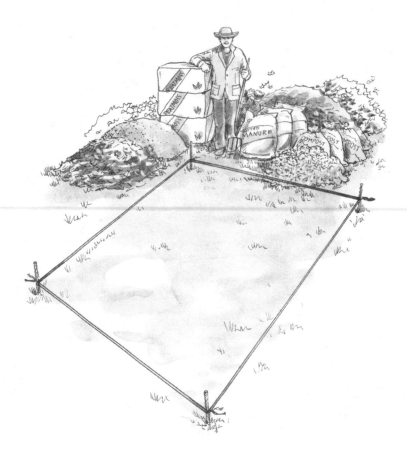

My resources for that first lasagna herb garden were grass clippings from 7 acres of fields surrounding the inn, composted kitchen waste from the inn, aged barn litter from my neighbor's horse, leaves from the village, and sawdust, wood chips, and triple-ground cedar mulch from the sawmill in the village. In addition, I had large bales of peat moss delivered from the farm store.

HERBAL HINT

If your lasagna garden layers include pine needles or wood chips, sprinkle about half a cup of lime over each layer. This will help counteract the acidity of these ingredients.

All this was more than enough, but I couldn't resist a sale on soil amendments and came home with my pickup truck full of 40-pound bags of humus, topsoil, and composted cow manure.

BUILDING THE BEDS

First I laid thick pads of wet newspaper on the garden beds and cardboard on the paths. Once I covered the cardboard with 4 inches of chipped bark, they looked like the finished paths they were meant to be.

Power Tools Lite

Ever since my terrifying experience with our tiller, I've eliminated most power tools from my gardening routines. With the lasagna method, I just don't need them. I don't dig, till, weed, or run gas-powered tools with the exception of my John Deere mower. (Even this I don't need at the Potager because I covered all the grass there with gardens and paths in 1996.) In 1990 I purchased 700 feet of extension cord to run all my electric tools. These have the advantage of being smaller, lighter, quieter, and easier to use than their gas-powered equivalents.

Because I keep my mower where there's grass to be mowed, I needed a way to deal with the wealth of leaves at the Potager. The leaves have to be gathered and chopped before returning them to the gardens in layers. For this I purchased a Vac N' Shred, which handles the job nicely and can go anywhere in the gardens with my ample extension cord.

HERBAL HINT

Next fall, think ahead and stockpile 20 or more bags of leaves in an out-of-the-way place. Better yet, pick a spot for a new garden and set the bagged leaves on the site. By spring, the ground under the bags will have no grass or weeds and will be softening up as earthworm activity increases. Remove the bags and start a new lasagna garden, using the partially decomposed leaves as layers.

I began the gardens beds with 2 inches of peat moss on the wet newspaper, then 4 inches of grass clippings and another inch of peat moss. By the time this was all layered on the beds, they looked as though they were freshly dug.

I continued the layering with 4 inches of chopped leaves and another inch of peat moss, then 4 inches of compost, an inch of peat moss, an inch of barn litter, and another inch of peat moss. By this time I had 17 to 18 inches of material on top of wet newspaper, and the weather had turned cold and smelled like snow.

I decided to sprinkle an inch of each of the bagged amendments, alternating with an inch of peat moss: topsoil, humus, and composted cow manure. This brought the garden beds to about 24 inches high. I remembered some wood ashes I had been saving and dusted the tops of the beds with a fine coat of ashes like the Parmesan cheese on real lasagna.

As I stood back to savor the view of a very large garden, prepared without lifting the sod and without digging or tilling, I was pleased with the way it looked. If my theory worked, I would have an army of earthworms under the paper, digging their way up to an endless buffet of food.

WAITING FOR SUCCESS

Waiting for spring took on a whole new meaning that year. I left the garden in the middle of November at the beginning of the first snow. Before May it had snowed many times with a total accumulation of several feet. At times I felt winter would never end. It was past the fifteenth of May before all the snow melted off the new garden, and I could see that only about 6 to 8 inches of the 24 inches of layered material was left. I scooped through dark rich soil down to the paper and could see it was riddled with holes. Down below the paper was another 4 to 6 inches of worm-dug soil.

There was no doubt the garden lasagna theory had worked. And it had worked far better than I ever hoped. I waited until Memorial Day and planted pots of herbs. It wasn't until July that I was sure there were no weeds in my new soil layers, and I hadn't had to water once. As the plants grew, I added layers of grass clippings, an inch or two at a time. When I had compost, I added an inch of that and, in fall, I added a foot of chopped leaves.

SEEDS IN THE SECOND SEASON

The perennial herbs I planted that first year survived our harsh winter. In the spring of the second growing season for the garden, I planted annual seeds right into the lasagna layers. It was easy in the loose, weed-free, fertile soil, and the seedlings didn't have to compete with weeds when they came up.

Getting Started: Think about It!

Preparing for a new garden involves taking stock of your resources and answering some important questions. Put on your thinking cap. Consider these questions and resolve them to your satisfaction before you begin. I've pro-

Lasagna Gardening in 50 Words or Less

If all this thinking has you worried that lasagna gardening is too complicated, relax. Here's everything you need to do to get started, described in fewer than 50 words:

Pick a site. Cover site with wet newspaper. Cover paper with peat moss and other organic materials. Layer materials using 1 part green stuff (nitrogen) to 4 parts brown stuff (carbon) until your garden is deep enough to plant in. Pull back the layers and tuck in plants. Water.

vided a list of the kinds of questions you should think about as you plan your lasagna garden. Thinking—not digging—is a big part of lasagna gardening.

- Where will your new garden be located?
- How much light will your new garden get?
- Is there a water source near the garden site?
- Is the garden site in a location where you can enjoy it daily?
- What organic materials—things like newspaper, grass clippings, peat moss, composted manure—are readily available to use as lasagna garden layers?

LASAGNA GARDEN HOW-TO: THE SLIGHTLY LONGER VERSION

This method of making gardens is really simple enough to explain in 50 words or less, but a little more information will reassure you that you're really doing it right—and it really is that easy!

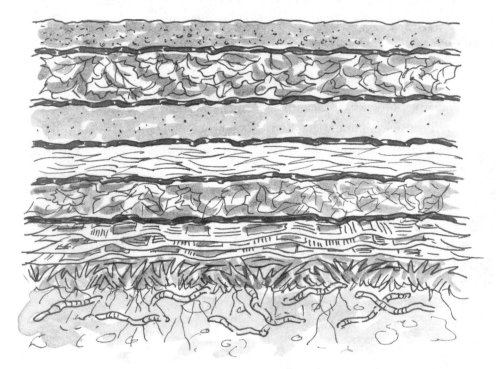

Choose your garden site carefully, keeping in mind how much sun the garden will receive. Mark off the site and cover it with thick pads of wet newspaper, overlapping the edges of the papers. Cover the paper with 1 to 2 inches of peat moss or other organic material. Begin layering with 2 to 4 inches of organic material, using 1 inch of peat moss (or other dry, brown material) between each layer. Build your layers to a height that will accommodate the roots of the plants you want to install. If you're planting seeds, you need to build your layers to a depth of only 5 to 6 inches.

Following these directions, you may have as much as 12 inches of layered organic material. You can plant just about anything in that much material, even large perennials or small shrubs. Just pull the layers aside and insert the plant's roots down to, but not through, the paper. Set the plant's rootball right on top of the paper and pull the layers of materials around the roots. Water your newly installed plants.

(Almost) Instant Gardens

The secret to installing and planting a lasagna garden with ease is having all your layering materials collected and ready in a handy place. You also need a nearby source of water and all your plants or seeds ready. This preparation enables you to have an almost instant garden.

MATERIALS

- Newspaper
- Water bucket or tub to soak newspaper
- Water hose
- Peat moss
- Grass clippings
- Chopped leaves
- Compost
- Plants and/or seeds
- Water source

(You'll find a more complete listing of potential lasagna garden layer materials starting on page 20.)

LASAGNA GARDEN Q&A

Here are the questions most people ask as they prepare to build their first lasagna garden:

Q How much wet newspaper should I use?
A Whole sections overlapped.

Q Where can I get extra newspaper if I run out?
A Take your neighbors' papers. It's easy to go out before the recycling truck makes its rounds and gather up the nicely bundled papers people have put by the curb. If you're doing a really big project, you can get all the bundles of paper you need with a trip to your local recycling center.

Q What kind of organic materials should I use for the layers?
A Peat moss, compost, grass clippings, chopped leaves, old hay or straw, etc. (See page 20 for a more complete list.)

Q Do I dig through the paper?
A No! Don't dig! Pull the layers aside and set the plant on top of the paper, then pull the layers back to cover the roots. Press firmly around the base of the plant to push out any air pockets.

Q How deep should my finished lasagna bed be?
A Measure the depth of the largest pot your plants come in and add an inch. For example, a plant in a 4-inch pot needs 5 inches of layers; a plant in a 6-inch pot needs 7 inches of layers.

HERBAL HINT

When you don't have enough leaves of your own, take bags of leaves your neighbors put at the curb. Open the bags on the lawn or the driveway and mow over them to chop them up before layering them on your garden.

Q Do I need to add additional layers of newspaper?

A Not for about 3 years. By then you will begin to see some weeds from seeds that have blown into the garden or been dropped by birds. Such unwanted visitors usually are easy to pull from the loose soil of a lasagna bed; then you can layer several sheets' thickness of wet paper around existing plants and cover the paper with a layer or two of organic materials.

Q Where can I get enough materials to make my garden?

A Do you have a neighbor—or more than one—who still puts garden waste (grass clippings and leaves) at the curb? Take it and use it to put more layers on your gardens. As you pile on the layers, your plants will be growing and reaching above the layers.

Q If I want to build a lasagna garden in the spring, where will I get leaves?

A Spring garden cleanup usually reveals loads of leaves that were blown in and around plants and buildings. Gather these around your property and watch for bags of leaves put out for collection by your neighbors. Be quick and take as many bags from the curb as you think you'll need for spring and summer layering. Open the bags on the lawn or the driveway and mow over them to chop them up before layering them on your garden.

Q How do I mark the outlines of my new garden?

A If your garden will have straight edges, stakes and string work great. For curved garden beds, you can use a length of rope or garden hose to help you visualize the finished shape, then sprinkle flour or garden lime along the shape marked by the rope to outline the area where you'll make your layers.

Q How do I plant potted herbs in my lasagna garden?

A When planting potted herbs, use your fingers or a digging tool to tease roots out of their pot-shaped growth pattern. Gently pull them apart and outward so they'll reach out laterally into the layers of organic material.

DO HERBS REALLY NEED A LASAGNA BED?

Because so many herbs come from places where the soil is dry, sandy, and well-drained, many people ask me if lasagna gardening is necessary—or even good—for herbs. Maybe some herbs grow well in poor soil, but most herb plants respond to the good soil in garden lasagnas by producing wonderful green foliage and an exuberance of flowers. Bigger, healthier plants also tend to be more fragrant. There are a few exceptions—plants such as nasturtiums and yarrow put too much energy into growing foliage when they're grown in rich soil. For these, I create lasagna beds with layers of peat moss, sand, chopped leaves, finely chipped bark, and other dry materials that provide good drainage but don't add a lot of nutrients. Lasagna gardening makes it easy to customize garden beds for your favorite plants, too!

Think about why you're growing herbs in the first place. Do you want herbs for cooking or crafts? Is your goal to have gardens full of fragrance and interesting foliage? Are you interested in the calming effects of gardening and of the herbs in your garden? Perhaps all of these things are results you hope to achieve.

Building lasagna gardens is fast and easy. It doesn't add to your stress and workload in the way traditional gardening practices do. If you want to enjoy the benefits of herb gardening without the pressures of digging, tilling, and weeding, lasagna gardening techniques can help you reach your goal.

Knowing something about herbs will come in handy when deciding what will go where. In Chapter 2 you can make good use of the herb profiles I've provided to give good basic herb information.

I grow nasturtiums and yarrow together because they both do better in average-to-poor soil. If you plant them in the rich soil of a typical lasagna garden, you will get great foliage but few flowers. Instead, I create gardens that are mostly sand and dry materials like leaves and peat moss with no added nutrients.

Crazy about Cosmos

One of the first people to "get" the idea of lasagna gardening was a woman from Fairhaven, New Jersey. In 1989, long before there was a book on the subject, she visited my gardens at the farm on Shandelee. She joined a group that was touring the gardens and listened to my instructions. Then she went home, marked out her sites for new gardens, and covered her front lawn sites with wet newspaper and peat moss. She added enough material to make her garden about 4 to 6 inches high, planted cosmos seeds, and waited.

Her efforts didn't go unnoticed. During the time she waited, her neighbors voiced their doubts as to her sanity. Why would she lay out newspaper on the lawn, and why would she think she could grow a garden in a few inches of peat moss and other weird and natural stuff? Still she waited. When the plants were up high enough to begin adding more layers, she did just that, placing inches of grass clippings and another inch of peat moss around the plants. Again she waited, while her neighbors laughed at her strange practice.

It wasn't until the first blooms began to appear on the cosmos that the lady's neighbors began to take notice without making fun. At the height of the season, with cosmos blooming on 5-foot stems, she had her husband take a picture of her standing in the cosmos bed.

I received her charming letter of thanks and the cosmos picture in early fall of that year. I keep it in my collection of notes and pictures from gardeners who believed what I told them about the lasagna gardening method.

LASAGNA LAYER MATERIALS

Mother Nature is the best gardener. She drops layers of debris and lets them decompose in their own time. Gradually, the debris becomes humus. Into this nature-made humus she drops seeds that germinate and grow into trees and wildflowers. Mother Nature is a bit slow and her process can take years. Nevertheless, her method is good, and it's what I use to make lasagna gardens where I grow herbs.

You may have heard that herbs will grow anywhere and that they don't need anything special, but I can tell you they do much better in lasagna gardens than in hard-packed clay soil. This list of materials is to encourage you to look around: See what you have handy that can improve your soil and give your herb plants a good place to grow. You can have a wonderful garden with little effort if you use readily available materials to build your garden. After you have layered enough material, just let Nature take her course.

Material	Where to Find It	How to Use It	Comments
Barn Litter (manure mixed with stall bedding: wood shavings, hay or straw, or shredded paper)	Race tracks, horse farms, dairy farms, barns, small animal farms, rabbit hutches	Use carefully to avoid burning plants. Place several inches away from plants or put in trenches and cover with soil. Side-dress plants or rows. Use as a layer in a lasagna garden that can be allowed to over-winter before planting.	Aged barn litter may be applied at any time. If you are lucky enough to have access to aged barn litter, you can use it freely around the herb garden as a top mulch.
Buckwheat Hulls	In better garden centers or directly from flour mills. Buckwheat hulls are left from making buckwheat flour.	Use as a top layer on a finished herb garden. The taupe-colored hulls are very attractive (and a bit pricey).	Once I have applied a 1-inch layer to the finished herb garden, I only have to touch up the mulch in following years. Buckwheat hulls are my favorite top mulch for the herb garden. They are pretty, lightweight, and all natural.
Coffee Grounds and Filters, Tea Bags	Coffeehouses, tearooms, restaurants, your kitchen	If you have small amounts of coffee grounds or tea leaves, they can go directly onto the garden. Filters, however, should go underneath other layers, as they have a tendency to blow away.	When using a lot of coffee grounds, sprinkle a little lime on each layer to moderate their acidity. Coffee grounds look good as a top mulch in the herb garden and rarely pose any problems related to their acidic nature.

Material	Where to Find It	How to Use It	Comments
Compost	Make your own, get as much as you need from municipal composting areas, or buy in bags at garden centers.	Apply as layers to entire growing area; spread finely screened compost over your lawn; side-dress around individual plants or between rows in vegetable gardens.	Try using a tomato cage to hold small amounts of kitchen and garden waste for composting right where you'll use it. Place cages behind tall plants to mini-mize their presence. Compost bene-fits herbs that need a nutrient boost; a single application typically supplies enough nourishment to last all year.
Corn Cobs or Stalks (chopped)	Farms that have chop-ping machines and use the chopped material as animal feed	Not the most attractive mate-rial, but fine as a top layer for a vegetable garden. Good as a coarse layer in a lasagna garden.	When dealing with farmers or other busy people, it's important to avoid getting in their way. If they are willing to give you what want, bring your own tools and bag it yourself.
Fruit Pulp	Cider mills, juice bars, natural food stores, your kitchen	Tuck any fresh fruit pulp under-neath other layers of material to avoid attracting insects.	Carry a plastic bag with you to take advantage of fresh fruit pulp finds. Keep fruit pulp on the bottom of the compost pile—it usually works better as a compost ingredient than as a lasagna garden layer.
Garden Waste (chopped weeds, stalks, leaves, clip-pings, dead flowers)	In the garden, lawn, and landscape	Once the coarse material is chopped (use the lawn mower, a leaf chopper, or a shredder), use as a layer in a lasagna garden. Something more at-tractive should always be on top. Add to the compost pile.	Place this kind of material in the tomato cages hidden around the garden. I don't usually use material this coarse on the surface of the herb garden; I keep it in the com-post heap.
Grass Clippings (fresh)	From your own yard, from your neighbor, or from a lawn care company. If you have a grass catcher on your mower, deposit the clip-pings right where you want them. If you have a mulcher on your mower, take it off (the grass has had enough clipping). If you have a lawn care company, have them leave the clippings or spread them on your garden.	Apply fresh clippings in 1- to 2-inch layers. After each mowing, I give all my gardens an inch of nitrogen-rich clip-pings, followed by an inch of peat moss or chopped leaves. Don't use grass clippings that have been sprayed with chemi-cals, especially weed-killers, on your gardens.	High in nitrogen, fresh grass clip-pings should be used as a 2-inch layer in a lasagna garden or as a 1-to-2-inch-thick top mulch. I usu-ally add an inch of peat moss after each layer of grass. Herbs benefit from layers of fresh grass clippings because the nitrogen helps them grow lots of fragrant leaves. Don't pile fresh grass clippings up and leave them— they can get smelly and disagreeable in a short time. This doesn't happen with just an inch or two.

(continued)

LASAGNA LAYER MATERIALS—CONTINUED

Material	Where to Find It	How to Use It	Comments
Hay (spoiled)	From farms that stock hay as feed for cattle or horses. The leftover hay spoils when left wet too long, making it no good to feed stock but great for the garden.	Unless you don't care what your garden looks like, keep spoiled hay underneath other more attractive layers. I use it to cover paths in out-of-the-way vegetable plots.	One of the main differences between Ruth Stout's method and mine is she just used hay as a mulch and threw her garden and kitchen wastes into the hay. We both achieved great soil, but mine is nicer to look at and uses materials more available to modern gardeners. Hay is too coarse for my herb garden, but I do use it to improve the soil.
Hops (spent)	Microbreweries	Spent hops are rich, full of nitrogen, and smell really bad. Use in your compost pile or as a bottom layer in a lasagna garden.	Hold your breath when you open the bag of spent hops. Don't use spent hops directly on the herb garden or your herbs will have all leaves and no flowers.
Kitchen Scraps	Your own kitchen, restaurants, food markets	Compost food scraps with lots of carbon-based materials like leaves and peat moss. Turn the compost often to let air into the pile. When material is dry and dark brown with no pieces of lettuce or cabbage leaves showing, apply to top of lasagna garden and around all plants.	Keep your compost pile small and easy to turn. Fresh vegetable waste gets heavy. Be careful about using table scraps, and monitor the waste to keep out butter, oil, salad dressings, and other materials that slow decomposition and attract pests.
Leaves	Mother Nature gives us tons of leaves each fall. If you don't have enough trees to furnish all the leaves you need, take your neighbors'. If necessary, go on a leaf-hunting expedition on days when municipal leaf pickup is scheduled and gather the bags placed by the curb until you have what you need.	When leaves begin to drop, mow over them just as you would grass. Each time you mow over a pile of leaves, the pieces get finer and finer. Cover your gardens with as many inches as you can—at least 8 to 12 inches. Tuck chopped leaves around shrubs, perennials, and rose bushes. Leaves provide the carbon you need to balance nitrogen-rich grass clippings and should be applied at a ratio of 1 part grass clippings to 4 parts chopped leaves.	Mow oak leaves until they're very finely chopped and use them in 3- to 4-inch layers with a sprinkling of lime to moderate their acidity. Herbs look especially healthy and green with a layer of chopped leaves as mulch.

Material	Where to Find It	How to Use It	Comments
Manure, Animal	Farms, racetracks, riding stables, mounted police stables, zoos, and farms where they raise rabbits, llamas, or petting animals	Add to the compost heap and allow to mature; dig trenches and place inside trench; or use at the bottom of a lasagna garden.	Don't allow fresh animal manures to touch your plants as they will burn. Concerns about bacterial contamination suggest that animal manure should be thoroughly composted before applying it to the garden. Use as a layer in fall for lasagna gardens that will "cook" over winter.
Spent Mushroom Compost	Mushroom farms	Spent mushroom compost is black and rich; I can't think of anyone who wouldn't want to spread it on top of the lawn or on their gardens.	Avoid mushroom compost that has been treated with chemicals. Mushroom compost is a pretty top mulch for an herb garden and can be added each year in 2- to 3-inch layers to keep the garden looking good.
Newspaper	On your doorstep, in your mailbox, or on the curb. (Your neighbors don't care if you take the bundles of paper they put at the curb.)	Wet thoroughly, lay over sod, weeds, rocks, etc., to form bottom layer of new garden bed. Overlap sections so no light can get through to weeds and grass.	Use a large container that will hold a lot of water and paper so you soak the paper thoroughly. You don't have to separate individual sheets of paper but can leave the paper folded the way it came to you. Do remove all slick or glossy sections. Herbs need a weed-free environment to grow in just like any other type of plant. Newspaper helps keep the garden weed-free for a long time.
Peat Moss	Garden centers, hardware stores, lumberyards, nurseries	Spread an inch between each layer of a lasagna garden: paper, peat, grass clippings, peat, leaves, peat, manure, peat, and so on.	Trying to wet a bale of peat moss is almost hopeless, but if you buy it in fall when prices are cheap, take it home and place each bale where you think you will use it. Cut away a large section of the bag and let nature wet it. Rain, snow, ice, whatever—it will be wet by next spring. Peat moss looks good and can cover a lot of mistakes or less attractive layers. Herb gardens are usually pretty gardens, and a 1-inch top layer of peat moss gives a finished look to the garden.
Pine Needles, Pine Straw	Under pine trees, sold in bundles at southern garden centers	Use several inches as a decorative mulch under planting beds and under acid-loving plants such as blueberries and rhododendrons.	To use in a lasagna garden, run the needles through the chipper and add a sprinkling of lime to moderate the acidity of the needles. A good-looking top mulch for herbs.

(continued)

LASAGNA LAYER MATERIALS—CONTINUED

Material	Where to Find It	How to Use It	Comments
Salt Hay, Seaweed, Kelp	At the shore, along beaches or lake fronts	Apply underneath other more attractive layers. Allow a winter season for it to break down.	Take buckets or baskets along when visiting the water. You never know when you'll find a supply of this nutrient-rich material. Seaweed is too coarse to use on top of an herb garden and usually not available in large enough quantities for layering, but it's a wonderful addition to your compost pile.
Sand	Garden centers, building supply stores, where mason supplies are sold	Add a layer of sand to help loosen heavy soil. Use to set stones in the garden path.	Sand is very heavy, so move it in small amounts. I carry a small pail in the car and use it to carry sand from the bag in my trunk to my garden until the bag is light enough for me to move. Sand is a valuable soil additive for herbs that need good drainage, but you need to use a lot to make a difference in heavy soil.
Sawdust	Lumberyards, carpenter shops, mills	Use as a regular layer in your lasagna garden or throw it on as you find it.	Use fresh sawdust in thin layers in the garden so it will break down quickly. Mix aged sawdust with equal parts peat moss and lime and apply directly to the soil in the herb garden.
Stone Dust, Stone Grit	Quarries, garden centers where rock bundles or mason supplies are sold	Use as a regular layer in a lasagna garden or as a top layer and mulch in an herb garden. Use to loosen heavy clay soil.	When building gardens in Texas or Georgia (or any place with difficult clay layers), order grit or stone dust in large amounts and use it freely. Grit makes a wonderful topping for paths around herb gardens.
Straw	Garden centers, farm stores, farms	Straw makes a pretty mulch around strawberries, spinach, lettuce, or other low-growing crops. When it is no longer needed as a groundcover, pile it in the path or add to a lasagna garden.	To keep the seeds found in straw from sprouting, cover the layer with 1 or 2 sheets of newspaper. Cover the paper with peat moss or other material to keep it from drying out and blowing away. Except for special plants like strawberries, keep the straw in the vegetable garden.
Wood Ashes	Wood-burning stoves, bonfire sites	Use a fine layer of wood ashes when using oak leaves or pine needles to balance the acidity of these ingredients.	Sift ashes before applying to garden. Don't use too often or in large quantities.

CHAPTER 2

My history with herbs does not date back nearly as far as my history as a gardener, but over the past 25 years I have come to see herbs as an essential part of any garden. Where I once knew only salt, pepper, and sage as the primary seasonings for food, I've come to enjoy the wide range of flavors that herbs add to everything from soups and salads to beverages and desserts. I've also gotten to know herbs as sources of soothing—or refreshing—fragrances, as useful friends in the first-aid kit, and as beautiful, easy-care plants that enhance my gardens in so many ways.

Herbs in Your Lasagna Garden

Getting to Know Herbs

Although I had been a gardener nearly all my life, I didn't *really* begin growing herbs until my husband retired from the navy and we became the proprietors of a country inn in the Catskill Mountains. The little herb garden next to the door of the taproom at Shandelee became an important part of the inn's character, as well as an entry point for me into the wonderful world of herb gardening.

Visitors to the inn passed by that herb garden (such as it was in the beginning) and either took pity on it or decided to give me a nudge in the right direction. They began to bring me plants from their own gardens: lemon thyme from Judy, angelica from Birdie, roses from Irv, rhubarb from Frank, and sage from Reverend Smith. The list of gift plants grew longer than my memory for the names of all the gift givers, but I can still see their faces when I'm in my garden and encounter a plant that first came to me as a gift from a friend.

With new plants from gardening friends and neighbors—and with additions like the basil that I used to enhance the menus at the inn—my gardens expanded rapidly. Of course, the inn kept me plenty busy most of the time, and I found myself increasingly frustrated by the lack of time I had for tending my gardens. Still, I kept gardening and planting more things because my gardens were refuge from the nonstop work of running an inn. Eventually, the demands on my time led me to the "ah-ha!" moment when I recognized the ease and simplicity of gardening lasagna style. I feel fortunate that this happened before I "threw in the trowel" on my gardens because they have come to play a central role in my life after innkeeping.

Using the layering method of lasagna gardening was the energy- and timesaver I needed to keep my gardens growing. Yes, I did find time and energy left over when my innkeeping chores were finished to devote to my growing passion with herbs. (What am I saying? Innkeeping work is never finished. Truth is, I stole time from other things for gardening, but I did have more energy.)

Herbs on the Move

The years passed as I spent my time as a full-time innkeeper and part-time gardener. All too soon it was time for retirement. The years between a chance visit of the couple from Williamsburg (see opposite page) and the time for me to leave the inn had been spent purchasing and renovating the old Rose home across the road. It was my first home in 14 years, and I had to pinch myself to be sure I was out of the one-room-with-bath at the inn. I began packing for the move across the road.

A Chance Meeting

It was a chance meeting with some guests from Colonial Williamsburg, Virginia, that really sparked my interest in growing herbs. Our guests were on their way to Caprilands for a visit with Adelma Grenier Simmons. They were staying one night with us before continuing on to Coventry, Connecticut. I didn't meet them when they checked in, but I was the breakfast cook the next morning. After breakfast, we chatted about my gardens, and they wanted to talk about the angelica they had seen growing by the back door.

I was intrigued because not many of my guests recognized angelica. The couple told me they were writing a book about the culinary herbs of Colonial Williamsburg and were traveling to meet with Simmons as part of their research for that book. I didn't know then of her reputation as a leading authority on herbs in America, but my interest was certainly piqued.

I shared my angelica plants with the couple and gave them some tips on growing it in Virginia. Two weeks after their visit, I received a signed book in the mail: *Herb Gardening in Five Seasons* by Adelma Grenier Simmons. The couple sent the book as a thank-you for the plants.

That winter I read the book. I loved the way it was put together and Simmons' stories about the herbs in her gardens. I began to feel a kinship with Simmons when she talked of her saltbox home where she hosted herbal luncheons and lectures.

In the spring I traveled to Coventry, Connecticut, to visit Simmons' herb farm. During lunch there I could see my own dining room at the inn full of guests eating herbal fare. Simmons gave a 15-minute lecture after lunch, then retired to her little bookstore to sign copies of her many books. I walked the gardens, made my way to the bookstore, and purchased several of her little books before heading for home.

Back in the mountains at the inn, I would catch myself looking across the road at my own saltbox, wondering if it wasn't possible to have my own small version of Caprilands.

> ### HERBAL HINT
>
> *Keeping a journal is one way to extend the pleasure of gardening: You garden, write about the garden, then go back and read about your gardens in your journal. Include notes about plants you're trying for the first time, when things bloom, and plants that didn't do what you'd expected. The point is to keep track of things that matter to you, not to follow any prescribed format. During one of my moves, I was pleasantly surprised to find a stack of notebooks that contained, among other things, all the plant descriptions and designs of my herb gardens at the inn. Paging through them was like visiting with an old friend.*

The movers moved furniture, but I moved plants. I took my first lasagna herb garden with me across the street—first the plants, then, using a flat shovel, I took the soil. (Don't think I was being greedy or spiteful—the new owner didn't want a garden in that spot and was planning to replace the garden with grass.)

On moving day, I walked across the road from the inn to the farm and began my new life. In the weeks that followed, I put my house together, and then I began making lasagna gardens. I planted herbs, perennials, and small fruits the first year. The second year, I added shrubs, vegetables, ornamental grasses, and more herbs. I had walked away from a job as a full-time innkeeper to another kind of life—a full-time gardener.

The second year at the farm was as busy as the first, and lots of folks who had been customers at the inn came to see me. One was a woman who owned a weekly paper in the area. She had heard about my gardens and wanted me to write a garden column for her paper. I had never written for anyone before, but it seemed to be a good idea. Anyway, how hard could it be?

I wrote 54 lines a week, 52 weeks a year for 8 years. I called my column "Down the Garden Path" and filled it with stories of my gardens and the gardens of friends and family. I had always wanted enough time to garden, and I also found out that I enjoyed writing about gardening and sharing what I learned in my gardens with others.

Pat's A-List of Herbs

From the Tennessee mountains to the mountains of New York, and in all the states and homes I've known in between, I have had a blast growing and using more than 100 different herbs. I grew them to use in recipes, to make handcrafted accessories for my home, and to give as gifts for friends and family. I grew them because they were interesting or because growing them made me feel good: I still grow large quantities of sage because it makes me think of my grandmother. While I still enjoy doing some things my grandmother did, the memory of how labor-intensive life was in her time inspired me to find easier ways to garden. Modern lives, including mine, are overfull, stressful, and focused on instant gratification.

Even though my living and gardening situation has changed, I still grow many of the herbs I've listed in this chapter. The information is meant to help you choose herbs for your own garden. It would be nearly impossible for me to choose a single favorite from among all of these, but as you read along, you will notice that I do have favorites, each for a particular reason. There may be other uses, other points of view on the plant's history, and other ways to grow these herbs. What follows here is my own experience. For perennial herbs, I've included the USDA Plant Hardiness Zones they grow best in; check the map on page 278 to see which zone you garden in, and pick plants that are compatible with your area. I hope you'll be inspired to try many of these herbs in your own garden and to discover your own personal favorites.

AJUGA (*Ajuga reptans* and cultivars)

This easy-to-grow groundcover features tidy rosettes of lobed leaves that spread gradually to form a reasonably good barrier against weeds and a pleasant underpinning for taller plants of all sorts. The unimproved species, *Ajuga reptans,* has medium green leaves and beautiful deep blue flowers in spring, but it is surpassed as an ornamental plant by its many offspring that offer features such as more colorful foliage and larger flowers. 'Alba' has white flowers. My favorite ajuga selections include the large bronze leaves of 'Caitlin's Giant', and 'Burgundy Glow', which has deep red leaves that contrast wonderfully with its blue flowers.

Although its modern-day use is almost entirely as an ornamental, ajuga has a long history as a medicinal herb. English herbalist Nicholas Culpeper mentions it in *The English Physician Enlarged* (1653) as an herb to apply to wounds and to cure a hangover; its leaves are reputed to have a mild narcotic affect.

How to Grow: Ajuga spreads readily on its own and is easily divided if you want to add its color to another spot in your garden. Seedlings of varieties with colorful leaves may have green foliage, but mature divisions will resemble the parent plants. Ajuga grows best in moisture-retentive soil in sun or shade. In my experience, the colors of both leaves and flowers are bolder if grown in part shade.

Uses: Plant ajuga around trees and perennial beds as a groundcover, on slopes to hold soil in place, and as a companion to late-blooming bulbs, especially daffodils and tulips. Its blue, pink, or white flowers are a welcome sight in spring.

HERBAL HINT

Try growing 'Burgundy Glow' ajuga with creeping Jenny (Lysimachia nummularia). The lime green leaves of the creeping Jenny wander amid the rounded burgundy leaves of 'Burgundy Glow' to create a truly spectacular living carpet for any garden. I guarantee that you'll love this combo!

ALOE (*Aloe vera*)

A succulent perennial of the lily family, aloe is native to Africa, where it has been used for thousands of years to smooth, soothe, and soften skin (it was reportedly part of Cleopatra's beauty regimen). The gel-like innards of aloe's fleshy leaves are still used today to treat minor burns and other skin irritations, and the plants are widely cultivated for inclusion in lotions, soaps, and all manner of natural beauty products.

Aloe's historical use as an important medicinal herb is well documented: It appears in South African cave paintings dating back to the Stone Age, and it is mentioned in the Bible and in fourth-century Greek writings.

How to Grow: Easy and undemanding, aloe makes a near-perfect houseplant that thrives on neglect. Its best location is near a bright window where it receives indirect sunlight. Overwatering is its nemesis—sandy, well-drained potting soil is best—and it thrives on neglect. Once-a-month watering is usually sufficient to keep aloe happy, and happy aloe will produce small side shoots that can be broken off and potted up as new plants to share with family and friends.

In the southern states, in Zones 9 and 10, winter temperatures remain warm enough for growing aloe outdoors, and plants can grow up to 2 feet tall. In cold-winter areas, aloe will enjoy spending summer days outside and returning to the comfort of your house before the first frost threatens.

HERBAL HINT

Every once in a while, I break off an aloe leaf, slice it open lengthwise, and scoop out the gel. I apply it to my face, neck, and hands to soften and heal my overexposed and abused skin.

Uses: It's handy to keep your potted aloe in or near the kitchen, where its leaves can serve as speedy first aid for minor burns and chapped skin.

ANGELICA (*Angelica archangelica*)

Being an innkeeper is a rewarding and fun way to make a living, not the least of which is the wonderful people you meet. As soon as I began working on the inn's first herb garden (the one outside the taproom door), one of my customers, Birdie Geiger, brought me some angelica plants. I had never seen them before and knew nothing about growing or using them, but I stuck them in with the chives and oregano. In the first year, I was surprised to see one plant grow to a height of 5 feet; I figured I must have done something right! Over the next few years I learned about angelica and its uses, and I came to appreciate both the height it added to my herb gardens as well as its culinary uses.

In many parts of the world, angelica blooms on or around May 8, the Day of St. Michael the Archangel. All parts of the plant are believed to impart a more angelic temperament to those who eat it.

How to Grow: Angelica is a hardy biennial that is sometimes grown as a perennial by cutting off the flowerstalks before they set seed. For best results, sow angelica seeds in fall—you'll probably need to do that only once, as it will self-sow thereafter from any flower heads left in your garden. Angelica requires rich, moist soil and partial shade; it grows best in cool climates. You can move seedlings when they are small, but angelica starts to resent relocation as it approaches its full height of up to 7 feet.

HERBAL HINT

To candy angelica stems, cut them into 2- to 3-inch lengths, then slice the pieces in halves or quarters lengthwise, depending on the thickness of the stems. Bury each piece in coarse ground sugar and leave it there for 2 or 3 days. Store candied stem pieces in airtight jars or lined tins.

Uses: Angelica seeds are used to flavor vermouth, Chartreuse, and wine. The plant is used in perfumes. Angelica stems can be candied to decorate cakes and pastries, and they also can be made into jams. The plant's imposing height makes it a good candidate for a focal point in the garden.

ANISE (*Pimpinella anisum*)

Anise is a popular annual herb whose seeds are used to season sausage, cakes, candy, and breads. Its flavor is generally associated with Italian food. During the time when Rome ruled the world and gastronomy was the order of the day, anise was used to flavor little cakes that were eaten to improve digestion after a meal. The seeds also were used to pay taxes, and when worn in little bags around the neck, they were thought to ward off the evil eye.

How to Grow: In rich, moist soil and full sun to part shade, anise typically grows 1 to 1½ feet tall.
This annual grows freely from seed sown in spring and will self-seed for the next year. Plant it once and ignore the seeds, and you'll have it in your garden forever!

Uses: Anise seeds give a pleasant licorice-like flavor to baked goods and candies. Anise also adds fragrance to soaps, perfumes, and potpourri.

ARTEMISIAS (*Artemisia* species and cultivars)

When I look at a planting of 'Silver King' artemisia, I see a silvery gray background that helps tie together the colors of other plants. I also see artemisia as a reliable source of base material for wreaths and swags and as a filler in dried arrangements, although its history includes medicinal uses, too. In parts of Asia, artemisia has been used as an antimalarial medicine for more than 2,000 years. In Europe, southernwood (*Artemisia abrotanum*) was long used to repel both insects and contagion: It was an important herb to include in a nineteenth-century nosegay (a small bunch of flowers and herbs used to ward off infectious disease and unpleasant smells).

How to Grow: Artemisias do best in full sun and well-drained, neutral to alkaline soil. While they can be invasive, artemisias are easy enough to keep

HERBAL HINT

After 25 years of growing several different artemisias, I still can't have too much of any one kind. I use artemisia to back up and show off other plants that have vividly colored flowers or foliage, and I'm sure the planting of artemisia around my roses has kept them free of insects and diseases. In late summer or early fall, I cut 'Silver King' or 'Silver Queen' and hang the leafy stems to dry. When business slows down at the Potager, I get busy making herbal wreaths with artemisia as the main ingredient.

in check in the garden, and you can divide them when you decide you need more in another spot in your landscape. Cut back the woody stems in late fall or early spring to keep plants full and attractive. Artemisias are hardy in Zones 4 through 9, but they are not fond of summer heat and humidity. Very rich soil can make them look puny.

Uses: The silvery foliage of most artemisias makes them excellent "blenders" both in and out of the garden. Artemisias are essential plants in a white garden and supply useful material for making wreaths. Tarragon (*A. dracunculus*) is an artemisia used for cooking and is described separately on page 92.

BASIL (*Ocimum basilicum* and other species and cultivars)

Sweet basil is a familiar and favorite annual herb with a clovelike flavor and a pleasant, spicy aroma. Although basil is associated with Italian food—the Italians call it *basilico*—its sweet-spicy flavor and many different forms make it a feature of many different cultures and cuisines around the world. In France the plant is known as *basilic*, and in Japan it's called *bajiru*. The Dutch use lots of *bazielkruid*, and the Portuguese have *mangericao*.

Native to Asia, Africa, South America, the Caribbean, and the Middle East, basil didn't arrive in Europe until a little more than 2,000 years ago. First associated with sacred rites and Christian legend, basil wasn't always a culinary herb. In Greece, it was considered sacred, and plants were taken to the church to be blessed on the first day of the New Year—St. Basil's Day. From Greece, basil lore spread through Eastern Europe to North Africa and Spain. Gerard's famous herbal, published in England in 1597, recommended basil only as a medicinal herb and admonished people not to eat it.

How to Grow: Sow basil seeds in a prepared bed after all chance of frost is past. Once the seedlings are up, thin them to 15 to 24 inches apart and replant the thinnings in another spot. Basil grows best in full sun to partial shade in moist, well-drained garden soil. Cuttings with a few leaves will root quickly in water: Take several long cuttings in late summer or early fall, before the first frost. Place the cuttings in a container with 3 to 4 inches of clean water in a sunny window. Pot up rooted cuttings, and keep them in a warm, bright location. New leaves will grow and you can harvest fresh basil all winter.

Uses: Basil leaves and flowers can be used in salads, vinegars, and sauces, as well as with fresh vegetables, especially tomatoes. Large-leaf varieties tend to have milder flavors and make pleasant additions to mixed green salads; sometimes referred to as "lettuce-leaf" basils, these leaves are also excellent on sandwiches in place of leaf lettuce.

There are more than 150 different basils; here a few of my favorites:

- **'MAGICAL MICHAEL'** has attractive flowers and a refined plant habit. If for no other reason than it bears the same name as my oldest son, it has been a welcome plant in my gardens.

- **'NAPOLETANO'** sports large, flavorful, puckered leaves for use fresh or dried. Pinch off flowers to promote bushy, branching growth and to keep large leaves forming continuously. This is a favorite in Naples, Italy, and it's one I'm sure to grow every year. Just one extra-large leaf can flavor a pot of sauce.

- **'PURPLE RUFFLES'** has a mild basil flavor and frilled purple-and-green foliage. Introduced in 1987 and recognized by the National Gardening Bureau as an All-American Selection, 'Purple Ruffles' became an instant favorite among basil lovers. Its leaf color gives vinegar a beautiful pink hue. Plants grow to 2 feet high and 18 inches wide.

- **'TRUE THAI'** has a fine anise flavor and deep purple flowers. This is one of the most attractive basils, and I love to let it flower because it adds so much to the garden. The flowers are just as flavorful as the leaves and look wonderful sprinkled on cold foods. Also sold as 'Siam Queen'.

BAY (*Laurus nobilis*)

In its native Mediterranean region and other places with similarly mild climates, this broad-leaved evergreen can grow to heights of 60 feet or more. Where winters grow cold (Zones 7 and colder), bay is typically grown as a potted plant by cooks who prize it for its culinary uses.

How to Grow: Bay has a reputation for being tough to start, and it needs some coddling to get it going. Cuttings rooted in moist sand and peat moss tend to be most successful; keep them in the shade, and mist them frequently. Even with plenty of TLC, bay cuttings may take 6 months or longer to root. Buying a small plant is an easier way for most gardeners to get started, but bear in mind that bay's finicky disposition will contribute to a higher price tag than that of many other herbs. In a large container, bay may reach 3 to 6 feet tall.

Uses: Bay leaves provide essential flavor to soups and stews. The sturdy evergreen leaves may be dried and made into wreaths.

Warning: Only *Laurus nobilis* is safe as seasoning for food. All other laurels are poisonous.

HERBAL HINT

Be prepared to fish bay leaves out of the pot before serving your soup or stew. The tough, woody midrib of a bay leaf is indigestible and presents a choking hazard if swallowed.

BORAGE (*Borago officinalis*)

Borage wins many a gardener's heart with its beautiful blue flowers—and its positive attributes are usually enough to earn forgiveness for its tendency to self-sow with abandon. In the old herbals (historical guides to the medicinal uses of plants), you can find recipes for borage tea, which was used to treat fevers and impart courage to its drinkers. Eating raw borage leaves to cleanse the blood was common practice. I think one would have to have courage to eat the hairy leaves of borage!

How to Grow: Sow borage seeds in spring in a sunny spot with moist, well-drained soil. This hardy, fuzzy-leaved annual grows from 1 to 3 feet tall and is pretty enough to include in a flower garden. Once you've grown it for a season, borage will self-seed freely, and you'll find new plants coming up in strange places forever after.

Uses: Use starry blue borage blossoms as a showy and edible garnish for punch or juice, or candy them for use as cake decorations. Cut fresh flowers and dip them first in beaten egg white, then in superfine sugar, and let dry. They are a divine shade of blue. Although some sources recommend chopping the young leaves into salads for their mild cucumber flavor, this practice is not recommended because of liver-damaging compounds found in borage.

Burgundy Punch with Borage Flowers

1   pint fruit punch
1   gallon burgundy wine
1   quart seltzer or club soda
1   pint raspberry tea

1   pint orange juice
1   orange, sliced into thin rings
Approx. 2 dozen borage flowers

Freeze the fruit punch in a ring-shaped form. Combine wine, seltzer, tea, and orange juice in a large punch bowl. Add orange slices and fruit punch ice ring, and float the borage flowers on top.

BURNET (*Sanguisorba poterium*)

Also known as salad burnet, this edible herb is invaluable in the cook's garden—not only for use in salads and sauces but also as a pretty garnish. Burnet's attractive little mounds of tender serrated green leaves have a fresh cucumber taste and pop up in early spring before most other greens.

Burnet is of Mediterranean origin but is also at home in Asia and England. Pilgrims brought burnet plants and seeds to America, where it naturalized.

How to Grow: Burnet is a hardy perennial in Zones 4 to 9. Grow it from seed sown in either spring or fall or, for a more relaxed method, let one or two plants flower and set seed. They will sow themselves, and little plants will appear the following spring. Dig small plants and replant them where you want them to grow. Although burnet can survive in full sun, I prefer to grow it in part shade, where the leaves are greener and stay tender longer.

Uses: Burnet gives a subtle cucumber flavor to salads and vegetable dishes. For salads, harvest young, tender leaves and add to lettuce and mixed greens. Harvest whole stalks with flowers to garnish plates or for use in tomato-juice drinks in place of celery.

The Potager's Vegetable Cream Cheese

Combine ¼ cup each minced carrots, scallions, and burnet leaves with 1 pound cream cheese. Great on bagels, toast, and sandwiches; for extra flavor, add walnuts, raisins, or dill weed.

Herb Butter

Combine ¼ cup each finely chopped flat-leaf parsley, dill weed, and burnet with 1 pound soft butter. Divide into four portions; roll each portion into a cylinder, cover with plastic wrap, and chill. Freeze for later use.

Burnet Herb Vinegar

Add 1 cup bruised burnet leaves to 1 quart hot—not boiling—white vinegar. Let stand in covered container in a dark place for 2 weeks. Strain and discard leaves; pour into decorative bottle(s) with 1 or 2 leafy stems of burnet. Use as a dressing for fresh salads or cooked greens.

CALENDULA
(*Calendula officinalis*)

Sometimes called pot marigold, calendula is a hardy annual that freely self-sows in your garden. An old herb that was used by the ancients much as it is used today, calendula is used to treat cuts and bruises as well as in the kitchen.

How to Grow: Take a few transplants from a gardener friend, or buy seeds or plants and start your own patch—either way, calendula's ability to re-seed itself means you'll never need to worry about planting calendula again. Calendula grows easily in full sun from seed planted in spring or fall.

Uses: Use fresh or dried calendula petals to add a yellow color to rice or other foods; it has been called "poor man's saffron." Fresh petals have a slightly bitter—but not unpleasant—flavor. The bright yellow petals are beautiful in summer salads; use whole flowers as a garnish.

CARAWAY (*Carum carvi*)

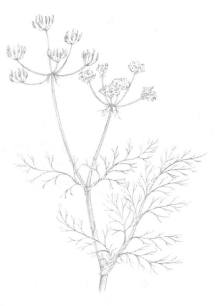

Caraway is an edible herb with a long history of use in cuisines from Asia and the Middle East to Europe and Scandinavia. Long believed to improve vision and enhance memory, caraway is widely used as a digestive aid and to relieve flatulence. In medieval times, peasants could not afford the expensive spices available to the ruling classes, so they used common herbs such as caraway to flavor their foods (caraway brought out the best in goat's cheese and boiled cabbage).

How to Grow: Caraway is a hardy biennial that grows to 3 feet tall. It self-sows readily and, once allowed to flower and set seed, will be a constant presence in your garden if you don't intentionally weed it out. I sow seed directly in the garden in either spring or late fall; it likes full sun and moist, well-drained soil. The plants produce foliage in their first year of growth, then bloom the following year. The seeds form in late August and need to be harvested before they fall to the ground. Hold a paper bag under the seeds to catch them.

Uses: Caraway seeds are commonly used in rye bread, sauerkraut, and the liqueur called *kümmel*. Many recipes for cakes, cookies, and breads call for caraway seeds, and they're also used to flavor fresh goat cheese. All parts of the caraway plant are edible; add the leaves to soups, stews, and fresh salads.

CATNIP (*Nepeta cataria*)

Native to Europe and naturalized across North America, catnip is so widespread that it's considered more of a weed than an herb in some circles. No matter what we humans think of it, catnip is irresistible to cats, who appear to enjoy the all-natural high it gives them. Bees like catnip, too, and beekeepers often find a place for catnip in their gardens.

How to Grow: Catnip is a hardy perennial that grows best in partial shade in sandy or well-drained soil. It tolerates dry conditions and grows 2 to 3 feet tall. If you cut the plant back after it blooms, it will produce new flowers for the remainder of the growing season.

Uses: Catnip leaves and flowers can be brewed into a calming tea for human consumption, but the herb is most often used in dried form for the amusement of cats.

HERBAL HINT

To dry catnip leaves, strip them from their stems and place in a large paper bag. Give the bag a daily turn or gentle shake to move the leaves around. Once dry, store the leaves in a covered container in a dark place to prevent fading.

GERMAN CHAMOMILE and ROMAN CHAMOMILE (*Matricaria recutita* and *Chamaemelum nobile*)

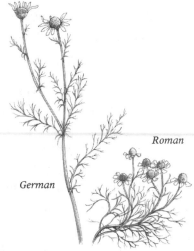

Roman

German

The two chamomiles—annual German chamomile and perennial Roman chamomile—have rather different growth habits, but both produce characteristic-looking flowers: smallish, white-petaled daisies with prominent yellow centers. Gather and dry the flowers of either chamomile to make soothing chamomile tea. Low-growing Roman chamomile was a popular feature of castle lawns in old England, during the time when castles had plenty of staff available to care for such plantings.

How to Grow: German chamomile is an upright and slightly weedy-looking annual that grows 2 to 3 feet tall. Roman chamomile is a low-growing (to 9 inches tall) perennial with a gently spreading habit. Both prefer neutral to slightly acid, moist but well-drained soil. Roman chamomile tolerates cold winter temperatures but can fade in prolonged summer heat and humidity. Sow tiny seeds of Roman chamomile into well-prepared lasagna beds in

HERBAL HINT

If you decide to plant a mini herbal lawn of Roman chamomile, select a small area that you can edge with stones or other border material. A feature like this makes a nice surprise at the end of a path. Choose a level site in part sun and part dappled shade. A lasagna garden, about 6 inches high and watered well, is perfect and allows you to plant instantly. Keep your eyes peeled for any competing plants that try to move in, and weed them out while they're young.

spring. Sow German chamomile seed in spring or fall; plants will reseed if a few flower heads are left unpicked in the garden.

Uses: Harvest and dry the flowers of either chamomile to use in tea and potpourri—the flowers have a pleasant apple fragrance. Some garden-supply companies even offer a rake made specifically for harvesting chamomile flowers. Roman chamomile makes an attractive and fragrant groundcover, but it isn't always as care-free as is desirable for this purpose—the plants need consistent moisture to truly thrive and may not fill in quickly enough to keep out competing weeds. Unless you have time to maintain a large planting of chamomile in a lawn area, you'll probably be more satisfied if you grow it in a more manageable situation, such as between stepping-stones or as the seat of a garden chair or bench.

CHERVIL (*Anthriscus cerefolium*)

Chervil is a hardy annual that, once established in your garden, will come back from self-sown seed for years. Native to Europe and Asia, chervil will grow in shady sites where other herbs will not.

How to Grow: Sow chervil seed where you want it to grow, as it rarely withstands transplanting. Chervil prefers moist, improved soil and part to full shade. Rake a planting bed, then broadcast seed on top of the soil. Gently press the seeds into the soil, but don't cover them.

Uses: Chervil has a subtle flavor. Use it as you would parsley, chopping it finely and adding it to vegetable, fish, or chicken dishes just before serving. Chervil's flavor goes especially well with eggs and cheese. Along with

HERBAL HINT

In cold-winter areas, sow chervil seed in fall by broadcasting it in the place the herb will grow. Chervil is a cool-weather crop that tends to bolt (flower and set seed) in the heat of summer, but it can be grown in warm areas in early spring and late fall.

parsley, tarragon, and thyme, chervil is part of French cuisine's *fines herbes* (in France, chervil plays a larger role in the kitchen than parsley).

CHIVES
(*Allium schoenoprasum*)

Mildly oniony chives are among the most widely known and used herbs. Every part of the plant, including its flower, is edible.

How to Grow: Chives are hardy perennials that grow best in a sunny site with well-drained soil. Sow seed in spring or fall; divide clumps of chives every 2 or 3 years. Plants grown in dappled shade produce fewer flowers, but those flowers are darker pink, while their leaves and stems are deeper green and more flavorful.

Uses: I use chives as a border plant in my cutting garden for its beautiful lavender flowers. I also use the flowers in dried arrangements. From the time chives first appear in early spring, I include the leaves—and later, the flowers—in most of my food preparation. Soups get large snips; salads get flower petals and stems. Snipped chives improve the flavor and appearance of baked (and other) potatoes. Lovely pale pink chive blossom vinegar is delicious.

GARLIC CHIVES
(*Allium tuberosum*)

This species of chives is sometimes called Chinese chives. It has flatter stems and tall white starlike flowers and is very fragrant. I love the way it looks among other perennials in my white garden. The flavor of garlic chives is a bit milder than regular chives, with just a hint of garlic. The plants do re-seed into other gardens, and I find the surprise of a new clump of garlic chives growing anywhere a pleasant thing.

How to Grow: Like their oniony relatives, garlic chives prefer dry, sandy growing conditions. They also like full sun and, from time to time, a bit of organic fertilizer.

Uses: I grow garlic chives in my white garden for the surprise of those lovely white flowers. Use the leaves, stems, and flowers as you would regular chives.

HERBAL HINT

When snipping chive stems, use a pair of really sharp scissors, not the bulky kitchen shears that you use for other chores. To use the blooms, pull each little floret from the base. When making chive blossom vinegar, use white vinegar and steep lots of stems and whole blossoms in it. After a couple of weeks, strain the liquid into a new bottle, discard the old stems and blossoms, and add fresh blossoms and a few new stems to the finished product.

COMFREY (*Symphytum officinale*)

You're not likely to lose comfrey beneath the leaves of other plants in your gardens: This big—3 to 5 feet tall—plant sports large, hairy leaves and pretty pale pink-to-purple flowers. I first planted comfrey just to have it in a garden dedicated to growing healing plants. A comfrey nickname, "knit-bone," comes from its use throughout history as a poultice to treat broken bones. Soon, however, I was planting comfrey to have plenty of leaves to help my compost "cook." Finally, it earned a place in a production garden to answer a growing demand for the plants.

How to Grow: Comfrey is a member of the borage family and is easy to propagate by division. It responds well to part-shade and wet areas, but I have grown it in full sun in a rich lasagna garden. It will seed itself in paths and other parts of the garden and can be easily transplanted—if anything, comfrey spreads a little too readily, and you need to be on guard to keep it out of areas where you don't want it. Start it from seed, or buy a few starter plants from an herb nursery; plant comfrey where it has plenty of room to grow.

Uses: I use comfrey leaves to accelerate the breakdown of compost in my containers. Place a layer of leaves after every 2 feet of other material. Although its days of treating broken bones are over, comfrey is still recommended for treating bruises and injuries to the skin. Make a poultice of chopped leaves and use on stubborn sores to help healing. Because it contains compounds that may cause liver damage, internal use of comfrey is not recommended.

CONEFLOWER
(*Echinacea angustifolia*)

Not only people stop to stare and sometimes touch the purple coneflowers in my gardens. Bees and butterflies are drawn to the beautiful wide petals with the prickly center. Coneflowers are native to the northern and central plains of North America, where they were widely used by the Plains Indians. Tribes such as Crow, Comanche, and Cheyenne used the fresh root, the fresh juice from the root, and an infusion made from the whole plant for a variety of ills, including snakebite, toothache, colds, and mouth sores.

How to Grow: Purple coneflower likes moist soil, especially areas around small streams and other naturally wet spots, but is quite tolerant of dry conditions, too. Belying its open prairie origins, this hardy perennial also tolerates dappled to partial shade. I grow purple coneflower in front of some old roses in the center garden at the Potager, in full sun and with little additional water. Sow seeds in any rich, well-drained soil in late spring after all danger of frost is past. Purple coneflower will self-sow in your gardens if you leave a few seedheads behind at the end of the growing season.

Uses: Purple coneflower is a lovely, long-blooming plant to include in ornamental gardens and is a valuable addition to flower arrangements. I use it fresh until all the petals fall, then dry the central "cone" for use in dried arrangements. Extracts of the root are widely sold under the plant's botanical name, *Echinacea,* as an herbal immunity booster and remedy for all manner of ailments. Leave the seed-filled spiky centers in your garden as fall arrives, and finches and other small seed-eating birds will perch on the tall dried stems to dine.

CORIANDER and CILANTRO
(*Coriandrum sativum*)

While its two names sometimes cause confusion, it's actually fairly easy to sort out the multiple personality of this herb: The foliage is generally called cilantro, while the seeds are known as coriander. Coriander has been around for centuries and plays an important role in cuisines around the world. Native to the Mediterranean and southern Europe, coriander seeds add their flavor to everything from Moroccan dishes to Belgian beers. Cilantro is a key ingredient in Spanish and Mexican cooking, as well as foods from China and Southeast Asia.

How to Grow: Sow coriander seed in early spring or fall in the spot where it will grow—this annual has a long taproot that makes transplanting mostly unsuccessful. Coriander grows best in full sun and well-drained soil; it tends to fade when summer temperatures and humidity begin to climb. If this herb is among your favorites, you may want to make successive plantings to have a steady supply on hand.

Uses: Use coriander seeds in curries, cookies, and candy. The seeds also add a citrusy note to potpourri. Cilantro adds authentic flavor to salsa and Asian-inspired dishes.

DAYLILIES (*Hemerocallis* spp. and cultivars)

We all know the cheery orange roadside daylily (*Hemerocallis fulva*) that many people mistakenly call a tiger lily. Those familiar orange flowers were brought to this country by early settlers and planted in their gardens; from there, the vigorous immigrant escaped to suitable growing sites everywhere.

HERBAL HINT

When you want a longer growing season for herbs—or any plant, for that matter—try floating row covers. Made from spun-bonded polyester, they let light, air, and water through to your plants but raise the air temperature a few degrees to ward off late spring or early fall frosts (and keep bugs away from tiny seedlings).

Today this wild daylily is found across North America, growing in a variety of conditions.

Native from Asia to central Europe, daylilies have received plenty of attention from plant breeders, and the resulting array of colors, sizes, and shapes of the flower appear in gardens around the world. Every part of the daylily plant is edible, from the fleshy roots to the trumpet-shaped flowers.

How to Grow: The cheerful and carefree attitude of those roadside daylilies attracts many people to attempt to dig up clumps to take home to their gardens. It's hard work, and the results of such efforts aren't nearly as satisfactory as those obtained by planting more refined daylily species and hybrids from reputable nurseries. Daylilies thrive in my lasagna gardens and provide a spectacular display with almost no care. Nice, loose lasagna beds make planting daylilies ultraeasy, too—I just pull back the layers and tuck in the roots of my new purchases. Once they get going, daylilies are reasonably drought-tolerant, and they bloom well in full sun to partial shade. Most daylilies are hardy in Zones 3 to 9.

Uses: In addition to the easy-care beauty they bring to your garden, daylilies can add pizzazz to your table, too—and not just as cut flowers. Cleaned and thinly sliced, the roots taste like bamboo shoots; young leaves can be cut into 1-inch pieces and stir-fried, dropped into soup stock, or added to salads. Fresh buds may be used in stir-fries, salads, or soups; whole flowers—with the pollen-bearing stamens removed—can serve as an edible garnish or be stuffed with fillings such as cream cheese or egg salad.

To dry daylily flowers, choose buds that are just beginning to open and shake them to remove any insects. Put a single layer of buds on paper towels on a cooling rack, and place the cooling rack inside a paper bag. Fold over the end of the bag and clip it shut to keep insects away from the drying buds. Set the bag in a warm, dry place; the buds should be dry in a couple of weeks.

DIANTHUS, PINKS, and CARNATIONS
(*Dianthus* spp. and cultivars)

I can't imagine a garden without dianthus (or cottage pinks, as my grandmother would have called them). These fragrant blossoms have been a feature of cottage gardens since the Middle Ages and are as at home in herb gardens today as they were in the abbey gardens of bygone centuries. With the exception of sweet William (*Dianthus barbatus*), a biennial often grown as an annual, most dianthus varieties are perennials, hardy in Zones 4 to 9. Although many dianthus bloom in shades of pink and red, the name "pinks" comes from the toothed—or pinked—edges of the flower petals, not their color.

HERBAL HINT

*Keep your pinks in the pink—and in bloom almost all season long—
by making a habit of promptly removing their spent flowers.*

How to Grow: Dianthus require full sun and will survive on moderate amounts of water. They are at home in alkaline soil, which explains their popularity in Texas, New Mexico, and other areas with similar soil conditions. Start seeds indoors about 3 months before your last frost date. Seedlings may be subject to damping-off, a soilborne fungus—avoid overwatering and keep a close eye on conditions while your seedlings are getting started. You can also root cuttings or take divisions from existing plants to have more dianthus for your gardens.

Uses: Besides their great looks in the garden, dianthus have wonderfully fragrant flowers, with scents ranging from clove to jasmine, depending on the variety. Dianthus flowers are edible, and a sprinkling of the pretty toothed petals makes an attractive addition to salads and desserts.

DIGITALIS or FOXGLOVE (*Digitalis purpurea*)

Foxglove is one of the most beautiful plants for cool climates and part-shade areas. In the Catskill Mountains, wild foxglove grows in the forest where trees have fallen and a shaft of light peeks through. In an area called Clear Lake, I have watched wild foxglove reseed (and relocate) itself over a period of 7 years, first by the side of a cabin, then across the road into the woods, and eventually down the side of the mountain. Foxglove heads for the light, so its seedheads fall forward and bring new plants ever closer to the road I travel.

> ### HERBAL HINT
>
> *If you think you have the right conditions to grow foxglove, buy fresh seed and wait until the ground is frozen. Mark the area where you will scatter the seed, and rake over it to loosen the soil. Sow the seed, using the back of a garden rake to press the seed into contact with the soil. Be patient—foxglove is a biennial (from seed to seed in two generations, or up to 3 years). Seed sown in winter will germinate the next spring, producing fuzzy green rosettes of leaves. The second year, tall flowerstalks will grow up from the rosettes. After blooming, the flowers produce seed for the next generation of plants.*

How to Grow: Foxglove is a hardy biennial or short-lived perennial that grows easily from seed tossed onto a prepared site. In ideal conditions, foxglove plants can grow up to 7 feet tall. The plants will self-sow, or you can plant the tiny seeds indoors and transplant your seedlings outdoors after all chance of frost is past. Foxgloves will tolerate full sun if they are well mulched to keep their roots cool.

Uses: In spite of its long use as a treatment for heart conditions, foxglove is highly toxic. Its uses in the home herb garden are strictly ornamental. Grow the tall, stately plants in the back of the garden in part shade. Rich, moist, well-drained, slightly acid soil will produce lush plants with sturdy stems to hold the showy bell-shaped flowers.

DILL (*Anethum graveolens*)

Native to Southwest Asia and widely naturalized in Europe and North America, dill is an annual that remains ever-present by freely self-sowing. I sow fresh seed only every 3 to 5 years to make sure I have plenty—I can't imagine an herb or vegetable garden without dill.

How to Grow: Dill is simply the easiest herb to grow. Grow it from seed sown in the place where you want it in the garden—a member of the carrot family, dill has a long taproot and generally does not transplant well. Once sown in the garden, it will self-seed for years. Dill isn't fussy about where it grows, so you will see it in part shade and full sun, wet and dry areas, and everything in between. It does like rich soil, and you can see the difference in the dark green foliage when it is well fed.

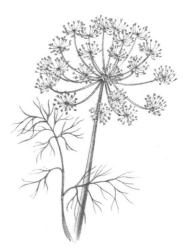

Uses: I use fresh and dried dill in many recipes, but the seeds also add robust flavor to dishes prepared in winter. One of my favorite ways to use fresh dill is to make dill-and-garlic pickles.

Pat's Next-Day Firehouse Bar-B-Q Chicken Salad Sandwiches

Remove the bones and skin from cold leftover barbecued chicken. Dice the chicken pieces and add ¼ cup each diced celery and red onion. Mix with mayonnaise, salt, and pepper to taste. Pile on slices of your favorite bread and add a layer of dill flower heads and lettuce before putting the "lid" on your sandwiches and cutting into serving-size pieces.

HERBAL HINT

Buy extra packages of dill seed for fall planting. Once cold weather has put the garden to rest, it's time to broadcast dill seed—just toss it out over the soil, the way the plants sow it when it falls from the seedheads. Once you have established dill in your garden, it will reseed itself. If you harvest lots of the flowers and seeds for use in your kitchen, you'll want to sow extra to ensure your supply.

EUCALYPTUS (*Eucalyptus* spp.)

If you've experienced eucalyptus only in its
dried form—or in cough drops—then you
have a pleasant surprise coming when you encounter the fresh, growing plant. On a recent
trip to California, I got up close and personal
with eucalyptus trees growing in backyard
gardens and in groves along the coast. The air
was pleasantly scented with their special fragrance, and I especially enjoyed the wide variety of bark colors and textures. Every part
of a eucalyptus tree carries the characteristic
aroma, so a piece of bark that has been shed
is as fragrant as the foliage.

Native to Australia and Tasmania, eucalyptus is equally at home in California and a few other sufficiently mild locations here in the States. There
are more than 500 different species of eucalyptus, a few of which lend
themselves to successful container culture.

How to Grow: While most eucalyptus trees can grow up to 75 feet tall,
don't let that scare you—these plants are easy to grow in containers, and
pruning keeps them container-size and promotes the growth of new
branches. This works out well because most gardeners want eucalyptus for
crafts, and the young clippings are the most useful for such purposes. A
couple of my favorites for growing in pots are lemon-scented gum (*Eucalyptus citriodora*) and *Eucalyptus alpina,* a dwarf species that grows to
about 3 feet tall in a container.

If you're just trying your hand at eucalyptus, you'll want to start with
a plant; these are usually available in 4- to 6-inch pots amid the herbs in
a well-stocked nursery. Transplant your purchase right away into a pot
(at least 8 inches in diameter) that will give the plant room to grow
undisturbed for a couple of years. Place a ½-page section of wet newspaper in the bottom of the pot, then fill the pot with alternating layers of

sand and compost. This will provide the well-drained, fertile soil eucalyptus needs. Water moderately during summer months, when the plant is actively growing. Otherwise, avoid overwatering; eucalyptus is susceptible to root rot. Keep the plant indoors during cold months, and put it outside after all chance of frost has passed. Bring it back inside before cold weather returns.

You can also start eucalyptus from seed with a simple technique called stratification. To stratify the seeds, place them in the refrigerator for 4 to 8 weeks. Sow stratified seeds in early summer in a sand-and-peat-filled rooting box and keep in the shade. Germination takes about 10 to 20 days. Once the seedlings are about 3 to 4 inches high, transplant them to quart or gallon pots. This is all a bit much if you don't have a heated greenhouse, but for those who do it's a remarkable experience, and it gives you access to a much greater selection of species.

Uses: Eucalyptus makes a handsome potted ornamental tree or shrub. Use the prunings in fresh or dried arrangements or in potpourri. Eucalyptus is an important bee herb in Australia, where its nectar and pollen are the main food of honeybees. In home gardens, a pot or two of eucalyptus can help lure honeybees and other insects to your fruit trees and other plants that need pollination. Commercially, eucalyptus is used to flavor cough drops.

FEVERFEW (*Tanacetum parthenium* and cultivars)

You might guess from this herb's name that its historical use was as a treatment for fevers. The pungent aroma of its leaves led many people to believe that feverfew had the ability to ward off disease, and it was commonly planted near houses to purify the air and prevent sickness from entering. More recently, feverfew leaves have been used to relieve migraines. Its small, yellow-centered white daisies are also called "bride's buttons" and were traditionally included among the flowers of a wedding celebration. You may

HERBAL HINT

*Golden feverfew (*T. parthenium *'Aureum') has attractive gold-green foliage that looks great next to purple-leaved plants like 'Purple Ruffles' basil. For greater effect in fresh and dried flower arrangements, try double-flowered feverfew cultivars such as 'Snowball' and 'White Pompon'.*

also find it offered under the names *Chrysanthemum parthenium* and *Matricaria parthenium*.

How to Grow: Feverfew is a hardy perennial that grows from 1 to 3 feet tall with light green leaves and white daisylike flowers. It grows well in average, well-drained soil in sun to part shade and is hardy in Zones 4 to 9. Feverfew self-sows readily and tends to pop up wherever it finds a spot to its liking.

Uses: Grow feverfew as a border around an herb or perennial garden, but don't plant it near flowers that need pollination—the strong scent of the leaves is believed to repel insects, including bees. Use the cheery daisies as cut flowers, or dry them for use in herbal wreaths and arrangements.

FRAISES DES BOIS (*Fragaria vesca*)

Wild woodland strawberries make you work to find their tiny fruits, but the excellent flavor of the berries makes the hunt worthwhile. Fraises des bois (pronounced frez day bwah), also called alpine strawberries, feature the same intense strawberry flavor as woodland strawberries but bear bigger fruits—up to an inch long—that are a bit easier to harvest. European

gardeners have used these petite cousins of
the more familiar garden strawberry (*Fra-
garia × ananassa* cultivars) as border plants
for hundreds of years. I first saw them offered at an astonishing price per dozen in a
catalog and became curious about a strawberry that could command such a figure.

How to Grow: Fraises des bois appreciate
the loose, improved soil of a lasagna bed
in full sun to partial shade and will reward
you with a steady supply of tasty little
berries. The small plants do not spread by runners like other strawberries, but grow into neat clumps that can be divided to increase the size
of your planting. Fraises des bois also self-sow, although not to the point
of being pesky, and you can start plants from seed, too.

Uses: When a friend gave me a dozen fraises des bois plants as a gift, I used
them as a border around my bean towers. Unless you really plant a lot of
these tasty berries, you're not likely to harvest enough fruit to make even
one batch of jam—but fraises des bois are almost too tasty for that, so enjoy
them fresh on your cereal or as a dessert. If you're making jam with regular
strawberries, toss in some fraises des bois for extra flavor. Use the leaves for
a fragrant herbal tea or in potpourri.

HERBAL HINT

*If you have children who visit your garden, invite them to pick
the fraises des bois. They will love hunting for and eating the petite
berries, and you will find that the more berries picked, the more
berries your plants will produce.*

GARLIC (*Allium sativum*)

Pungent and enticing, garlic's presence throughout history is recorded in the tombs of pharaohs, in the writings of early Chinese dynasties, and by early Greek historians. Modern gardeners enjoy garlic at least as much as those ancient garlic growers and can experiment with the various types favored by different cuisines and cultures. From strong and spicy to smooth and mellow, there are garlic flavors to suit almost every taste. Festivals held to celebrate this humble bulb feature everything from garlic-flavored oils and vinegars to garlic ice cream.

Garlic's uses have not been limited to the kitchen—this herb has a number of recognized medicinal properties, too. Allicin, the source of garlic's potent aroma, is an effective antifungal and antibacterial agent, and garlic has been used to treat everything from athlete's foot and influenza to internal parasites, whooping cough, and high blood pressure. This is one herb that truly is good for whatever ails you!

How to Grow: Wherever you garden, you'll enjoy better results if you start with garlic from a local source. Buy a few bulbs from a local grower and plant the largest cloves to start your crop. Lasagna gardens are perfect for growing garlic. Separate a bulb into individual cloves and push them, root-end down, 1 to 2 inches into the loose, rich soil of a sunny garden bed. Where you live will determine the timing of your garlic planting. In most of the United States, plant garlic in fall—like other hardy bulbs—for summer harvest, usually late June to early July. Most garlic grown in cold-winter regions is hard-neck garlic (*Allium sativum* subsp. *ophioscorodon*), characterized by the tall, twisty flowerstalks it produces in late spring. To encourage your garlic to form larger bulbs, cut off these flowerstalks before they start to bloom. Don't toss them out—chop them up to use in stir-fry or salads.

> ## HERBAL HINT
> *Save the largest unblemished cloves from your harvest to plant for the coming year's crop.*

In milder climates, soft-neck garlic (*A. sativum* subsp. *sativum*) is more common; this is the type of garlic that's usually sold in supermarkets, and it tends to keep better than hard-neck types. In California and in the South, plant garlic in early spring for late fall harvest.

Uses: Garlic's many uses are limited only by your imagination and your tolerance (and that of those around you) to its pungent aroma. Use it to season cooking utensils and salad bowls, add its flavor to vinegar or olive oil, roast it and eat it as a vegetable. You can even add a clove or two to your dog's food to help ward off fleas and ticks—if you can stand to have a dog with garlic breath! If you cure your garlic harvest with the tops intact, you can braid the bulbs into an attractive and useful rope or wreath to hang in your kitchen.

Roasted Garlic

Slice the top off a garlic bulb, and drizzle olive oil over the exposed cloves. Bake in a 350°F oven for 30 to 40 minutes or until the cloves are soft. You can also separate the cloves, spread them in a pan, and drizzle them with olive oil before baking. To use, simply squeeze the insides of the roasted cloves onto slices of crusty bread. Roasted garlic has a rich, mellow flavor that's also great for adding to sauces or soups.

GERMANDER (*Teucrium chamaedrys*)

Germander is a handsome herb with small, dark green leaves that resemble boxwood. Once widely used as a treatment for gout, germander is now more popular for the structure it provides as a low-growing hedge in formal herb gardens.

How to Grow: Hardy in Zones 5 to 9, germander is a shrubby perennial that grows 12 to 18 inches tall. Plant it in full to part sun in well-drained, moist soil. You can start germander from seed, but it may take up to 30 days to germinate. Cuttings taken early in the growing season are a quicker, more reliable way to get more of this useful plant. Germander bears loose clusters of a profusion of small magenta flowers, but most gardeners trim these off to help keep the plants dense and bushy. Mulch germander in fall to prevent winter injury.

Uses: Germander is most valuable as a little border hedge for herb gardens. I planted this small hedge around the perimeter of my herb garden at the Potager. In 2 years, I have trimmed the plants six times to form the hedge. Individual plants are short but bushy and incredibly healthy.

GOLDENRODS (*Solidago* spp.)

Sweet goldenrod (*Solidago odora*) is the official state flower of Kentucky and Nebraska, the official herb of Delaware, and my favorite roadside flower each fall. Combined with the purple hues of New York's state flower, the New York aster (*Aster novi-belgii*), whole acres of blooms brighten the way as I travel my usual 45-minute commute across upstate New York. At times, Queen-Anne's-lace joins the picture, giving me the impression that Nature has been doing some serious flower arranging.

How to Grow: A vigorous grower, goldenrod likes full sun and sandy soil and is hardy in Zones 4 to 9. Its preferred haunts along roadsides

and in fallow fields reveal its tough nature, and it actually tends to grow overly tall and floppy in too-rich soil. If you want some for your garden, leave the wild goldenrod where it is and choose from among the many improved varieties. These well-bred selections feature bigger, showier flower clusters and more compact stems that are less likely to flop over. I love goldenrod in my landscape, but I restrict it to flowerbeds where it grows with other vigorous perennials—I don't want it to get a toehold in my herb gardens.

Uses: Goldenrod is a showy standout in the perennial garden from late summer well into fall. In the garden or in a vase, the sprays of bright yellow flowers make striking combinations with asters, chrysanthemums, purple coneflowers, black-eyed Susans, and other fall bloomers. Dried to a more sedate shade of gold, the flowers look lovely in arrangements. During the American Revolution, goldenrod leaves were an ingredient in the "liberty tea" that was used to replace the much-taxed tea imported from England. Today, we're able to enjoy goldenrod's ornamental qualities while sipping cups of genuine tea. Among honey connoisseurs, goldenrod honey is a favorite, and the flowers have long been used as a source of yellow dye.

GOOD KING HENRY (*Chenopodium bonus-henricus*)

Good King Henry came to North America with early European colonists who treasured it enough to include it among the seeds and plants they carried over the ocean with them. A hardy perennial, good King Henry is a reliable source of edible greens in very early spring, just as our bodies begin to crave them.

How to Grow: Sow good King Henry seeds over a sunny prepared bed in spring or fall. Good King Henry is hardy in Zones 3 to 9, but prefers cool temperatures and tends to bolt (flower and set seed) when temperatures rise. Remove flowerstalks before they produce seeds to keep the leaves from becoming bitter.

Uses: Use the young leaves of good King Henry as a substitute for spinach in early spring. Add the young tender leaves to salads; cook older leaves alone or with other spring greens in a little water with some olive oil and salt. Young shoots, up to about 5 inches tall, are delicious peeled, boiled, and eaten like asparagus.

HOPS (*Humulus lupulus*)

Usually produced on an agricultural scale for use in beer production, hops have their place in the herb garden, too. My first experience with this fast-growing vine was a pleasant surprise. I wanted the hops vine to cover the lattice roof of my shade house but didn't want to give up garden space to plant it, so I installed the young plant in a half-barrel near a support post to give the vine something to climb.

The first year, the hops vine didn't do much more than settle into its new growing space. The second year, I had to get a tall ladder to help it up onto the shade house. As soon as the long vines touched the lattice, it seemed to take off. A fast grower, the vine turned out to be an excellent low-maintenance choice for this spot, providing cool, leafy shade every summer after it got going.

How to Grow: Hardy in Zones 3 to 8, hops grow best in loose, moist, enriched soil—they love lasagna gardens! Japanese hops (*Humulus*

> ## HERBAL HINT
>
> *Moisten the hops in an herbal sleep pillow with a little bit of water to keep them from rustling during the night and counteracting their gentle sedative effect.*

japonicus) is usually grown as an annual and is available in an attractive variegated form. For ornamental purposes, there is also a yellow-leaved variety (*H. lupulus* var. *aureus*) that is quite pretty, although not as hardy as its dark green parent.

Uses: Hops may have made their name as an ingredient in beer, but there are other reasons for growing this vigorous vine. Once established, hops grow quickly to provide a living screen over fences, lattice, or arbors. The unusual conelike flowers—the part used in beer-making—have a long herbal history of treating many ailments. Even my own grandmother, when caught drinking a bottle of beer, would swear it was on her doctor's orders! While most of their medicinal uses are no longer in vogue, hops flowers are still recognized for their calming effects. One of my favorite herbal remedies is a pillow containing dried hops flowers. Being an insomniac of many years, I enjoy the soothing effects the hops pillow brings to my often sleepless nights.

HOREHOUND (*Marrubium vulgare*)

Members of my generation remember the taste of horehound candy, but you would be hard-pressed to find a young person who knows the word "horehound," let alone the flavor. You can still find horehound candy in the gift shops of historic sites and museums. In Germany, the candy is still made and used to treat coughs and colds, as a digestive aid, and as an appetite stimulant.

Horehound has been used for centuries by herbalists to treat everything from fevers and respiratory ailments to snakebite and rabies.

How to Grow: Hardy in Zones 4 to 8, horehound thrives in dry soil and is prone to failure in poorly drained sites. Horehound is easy to grow from seed sown in early spring and will self-sow if you don't trim off its burrlike flowers, but it grows slowly and doesn't flower until the second year of growth.

Uses: I use horehound as an ornamental in my white garden. The fuzz on its gray, wrinkly leaves makes it appear almost white, and I enjoy having this traditional herb-garden plant in my gardens. Tea made from the leaves is still used to treat coughs and sore throats.

HORSERADISH
(*Armoracia rusticana*)

Few people feel indecisive about the flavor of horseradish—either you love it or you hate it. I'm quite fond of it myself, and I'm happy to have a healthy patch of it that started with a few roots left over at the end of the growing season at the Potager. Not wanting anything to go to waste, I decided to plant them. Their dried-up, dead-looking condition didn't deter me, and I'm so glad because I've enjoyed a steady supply of this flavor sensation ever since.

> ## HERBAL HINT
> *When preparing horseradish—cleaning and grating the roots—wear safety glasses and a dust mask to protect your nasal passages and eyes from the potent fumes. In commercial operations where horseradish is prepared, the workers are required to wear gas masks!*

Of course, anything as pungent as horseradish must be good for you, so it's no surprise that the fiery roots have been used in herbal medicine for hundreds of years—both externally to treat aches and pains, and internally to relieve coughs and sore throats and as a diuretic. Horseradish didn't gain wide acceptance as a condiment until the seventeenth century.

How to Grow: Plant horseradish roots in improved soil—lasagna gardens are perfect for this herb. Choose a site where you'll be happy to have horseradish as a permanent resident—the roots spread vigorously and new plants sprout from any piece of root left in the soil. Horseradish is a heavy feeder and benefits greatly from frequent applications of well-rotted manure or compost.

Uses: If my nose is stuffy, I open a jar of prepared horseradish and take a sniff to open my nasal passages—it works every time! But my favorite use is as a spicy condiment served with beef. After digging the roots, clean them thoroughly and peel or scrape them. Grate the cleaned roots into a small bowl. Add just enough white vinegar to cover, and store it in the refrigerator in a closed container for up to 3 months.

HYSSOP (*Hyssopus officinalis*)

This pretty, blue-flowered herb is perhaps one of the most underused plants in the flower garden. A member of the mint family, hyssop has a clean, slightly medicinal fragrance. Almost shrubby at 2 to 3 feet tall, hyssop can be trimmed into an attractive low hedge.

How to Grow: Hyssop is a hardy perennial that grows best in full sun in a light, dry soil that's slightly alkaline—go easy on the peat moss in lasagna gardens where you want to grow hyssop. In shade and rich, moist soil, hyssop tends to grow leggy and has less of its signature pungent aroma. In spite of its family ties, hyssop is better behaved than many of its minty relatives and is less likely to become a spreading nuisance in your gardens.

Uses: Grow hyssop in your vegetable garden to discourage cabbageworms, snails, and slugs. It makes a good companion plant in the vegetable garden and a showy plant in the flower garden. Bees find it attractive, so it's a worthy plant to grow near flowers in need of pollination. Add dried leaves and flowers in small amounts to potpourri for a sharp, fresh note in the fragrance.

HERBAL HINT

Cut hyssop back hard in spring after new growth starts to appear. This will let you see which stems are producing new green growth and which are dead. I cut my hyssop border back to the ground each spring to keep it growing evenly as a mock hedge.

LADY'S MANTLES (*Alchemilla* spp.)

Lady's mantle is one of my favorite plants for part-shade areas. Its downy, rounded leaves and low, spreading habit make lady's mantle a charming companion for tall, spiky perennials such as irises, while its clusters of dainty lime green flowers float just above the foliage in late spring to midsummer.

How to Grow: Don't let this plant's delicate appearance—or its genteel name—fool you. This perennial is hardy in Zones 3 to 9, is as tough as nails, and will grow and spread in a broad range of conditions. I purchased my first plants from a reputable nursery and have divided the original plants many times, and I dig and move volunteers from the driveway to other beds frequently. Lady's mantle prefers a cool, sunny growing location and moist, well-drained soil, but it also thrives in partial shade. Once it's established in your garden, lady's mantle needs little care.

Uses: One of the explanations for the name lady's mantle is its long-time use as an herbal medicine to treat female complaints; common lady's mantle (*Alchemilla vulgaris*) is the species most often used by herbalists. The lady's

---

HERBAL HINT

Dwarf or alpine lady's mantle (Alchemilla alpina) is a more petite species, with pretty, silver-edged lobed leaves. It appreciates the same growing conditions as its larger relatives, but grows to only about 8 inches tall. Miniature stems hold sprays of tiny yellow-green flowers in early spring. Alpine lady's mantle is particularly useful in rock gardens and as a border edging.

mantle most often found in the garden, *A. mollis,* makes a lovely ground-cover edging, and its leafless stems of chartreuse flowers add an airy touch to fresh and dried flower arrangements.

LAMB'S-EARS
(*Stachys byzantina*)

If children visit your garden, you'll want to make sure you have lamb's-ears to show them. Once you tell them the plant's name, they'll touch the leaves with the same awe they have for real lambs. For kids of all ages, the appeal of lamb's-ears comes from the silky hairs that cover the 4-inch-long gray-green leaves. The hairs give the leaves a silvery look—and make them pleasant to "pet" when you're puttering in your garden. In the past, the furry leaves were used to bandage wounds; some gardeners still use them as makeshift bandages for cuts and scrapes sustained while gardening.

How to Grow: A hardy perennial (Zones 3 to 9) that grows from 4 to 18 inches tall, lamb's-ears grow best in evenly moist, well-drained, sandy soil in full sun. The plant is a gentle spreader that produces side shoots that you

HERBAL HINT

*Before establishing a bed of lamb's-ears, plant autumn crocus (*Colchicum *spp.*) *bulbs, then plant the lamb's-ears over the bulbs. Autumn crocuses produce grasslike leaves in spring and then bloom in late summer and early fall. Their lovely lilac blooms stand on bare stems just above the silvery background created by the lamb's-ears leaves. My inspiration for this planting came from a visit to Brent and Becky Heath's Bulb Farm in Virginia.*

can divide in early spring. Tall spikes of purple flowers appear in summer above the leaves, giving lamb's-ears an untidy appearance. Cut off the flower spikes to keep plants looking neat and to limit self-sowing. 'Silver Carpet' and 'Big Ears' are two cultivars of lamb's-ears that rarely bloom, eliminating the need to worry about snipping off the flower spikes.

Uses: For a white garden in full sun, lamb's-ears make a wonderful edging that provides interesting texture and lovely silvery gray color. The leaves are also attractive in floral arrangements, and they make a perfect foil for bold flower colors.

LAVENDER (*Lavandula angustifolia*)

The classic fragrance of lavender seems to awaken echoes of romance in even the hardest of hearts. Every part of the plant carries the classic smell of this popular herb. Lavender originated in the Mediterranean; it was used to scent the baths of ancient Greeks and Romans long before it was called "English" lavender. The French also claim affiliation with the heady fragrance of lavender and grow fields of it to supply the fragrance industry. In the United States, commercial lavender production centers in California, where growing conditions are best suited to lavender's needs, but this herb remains popular in home herb gardens and perennial beds across the country.

How to Grow: English lavender is a hardy perennial that grows 2 to 3 feet tall on woody stems with 1½-inch-long lance-shaped leaves. Its fragrant lavender-purple flowers last most of the summer. Hardy in Zones 5 to 8, English lavender does best in Mediterranean-like conditions: full sun and improved, sandy, well-drained soil, with good air circulation around the plants (they are prone to rot in soggy soil so good drainage is a must). Plants benefit from winter protection.

French lavender (*Lavendula dentata*) is a tender perennial with narrow, fernlike foliage. It grows 1 to 3 feet tall and produces very fragrant flowers in spring. It needs fast-draining soil and full sun.

Uses: Although lavender is edible and has a history of medicinal use, most modern-day uses of lavender are related to its clean, fresh fragrance. The scent of lavender shows up in all manner of commercial products, from perfumes and cosmetics to drawer liners and laundry products. Use your home-grown lavender in fresh or dried arrangements, potpourri, or sachets destined for your linen closet or dresser drawers. In the kitchen, lavender is sometimes used to flavor vinegar or jelly; the leaves and flowers may be used in small amounts in salads. Along with marjoram, thyme, summer savory, basil, rosemary, and fennel seeds, lavender is an ingredient in *herbes de Provence,* a traditional blend of herbs from rural France; the dried herbs are combined in a small cloth bag that is added to soups and stews during simmering and cooking.

LEMON BALM (*Melissa officinalis*)

Fragrantly lemony with just a hint of mint, lemon balm is an herb more people should get to know. In the garden, brush against its leaves to release a refreshing breath of lemon.

How to Grow: Lemon balm grows best in full sun to partial shade in rich, moist soil with good drainage. A perennial that's easy to grow from seeds or divisions, lemon balm can reveal its invasive mint-family tendencies when it spreads throughout your garden. To limit self-sowing, trim off the flowers before they produce seeds.

Uses: Dry lemon balm leaves to make delicious hot or cold teas. Medicinally, lemon balm has been used as a treatment for cold sores and is sold in

Germany as a cream for that use. Add small quantities of chopped leaves to salads, or use them to season fish or chicken during cooking. Lemon balm carries big flavor in a small leaf.

LEMONGRASS (*Cymbopogon citratus*)

An evergreen grass from Africa and Asia, lemongrass is perhaps best known for its role in the cuisines of Southeast Asia. The essential oils that give lemongrass its bright lemony flavor and fragrance are also used in perfumes, teas, and aromatherapy. Commercial crops of lemongrass are grown in Florida and Texas.

How to Grow: Lemongrass is a tender perennial that's hardy only in the southernmost regions of the United States (Zone 10). It typically grows to about 3 feet tall; in perfect conditions, it can reach up to 6 feet. In most parts of the country, lemongrass needs to spend the cold months indoors, venturing outside only during the frost-free summer months. Fortunately, it makes an attractive container plant, and its wonderful flavor and scent make it worth the extra effort to have around. Start from seeds or plants from a reputable nursery and a good-size container. Lemongrass rarely reaches its full height potential in a pot. Fill your container with lasagna layers to promote good drainage, and keep the soil evenly moist during the growing season. Cut back on watering during winter months. Inside or out, lemongrass needs a sunny spot.

Uses: Lemongrass is a favorite with cooks from Southeast Asia, who appreciate its clear lemony flavor with flowery overtones. Use the leaves and the somewhat fleshy leaf bases to flavor fish, chicken, vegetables, and tea. Cut a few leaves to add to fresh arrangements; add dried lemongrass leaves to potpourri. Medicinally, this herb is used to reduce fever and to alleviate cold symptoms, headaches, and upset stomachs. Lemongrass oil gives lemon flavor and fragrance to a wide array of cosmetics, foods, and bath products.

LEMON VERBENA

(*Aloysia triphylla,* also sold as *A. citriodora* or *Lippia citriodora*)

A deciduous shrub from Chile and Argentina, lemon verbena has a delightful lemon fragrance and flavor. This herb is cultivated commercially in Europe and Africa for its oil, which is used in bath products and colognes.

How to Grow: In its native South America and in the warmest parts of the United States (Zones 9 and 10), lemon verbena may grow as tall as 15 feet. Where winter temperatures fall below freezing, lemon verbena needs the safe confines of a container that can be moved indoors before cold weather arrives. Container-grown lemon verbena tends not to grow nearly as large and may be easily cut back to keep it a manageable size. Start with a healthy plant from a reputable herb grower, or take a cutting from a friend's plant. Lemon verbena likes rich, moist, well-drained, sandy soil in full sun. When it loses its leaves in fall, reduce watering and keep things on the dry side until new growth begins to appear.

Uses: With its strong lemon flavor, lemon verbena makes a delightful lemony tea and can be used to flavor jellies, beverages, fruit salad, and desserts. Dry the leaves to use in tea or to add to baked goods, chicken, or fish. Use fresh leaves to flavor cold drinks, marinades, soups, and sauces, but remove them from food before serving—they're a bit too tough to eat. Place your pot of lemon verbena someplace where you'll brush against it often and release its lemon fragrance to tingle your senses.

LEOPARD'S BANE (*Arnica montana*)

Uncle Ernie Schleiermacher used to tell me stories about the old days. One was about his first wife: When she was down with sore feet, his concern was with getting her back to work. He would go to the pharmacy and get a little cardboard salve box full of leopard's bane to rub on her feet, and she'd soon be back at work.

In Germany and Austria, leopard's bane has a long history of use as a medicinal herb, but it is not approved for internal use in the United States. Leopard's bane was once freely used to treat the symptoms of old age and angina.

How to Grow: A perennial in Zones 5 to 8, leopard's bane grows best in partial or dappled shade in rich, well-prepared soil full of organic matter—so it thrives in lasagna gardens. An alpine plant, it does best in cool summer areas with low humidity.

Uses: I love having this wonderful little plant in the front border of my part-shade gardens. When its cheerful bright yellow blooms appear in late spring, they bring attention to an often-overlooked part of the garden. The sight of the daisylike flowers makes me feel good, so leopard's bane

HERBAL HINT

Grow leopard's bane in the front of a border, underplanted with small spring bulbs to create two layers of color. Leave room for annuals to add color after leopard's bane has finished flowering.

offers me health benefits just by being in my garden. Isn't that reason enough for me to grow it?

LOVAGE (*Levisticum officinale*)

Celery flavor without the hassles associated with growing celery is what you get from lovage. An easy-growing perennial that deserves to be included in more gardeners' repertoires, lovage was once considered indispensable in the herb garden, for both culinary and medicinal uses. One plant will supply all the celery flavor you need for any dish you are preparing.

How to Grow: Sow lovage seeds in late summer or fall in full sun to partial shade in rich, improved soil, or start with a purchased seedling or a division from a friend's garden. Hardy to Zone 3, lovage isn't fussy, but it prefers evenly moist soil where it can sink its deep root system and enough space to reach its full height of 5 feet. Lovage may reseed itself in your garden if you leave seedheads behind late in the season, but it's not aggressively invasive.

Uses: Every part of the lovage plant—leaves, stems, seeds, and roots—is edible and has a strong celery-like flavor. Add fresh or dried leaves or

> ### HERBAL HINT
>
> *Lovage is a large plant that discourages some gardeners with limited growing space from planting it. I grow this gentle giant in the back of a small garden bordered with a chain-link fence. The lovage grows under the links and into the fence, keeping itself upright and allowing me quick, easy access to harvest.*

chopped stems to soups, stews, stir-fries, vegetables, and salads. Harvest stems from plants at least 2 years old and use as you would stalks of celery, or cook and serve them like asparagus. The leaves can be eaten as cooked greens. Keep flowerstalks trimmed to promote bushy growth, but allow a few to set seed to dry and use as a flavoring much like celery seed.

SWEET MARJORAM (*Origanum majorana*)

Sweet marjoram is often mistaken for closely re-lated Greek oregano (*Origanum vulgare* subsp. *hirtum*), but there are noteworthy differences be-tween these herbs, particularly for gardeners.

How to Grow: A tender perennial from North Africa and Southwest Asia, sweet marjoram is hardy only in Zones 9 and 10, and as a result it is often treated as an annual. Like other tender perennials, sweet marjoram may be grown in a container and moved indoors in fall before frost arrives. Give it full sun and well-drained soil and it will grow into an attractive, bushy plant with a pleasant fragrance. Sweet marjoram seeds are small and slow to germinate, so this herb may be easier to add to your garden in the form of nursery plants. After planting, keep plants evenly moist; use an organic mulch to help keep roots cool. Tiny edible white, lilac, or pink flowers appear at the end of each stem (they taste like the rest of the plant).

Uses: Sweet marjoram has a sweeter, less pungent flavor than oregano. Use its fresh or dried leaves in any dish as a substitute for oregano. Sweet marjoram leaves add a pleasant note to potpourri, dried herbal wreaths, and dried arrangements.

MINTS (*Mentha* spp.)

Even an invasive plant like mint has many uses. During a lecture I was giving in Springfield, Illinois, a person asked about taming a difficult bank, and I suggested mint. I heard a few snickers from the audience and thought, "Here is another instance where folks know a little bit about a plant but not a lot about the whole family of herbs." Mint would put down enough roots to keep that unruly, wet bank intact—and would smell great while doing it.

Far from being shunned for its invasive tendencies, mint has been revered throughout history and is featured in Greek and Roman mythology, as well as in the foods of the Middle East, the Mediterranean, India, and North Africa.

How to Grow: What I refer to here as "mint" is actually several species and hybrids of mostly hardy perennials that feature varying degrees of minty flavor and fragrance. Most are hardy to at least Zone 5 and are not especially fussy about where they grow. They do look better in a bit of dappled shade, and they prefer damp, humusy soil conditions, but if you plant a mint in full sun it will quickly outgrow its space. Mints don't often "come true" from seed—that is, seedlings don't always resemble the parents. If you would like a particular kind of mint—apple, peppermint, spearmint—start with a plant from a reliable source or a division from your favorite mint in your friend's garden. As long as it's not crowding out less vigorous plants in your garden, mint's tendency to spread isn't unbearable, and if it wanders out into your lawn, it doesn't mind being mowed along with the grass.

Uses: Use mint as a garnish, for mint tea, and for mint jelly. Mint is regularly used in food, fragrances, bath products, cosmetics, and medications. It's not surprising that mint is a popular home remedy for bad breath, but it's also used—mostly in tea form—to treat flatulence, insomnia, colds and flu, fever, headache, toothache, sore throat, indigestion, and chapped skin.

HERBAL HINT

Growing mint in gardens surrounding the inn didn't come with the usual problem of containing the mint—we sometimes had trouble finding enough mint to fill 25 to 30 small vases for the dining room tables. The mint gave off a pleasant scent, and guests could pick a breath-freshening leaf after a meal. With the vases full of mint and other herbs, we needed only one flower per vase to add color to the arrangement.

An unexpected bonus was when the mint crept into the lawn. Mowing was much more refreshing after that and, during our outdoor concerts, guests sat on the lawn and were completely enchanted by the minty fragrance.

Clearly, folks appreciate an herb that's safe, effective, and pleasing to the nose and palate.

Mint Jelly

4 cups unsweetened apple juice	4½ cups sugar
¼ cup lemon juice	1 cup chopped mint leaves
1 package powdered fruit pectin	Green food coloring

Combine apple juice, lemon juice, and pectin in an 8-quart pot and bring to a boil. Stir in sugar and mint leaves; bring to a full boil for 1 minute, stirring constantly. Remove from heat, add food coloring, and stir. Skim foam and strain out the mint if desired. Ladle into six hot, sterilized half-pint jars. Cover with hot sterilized lids and process in boiling water for 5 minutes. Remove jars from water and cool.

OREGANO (*Origanum vulgare* subsp. *hirtum*)

There's a little bit of mystery surrounding the identity of oregano (also known as Greek oregano), that popular herb of pizza and tomato sauce. The ancient Greeks and Romans crowned themselves with wreaths of the stuff—the word "oregano" comes from Greek words meaning "joy of the mountain"—but they might have been using wild marjoram (*Origanum vulgare*), a pretty but rather flavorless herb. What this means to gardeners who want to grow their own supply of oregano is: buyer, beware. Oregano seedlings vary a lot in their flavor and fragrance; you're more likely to get the fragrant herb you want by purchasing plants or getting cuttings or divisions from a fellow gardener.

How to Grow: Grow this hardy perennial (Zones 5 to 10) in full sun in average garden soil that's a bit on the dry side and has good drainage. Prop-

HERBAL HINT

Golden oregano (O. vulgare 'Aureum') is a perennial with aromatic green-gold foliage accented with pink flowers. It has a mild oregano flavor and can be used in almost any casserole dish that calls for oregano. Golden oregano grows to 6 inches tall and is excellent in rock gardens or as a groundcover. Plant it in full sun or partial shade in well-drained, slightly dry soil.

agate by division or cuttings. Although oregano is winter-hardy, it benefits from a loose mulch during winter months. With a little care, one plant can last a lifetime.

Uses: Use oregano's leafy stems and flowers in fresh or dried arrangements. Along with basil, oregano is a major component of the Italian seasoning mixes sold in stores. Fresh oregano has a lovely mild taste, while dried oregano is more pungent and can be overpowering if you use too much. Add sprigs of fresh oregano to tomato sauces, salads, and vegetables; chop the leaves finely over fresh tomatoes.

PARSLEY (*Petroselinum crispum*)

Parsley is America's most-used garnish, but its routine appearance on the rim of the plate seems to have cost this wonderful herb the respect it deserves. I have always loved parsley for its fresh, clean flavor, but when you chop up a cup of fresh parsley and add four cloves of crushed fresh garlic and enough olive oil to cover in a covered jar, you are just a tablespoonful on hot pasta away from a delicious meal. Two types of parsley are typically seen in gardens: curly-leaf,

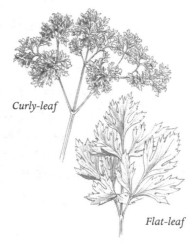

Curly-leaf

Flat-leaf

and flat-leaf or Italian parsley (*P. crispum* var. *neapolitanum*); both types have their advocates, and both work equally well in recipes calling for parsley. Flat-leaf parsley is reputed to have a stronger flavor and is thus preferred for drying.

How to Grow: A true biennial, parsley has a long taproot and will come back its second year, flower, set seed, and then die. Parsley's long taproot makes it hard to transplant successfully, so it's important to sow seeds where you want your parsley to grow. Parsley seeds can be slow to germinate; there are various tricks you can use to encourage it to get growing. My preferred methods are to either soak the seeds in warm water overnight before sowing, or freeze two or three seeds per ice cube, then plant the cubes into the garden. Choose a spot in full sun to part shade; parsley appreciates the rich, loose layers of a lasagna bed.

Uses: Loaded with vitamins, parsley is one of those foods that's good for you and that tastes good, too. Its pleasant mild flavor goes well with many other foods. Drop a few stems of parsley into the water as you're boiling potatoes, or add finely chopped leaves to cheeses, meats, soups, and vegetables. When dried, it's useful for adding flavor to your menu all winter.

HERBAL HINT

If you have a frost-free refrigerator, you can dry herbs easily without having to dodge hanging bunches of them for weeks at a time. In fact, I discovered this because many of the herbs I stored in my refrigerator dried out before I could use them. (Now I do it successfully on purpose.) Use small magnets to hang fresh herbs in plastic mesh bags (the kind onions come in) on the inside walls of the refrigerator. Most herbs take anywhere from 1 to 3 weeks to dry; chopped herbs—spread on a baking sheet placed on a shelf in the refrigerator—dry even faster.

ROSEMARY (*Rosmarinus officinalis*)

This tough evergreen shrub is native to the Mediterranean, where it grows wild. In warmer regions of North America, you can get an idea of how it looks in its native habitat: In California, it's common to see a rosemary "shrub" in the landscape. At Longwood Gardens in Pennsylvania, prostrate rosemary (*Rosmarinus officinalis* 'Prostratus') grows as a large weeping shrub hanging over a stone wall.

Where the year-round climate is less suitable for rosemary, home gardeners grow it in the herb garden all summer, then pot it up to bring inside for winter use. It is a wonderfully fragrant herb and can bring pleasure not only to your palate but also to your other senses. Each fall I bring in two or three small plants and conceal their utilitarian clay pots inside a pretty basket.

My most successful transplanted rosemary plants grow in indirect light, under a table lamp, away from heat. I set the pots on dishes filled with pebbles and water them from the bottom.

How to Grow: All rosemaries like full sun, well-drained neutral to alkaline soil, and protection from cold winds. Evergreen and hardy only in Zones 8 to 10, rosemary can't tolerate prolonged cold or wet soil; this much-desired herb is mostly limited to being an "indoor/outdoor" herb in places where winter temperatures fall below 10°F. Neither can it be deprived of water for long periods—a dry rosemary is a dead rosemary. But don't give up too soon: As long as your rosemary plant is green, it can furnish cuttings to root even though it may be dying. Rosemary is relatively easy to start from seed, but plants are slow to grow to garden size.

Uses: Culinary uses for rosemary, both dried and fresh, are many. Its piney, minty, almost citruslike flavor is especially good with lamb, pork, or wild game. Use rosemary to flavor sausages, stuffing, soups, stews, and vegetables. Cooks love to put fresh sprigs into oils, vinegars, and cooking wine, then use these for dipping (with crusty bread) and to flavor sauces and salads. Rosemary flowers, which range from pink to white to blue, are delicious and beautiful as garnishes and sprinkled over salads.

Rosemary leaves are tough, needlelike, and blunt-ended. Chop young leaves and add them directly to food; older leaves—and dried ones—are hard to digest, so enclose them in a cheesecloth bag before adding them to a recipe, then remove before serving. Or use a sprig of rosemary to flavor food during cooking, and remove it before the food is served.

Rosemary's fresh herbal fragrance is used in many cosmetics and bath products. Use the leaves in sachets to freshen your dresser drawers, or add them to potpourri.

There are several worthwhile varieties of *R. officinalis* for the garden, featuring different flower colors and growth habits:

- **'ARP'** is hardy in Zones 7 to 10 and can remain outdoors year-round in Zone 6 with winter protection. 'Arp' has an upright habit with lemon-scented leaves.

- **'BENENDEN BLUE'** bears large sky blue flowers amid narrow dark green leaves and has an upright to trailing habit.

- **'PINKIE'** has short gray-green leaves and bright pink flowers.

- **'PRIMLEY BLUE'** has an upright habit and blue flowers on stout stems.

- **PROSTRATE OR CREEPING** varieties have arching stems that trail along the soil. These are good in hanging baskets, containers, and rock gardens; along walls; or as bonsai.

HERBAL HINT

You are just a wire coat hanger and a creeping rosemary away from your own topiary. Plant your coat hanger and your rosemary plant in an attractive pot, and begin to train your plant to grow up the form by tying the stems to the hanger with a bit of raffia.

HERBAL HINT

To root rosemary cuttings, cut softwood stems about 3 inches long and remove an inch of leaves from the base of each stem. Using clean pots and new potting soil, fill the pots to within 1 inch of the top and moisten the potting soil. Dip the stem ends in rooting compound, and insert into filled pots. You can use one large pot to root 20 or more stems, then transplant them to individual pots. Keep the cuttings warm and consistently moist for about 2 weeks before checking for roots.

- **'ROSEUS'** has pink flowers.

- **'SEVERN SEA'** has trailing stems with violet-blue flowers.

- **'SUDBURY BLUE'** has blue-green leaves on upright stems and mid-blue flowers.

- **'TUSCAN BLUE'** is one of the fastest-growing upright selections, with dark blue flowers and glossy leaves. It can grow to 6 feet tall in suitable conditions and has good flavor for cooking.

RUE (*Ruta graveolens*)

Not everyone appreciates the pungent smell of rue, and some people have a downright alarming reaction to this attractive blue-green herb: Brushing against its leaves can cause a blistery rash at the points of contact. Once used as a medicinal herb to treat a wide range of ailments, rue is primarily grown as an ornamental in modern gardens.

How to Grow: An evergreen and somewhat woody perennial, rue is hardy in Zones 4 to 9

> ## HERBAL HINT
>
> *I have a small herb hedge bordering the front garden at the Potager.*
> *In the front, lamb's-ears lean out over the walkway. Behind them is*
> *a row of dark green germander that I clip to keep it looking neat.*
> *The next row is a planting of calamint (Calamintha sp.) with soft*
> *gray foliage that appears to weave in and out of the overall planting.*
> *For contrast I planted a row of blue-green rue, which I keep*
> *trimmed, and the resulting look of the hedge is pleasing to me and to*
> *others who walk its edges, admiring the only in-town herb garden.*

and tolerates a wide range of soil conditions. Rue will thrive even in highly alkaline soils where most plants languish, although it's at its best in average, well-drained to dry soil in full sun. You can grow it easily from seeds sown indoors in winter or from divisions or cuttings.

Uses: Rue is a great contrast plant in the garden. Its pretty blue-tinted foliage makes grays look grayer and greens look greener. The rounded spatula shape of its leaves contrasts well with the texture of other plants, making it a nice addition to a small herb-garden hedge.

SAGE *(Salvia officinalis)*

There's a lot more to like about common sage than what it does for a Thanksgiving turkey and family traditions. This hardy perennial herb with pebbly gray-green leaves and a slightly bitter but clean flavor makes an excellent accompaniment for all kinds of savory foods—meats, eggs, cheeses, vegetables—and it has properties that make it a useful home remedy as well.

Sage's gray-green foliage looks good in the garden, too; it helps mediate relations between hot flower colors and contrasts nicely with fine-textured foliage. I grow lots of sage each year for the kitchen and for wreaths. One wreath I make each year starts with a wild grapevine base. I plump it out with artemisia foliage and end with the addition of 50 or 60 little bundles of herbs. Sage is the primary herb I use, and the finished wreath is pale sage green with off-white (artemisia), and tiny bits of yellow tansy.

How to Grow: Common sage is hardy in Zones 4 to 8 and will thrive in full sun and well-drained soil. Sage is easy to start from seed but needs a couple of years to grow to reach harvesting size. Water seedlings and young plants well until they are established; after that, sage is reasonably tolerant of dry soil. Prune sage in spring to keep it from flowering and to keep the plants looking tidy. There are many different cultivars of common sage, including golden sage (*Salvia officinalis* 'Aurea'), purple sage (*S. officinalis* 'Purpurea'), and tricolor sage (*S. officinalis* 'Tricolor'); these selections are attractive in the garden and may be used like common sage but tend to be less winter-hardy.

Uses: Add fresh sage leaves to salads, egg dishes, breads, and vegetables. Lay sage leaves over roasts before cooking. Crumble dried leaves to use as

---

HERBAL HINT

*Pineapple sage (*Salvia elegans*) is a tender perennial that's usually grown as an annual in cold climates and is hardy only as far north as Zone 8 or 9. The entire plant, including its red, tubular flowers, has the scent of pineapple. Pineapple sage's showy red flowers borne on tall green leafy stems are a late-season treat for southern gardeners. Northern gardeners can also enjoy it, but they will need to bring it indoors before frost arrives in fall. Use pineapple sage in fresh flower arrangements, fruit salads, and breads; mince it into cream cheese; or dry it to make tea.*

seasoning. Sage leaves also make an attractive addition to fresh or dried floral arrangements. Sage has antiseptic properties and has been used as a treatment for minor cuts and bruises. Sage tea is good for colds; it's also recommended—when cooled to a comfortable temperature—as a footbath to help relieve sweaty, smelly feet. Bees like to visit sage flowers; their scent may repel other insects, including cabbage moths.

⌇

ST.-JOHN'S-WORT *(Hypericum perforatum)*

Described variously as a wildflower, a weed, and an herb, this humble plant was named for John the Baptist because it begins to bloom on St. John's Day, June 24. Over the years, St.-John's-wort has been used to drive out evil spirits, as a digestive aid, and to treat minor wounds and sores. More recently it has attracted attention as an effective antidepressant and sleep aid.

How to Grow: St.-John's-wort is hardy in Zones 5 to 9 and will grow just about anywhere with little or no special treatment. Plant it in a sunny, not-too-rich lasagna bed and it will grow less like a weed and more like a desirable, shrubby perennial with a long-lasting display of showy yellow flowers.

Uses: I first became a fan of St.-John's-wort after I saw it in a foundation planting in South Hampton, New York. The 2- to 3-foot shrub was still in bloom and very pretty in September. The flowers were huge and seemed to dwarf the shrub's leaves. I use it in my gardens to bridge the gap between perennials with shorter bloom seasons. Its bright yellow flowers never fail to cheer me up.

WINTER SAVORY
(*Satureja montana*) and SUMMER SAVORY (*S. hortensis*)

Winter savory

Summer savory

Both types of savory, winter and summer, have been used in Europe as culinary herbs for thousands of years. Fragrant and flavorful, these two related herbs have similar uses in the kitchen but require different treatment in the garden.

How to Grow: Both winter and summer savory prefer full sun and average, well-drained soil. Winter savory is a shrubby, somewhat woody perennial, hardy to Zone 6; summer savory is an annual that is very sensitive to cold. Both can be grown from seed, although winter savory is a bit slower to start this way and may be easier to start from divisions or cuttings.

Uses: Use savory in fish, game, meat dishes, stews, and soups. Savory contains properties that aid digestion and is a time-honored seasoning for all kinds of bean dishes, as well as for brussels sprouts, cabbage, and other vegetables. Use winter savory in the landscape as a rock-garden plant.

GARDEN SORREL (*Rumex acetosa*)

Garden sorrel is a tart, lemon-flavored herb, grown mainly for its bright green leaves, which are delicious when added fresh to soups, salads, and sauces. A vigorous, slightly weedy perennial, sorrel is high in vitamin C.

How to Grow: One of my more memorable gardening experiments was with sorrel seed. I grew a remarkable 400 plants with the seeds from one packet. Ten years later, I am still picking sorrel at the Potager from plants

originally grown on and moved from my farm. Needless to say, this hardy perennial (Zones 4 to 9) is easy to grow from seed!

Sorrel grows best in organically enriched moist soil, in part sun to part shade. Seed sown in early spring will be ready to harvest by late summer, but I get the best results from seed when I sow it in pots in a protected area and plant out established plants in fall. To extend your harvest of tender leaves, remove sorrel's flower stems as soon as they appear. 'Profusion' is a nonflowering selection that allows you to harvest tender leaves all season.

Uses: This lemony green is best in early spring when the leaves are young and tender. French sorrel (*Rumex scutatus*) has smaller leaves than garden sorrel and a more concentrated flavor. Culinary uses for sorrel are many; here are some of my favorites:

- Make a lemony sorrel sauce from flour- and butter-based roux; thin with chicken stock or milk, and flavor with finely chopped sorrel leaves.
- Add chopped fresh young spring leaves to salads, soups, sauces, eggs, fish, chicken, or soft cheeses.
- Puree the leaves with a bit of olive oil and add to sauces or mayonnaise to give them a fresh green color and tangy lemon flavor. This puree is also good drizzled on a plate before a main course of chicken or fish.
- Make an early spring sorrel soup (a tradition at our house).

SWEET ANNIE (*Artemisia annua*)

An annual artemisia with a sweet-as-can-be nature, sweet Annie is an herb that every crafter wants in the garden for its attractive, lacy leaves with their sweet, long-lasting fragrance. Wreaths made of Sweet Annie are just as sweet in appearance and smell as the name implies.

How to Grow: Grow sweet Annie from seed started indoors in late winter or sown directly in the garden in a sunny spot with average soil. Like most artemisias, sweet Annie tolerates dry conditions. Spacing is critical because sweet Annie can grow up to 6 feet tall and 3 feet wide; allow 3 to 4 feet between plants. If you let sweet Annie go to seed, it will self-sow and you'll always have enough to go around.

Uses: Harvest branches of sweet Annie in late summer after the tiny yellow, almost beadlike blossoms appear. Use sweet Annie in fresh arrangements, or hang in bundles in a warm, dark, dry place; use the dried bundles to make wreaths, swags, and garlands. Add sweet Annie to sachets to keep moths out of clothing; this herb is also reputed to repel mosquitoes.

TANSY (*Tanacetum vulgare*)

I grow tansy in several places at the Potager, planting it in spots where I think ants might have access to the building. Also known as "ant fern," tansy has been widely used as a repellent for ants, flies, beetles, and even mice. Knowing this, when I cut my tansy back several times a year, I use the cut branches to mulch plants growing close to the building at other points. My approach is far from scientific, but it seems to work—I've yet to see an ant inside.

Although it has a long history of use as a medicinal and culinary herb, tansy's modern-day role is as an ornamental and for its insect-repelling abilities—internal uses are no longer considered safe.

How to Grow: Tansy is a perennial, hardy in Zones 4 to 9. It thrives in sun to partial shade in any kind of dry soil, but it will not tolerate constantly wet soil conditions. I like to plant it near a fence in the back of a border. The fence helps protect the plants from too much wind (which makes them fall over). Tansy is a vigorous spreader, but it's not hard to control with frequent division and by weeding out unwanted seedlings.

Uses: Plant tansy near your house to help repel ants; use tansy in arrangements on picnic tables and windowsills to chase off flying pests. Tansy's clusters of small yellow button flowers add color to dried arrangements, wreaths, and swags.

FRENCH TARRAGON
(*Artemisia dracunculus* var. *sativa*)

Tarragon has earned a permanent place in my gardens. I brought one plant with me when I moved from the farm to the Potager, and it still grows in the original spot. Each year I take a few cuttings in case the old plant dies out, but I have not yet needed a replacement.

This anise-flavored herb is often overlooked by new cooks, but its distinct flavor is an essential feature of French cuisine. Flavor is a clue to tarragon's identity, too—French tarragon has a pronounced anise flavor and fragrance, while Russian tarragon (*Artemisia dracunculoides*) has almost none of the characteristic flavor or aroma.

How to Grow: Tarragon is a hardy perennial in Zones 4 to 8. Make sure you buy plants of French tarragon, or get cuttings from a friend's garden.

> ## HERBAL HINT
>
> *Tarragon vinegar is easy to make and very flavorful. Just drop sprigs of the herb into a bottle of white vinegar, add garlic cloves, cap tightly, and set aside for about 2 weeks. If desired, strain out the tarragon and garlic cloves and add a fresh sprig of tarragon to the bottle before serving. Tarragon vinegar makes an excellent salad dressing.*

This plant cannot be grown from seed—tarragon seeds offered for sale are the taller, weedier, and less flavorful Russian tarragon. Plant tarragon in full sun to part shade in the evenly moist, well-drained soil of a lasagna bed. Mulch around it to protect it from frost heaving during winter months.

Uses: This bitter and aromatic herb is best used on chicken or other poultry, on wild game and pork, in egg dishes, and in sauces such as béarnaise and hollandaise. The smell and flavor of licorice is intense when meat is roasted with an herb crust of tarragon, garlic, parsley, salt, and pepper.

THYME (*Thymus vulgaris*)

One of the most beautiful, unexpected sights I ever encountered was in the empty lot next to the house of Terry and Dave in Willowmoc. Dave had mowed a path through the field, and growing in the path was thyme in full bloom and full fragrance. We surmised it had escaped from a farmhouse that had been removed many years before and naturalized in the surrounding property. In full bloom, it formed a carpet of lavender flowers.

Of the more than 300 species and varieties of this agreeable herb, I've grown about 20 different types—a wealth of thymes to me, but a small fraction of the many that are available. Because of my love for rock gardens, stone paths, and rock walls, I have collected my thymes mostly because of their unusual leaves, fragrance, or flowers. Although there are shrubby, upright types of thyme, my favorites tend to be the low-growing groundcover kinds that are well suited for tucking into small cracks and crevices and for planting in pathways.

How to Grow: Hardy perennials (Zones 4 to 9), thymes grow best in well-drained soil in full sun to partial shade. You can grow plants from seed sown in spring, from softwood cuttings rooted in summer, or by division in fall. When installing a new path, I may purchase several thymes to plant right away, but I have had great results by sprinkling seed directly where I want it to grow. Most trailing thymes can be lifted with roots in place along the stems for easy replanting.

Uses: Thyme is most often thought of as a seasoning for soups, stews, and chowders—it's essential in Manhattan clam chowder—plus it is one of the main ingredients of "jerk barbecue," a Jamaican marinade. Thyme's flavor also goes well with meats and cheeses, vegetables, and other herbs—it's one of the *fines herbes* of French cuisine and also a regular ingredient in bouquet garnis. Medicinally, thyme has been used to treat respiratory ailments.

I think of thyme as an interesting groundcover to grow between stepping-stones and along the path. It gives off a pleasing fragrance when touched or stepped on. I also use thyme in all my herb baskets. Here are some of my favorite varieties:

- **CARAWAY THYME** (*Thymus herba-barona*): Rub this thyme's spiky leaves and you'll be reminded of a loaf of rye bread.

- **'DOONE VALLEY'** (*T.* 'Doone Valley'): This is one of the best path thymes because it forms a dense mat; its dark green leaves and bright pink flowers make a pleasing splash of summer color.

- **GOLDEN THYME** (*T.* × *citriodorus* 'Aureus'): This is the lemon-scented, yellow-variegated thyme I plant along the sides of the

---

HERBAL HINT

One of the first things I did when I moved from the inn to my house was to lay a fieldstone path and plant thymes and other creeping herbs between the stones. Each time I entered the front door of my home, I walked by (and on) some of my favorite plants.

---

walkway on the shady side of the herb garden. It thrives there and brings wonderful light to a rather dark place.

- **OREGANO THYME** (*T. nummularius* 'Fosterflower'): Oregano thyme serves as thyme and oregano, plus it produces a lovely blanket of white flowers.

- **SILVER THYME** (*T. × citriodorus* 'Argenteus'): This thyme has silver-edged leaves and is my favorite for my basket herb gardens and deck planters.

- **WOOLLY THYME** (*T. pseudolanuginosus*): I have loved the look of this lovely fuzzy gray thyme since I first saw it in a garden water feature setting, where it draped its woolly tendrils over rocks.

VALERIAN (*Valeriana officinalis*)

Also called garden heliotrope, valerian is an old-fashioned garden perennial with a long history of use as an herbal medicine. Herbalists swear by valerian as an effective natural tranquilizer, but commercial products based on this useful herb are not widely available in the United States. In this country, valerian is used mostly as an ornamental addition to perennial borders and historical herb gardens.

How to Grow: Hardy in Zones 3 to 10, valerian will grow just as well in sun as in shade, in any soil, although it thrives in rich, moist soil. In summer, its 3- to 5-foot-tall stalks are topped with clusters of tubular pink to white

sweet-scented blooms. Plant valerian toward the back of the border with plants 15 inches apart. Provide stakes while plants are small to keep mature plants from flopping onto the plants in front of them. Divide plants every 2 or 3 years. Valerian will reseed and, once established in your garden, will stay for years.

Uses: Commercially produced in Europe for medicinal uses and as a flavoring, valerian adds a tall, stately note to herb gardens, and its flowers are lovely in fresh arrangements. I use it in the back of all my gardens for its height and sweet fragrance. I also recommend it to my friends who are batty about their cats; felines are at least as fond of valerian as they are of catnip. If you plant valerian in your garden, you'll need to protect it from the affections of roaming cats, who will roll and tumble in it. Just like catnip, valerian makes a kitty-pleasing filling for a sturdy fabric cat toy, although humans tend to find the fragrance of dried valerian much less pleasing than that of dried catnip.

SWEET VIOLET (*Viola odorata*)

These dainty, pretty perennials will always remind me of my Aunt Violet, but that pleasant connection is just one reason why I enjoy keeping sweet violets in my gardens. Their dark purple, white, or pink flowers have a lovely sweet perfume, and I love to use these sweet, edible flowers to garnish all sorts of foods.

Sweet violet's heart-shaped leaves once earned it the name heart's-ease; it was used

> ## HERBAL HINT
>
> *Violets can be dried and used in many craft projects. Pressed-flower artist Pat Yelle uses old phone books to press all her flowers but can really maximize her efforts with violets. "Violets are so small and easy to press, they take up less room, so they can be placed in every page of a phone book," she explains.*

in love charms in Shakespeare's time. The flowers and leaves have also appeared in recipes over the years, and both are rich in vitamins.

How to Grow: Sweet violets will grow happily in Zones 4 to 8 in moist, woodsy soil in full to partial shade. You can start sweet violets by sowing seed outdoors in fall, or divide an existing clump to get your violet patch started. The plants will spread gently by stolons into suitable spots in your garden.

Uses: Although their days of being used for medicinal purposes are mostly in the past, sweet violets are still an important part of an herb garden. Whether used as an attractive border or a blooming groundcover, violets bring good cheer and happy thoughts. At the Potager, we use violets in our salads and cold dishes, as well as for decorations. They can be candied or used fresh on all sorts of desserts. My favorite way to use fresh violets is as a decoration on wedding cakes.

SWEET WOODRUFF (*Galium odoratum*)

I will always associate sweet woodruff with Adelma Simmons and her beloved Caprilands Herb Farm in Coventry, Connecticut. Adelma served her lunch guests a cup of May wine with sweet woodruff flowers floating in it in the appropriate month.

Sweet woodruff is common in Europe's deciduous forests, perhaps most famously as a groundcover on the floor of Germany's Black Forest. During the Middle Ages, sweet woodruff was used, with other herbs and wildflowers, as a strewing herb on castle floors to improve the air. The sweet, haylike fragrance of the dried plant was probably a pleasant relief from the stale, moldy odors that abounded at that time.

How to Grow: Sweet woodruff is perennial in Zones 3 to 9 and will thrive and spread in moist, shady, woodsy sites. Its pretty whorled leaves and clusters of dainty white flowers make it an attractive groundcover in a woodland garden. Sow sweet woodruff seeds outdoors in fall, but be patient: They may take many months to germinate. Purchasing plants or getting divisions from a fellow gardener may prove an easier way to enjoy this delightful shade dweller in your garden.

Uses: A key element in the preparation of May wine, in which sprigs of sweet woodruff are soaked in sweet wine a few days before it's served, this herb is not otherwise recommended for internal use. When dried, sweet woodruff has the sweet fragrances of vanilla and newly mown hay; it makes delightful sachets to freshen drawers and linen closets, as well as a pleasant addition to potpourri.

WORMWOOD (*Artemisia absinthium*)

Wormwood's rather loose, spreading habit makes it less useful in the garden than other, more shapely artemisias, but as the active ingredient in the infamous drink absinthe, wormwood boasts the most interesting history. Although true absinthe is no longer available in most countries, wormwood is still used to flavor vermouth and other alcoholic beverages. It was also widely used as a worming medication for livestock and people, but its internal use is no longer recommended.

How to Grow: A ferny, gray-green perennial that grows up to 4 feet tall, wormwood is not fussy about location and will grow as well in dry, poor soil conditions as it will in enriched soil. Like most artemisias, wormwood requires good drainage and prefers full sun to partial shade. Hardy in Zones 4 to 6, wormwood may be started from seed sown outdoors in fall or from cuttings or divisions taken in early spring or fall.

Uses: I use wormwood to repel insects both in the garden and in the home. In one of my gardens, wormwood grows near the roses and at the edge of the bean and tomato garden. It is particularly useful as a repellant against mosquitoes and black flies. Add sachets of dried wormwood to closets and

HERBAL HINT

Once I left the inn and moved to my farm, I had time, energy, and space to grow many herbs I had only heard about before. Southernwood (Artemisia abrotanum) was the first herb I planted to help me repel aggravating insects that might have kept me out of the garden. I planted it in places that allowed me to walk into the bush and rub the oil from the plant onto my exposed body parts. After making sure I had enough protection on arms and legs, I used the oil from my hands to apply it to my face. Finally, I stuck a sprig in my hatband.

After seeing me do this wormwood dance, a fly fisherman's wife asked me why. Once I explained my bizarre behavior, she bought several southernwood plants for their fishing lodge grounds. The word got around about southernwood and began a run on the fine-textured herb—I couldn't root new plants fast enough.

drawers to repel moths and beetles. I cut the stems back twice a year to keep the plants looking good and use the prunings fresh or dried in floral arrangements.

YARROWS (*Achillea* spp.)

Common

Hybrid

Yarrow earns its keep wherever you grow it, and it has an interesting history as a medicinal herb to boot! In the perennial garden, yarrow is a dependable performer with showy, long-lasting blooms. In the cutting garden, yarrow produces abundant, colorful flower heads that add pizzazz to fresh and dried arrangements.

Wild or common yarrow (*Achillea mille-folium*) plays a big part in my flower arrangements and in my cottage-style gardens. Its flat heads of small white flowers add great texture to fresh arrangements, and they dry to celadon green, a favorite color for my home. Common yarrow has smaller flower heads than most hybrid yarrows, so it takes more of its blooms to make a wreath or arrangement, but the results are worth it.

Yarrow hybrids top my list for full-sun perennial plantings and offer many different sizes and colors. Yellow is my favorite color, and there are so many shades of yellow yarrow that I would be hard pressed to pick a favorite, but 'Coronation Gold' is a definite contender. When I started my herb farm, I planted 3 gallon-size 'Coronation Gold' plants in one of the first lasagna beds. Every year, I dug and divided the plants in that bed, potting up all but about 12 plants that I replanted. In 5 years I must have potted and sold at least 100 gallon-size plants per year—a pretty good return on my initial investment!

How to Grow: Yarrow needs little care and is so good-looking and easy to grow that it should be in every garden. In the wild, yarrow grows along the roadside, in fields, and in waste sites and hayfields that have been allowed to go wild. Although it has few needs, it grows in lasagna gardens at a rate that keeps the plants strong and healthy. Full sun and sandy, well-drained soil are the keys to success with yarrow, and under those conditions, pests and diseases don't trouble it.

Uses: Cut yarrow stems before the flowers open completely. For fresh arrangements, strip off the foliage and stand the stems in warm water until you're ready to use them. For dried use, strip away foliage and either hang stems upside down to dry (for compact flower heads) or stand the stems in a dry vase (to produce more open, relaxed flower heads). The yarrow should be dry and ready to use after about 5 days.

While most of us have access to commercial bandages when the need arises, yarrow can be a handy remedy in a pinch. Try using a few yarrow leaves—placed directly on the wound—to stop the bleeding of small cuts or insect bites the next time you find yourself in the garden without your first-aid kit.

My favorite use of common yarrow and pale yellow hybrid yarrow is as part of a pale, almost white and celadon green herb wreath. See page 204 for directions on making a wreath yourself.

CHAPTER 3

When I think of edible flowers, I first think of nasturtiums, pansies,

and basil flowers. Because they are my favorites, I routinely plant them in easily

accessible beds and containers. The planters bordering the ramp that leads to the

front door of the Potager are attached to the handrails and are located at about

waist level for easy harvesting. Throughout the growing season I keep them

filled with herbs, flashy annuals, and plants with edible flowers.

Edible Flowers in the Lasagna Garden

Flowers: The Fun Parts of Plants

I've had people resist eating flowers for a variety of reasons: "They might not taste good" and "They're too pretty to eat" are the two most common. Of course, as the mother of seven (now grown) children, I have lots of experience in helping people overcome their hesitance about eating what's put before them. And frankly, flowers are a much easier "sell" than the vegetables I occasionally had to convince my kids to eat!

Although flowers seem exotic when they appear in food or as a garnish, there's really nothing new at all about eating them. Edible flowers, especially crystallized violets, were immensely popular in the Victorian era, and although the flower craze of that time faded long ago, there are a few flowers that are traditionally and widely eaten without anyone considering it the least bit unusual.

I used to think that there must be millions of people who had never eaten a flower of any kind until I started thinking about exceptions to that viewpoint. It's pretty hard to find a person of Italian ancestry who hasn't enjoyed a few batter-dipped zucchini blossoms fried in olive oil. And daylily buds are a popular ingredient in dishes served in China and across much of Asia. Dill flowers, used in pickling and eaten along with whatever else has been pickled, account for the flower consumption of another substantial part of the world's population. If you add in things like capers (the pickled flower buds of a Mediterranean plant) and saffron from saffron crocuses (*Crocus sativus*), you can see that eating flowers is actually much more common than most people realize.

Whether you consider edible flowers to be exotic or common, there's a certain amount of pleasure involved in eating bright petals, plump buds, and delicate blossoms. Flowers are the fun parts of plants, and the main reason, at least in my opinion, for eating flowers is for the enjoyment you get from their beauty and from the colors, flavors, and textures they add to other foods. You're not likely to make an entire

HERBAL HINT

The more you know about edible flowers, the more you will be able to enjoy them. If you are going to eat a floral garnish in a restaurant, it helps to know what flowers are safe to eat, as well as how the flower on your plate was grown. I have been served exotic flowers that have to be imported into this country or grown in greenhouses using lots of chemicals. When in doubt, ask. Since edible flowers are for fun, there's no reason to eat the wrong kind of flower or one that's been doused with pesticides. There's nothing fun about that!

meal of nothing but flowers, nor are they likely to become a staple in your diet. The point of eating flowers is pleasure—edible flowers are fun accessories that enhance the more ordinary foods around them.

From Herbs to Edible Flowers

After I retired from innkeeping and moved to the farmhouse across the road, I spent most of my time creating wonderful gardens without digging or tilling. It wasn't long before there were more than 30 gardens. These gardens were planted with a diverse collection of plants that could survive in Zone 4. Surprisingly, this was almost everything I ever wanted to grow: small fruits, vegetables, herbs, and ornamentals.

The four big beds outside the back door (see pages 108 and 109) were my favorite places to grow an ever-changing assortment of herbs and perennials. I could see every inch of those beds from my summer kitchen and tearoom windows. I could have coffee in the morning while sitting on the deck and be in the midst of the gardens. I built an instant patio in the middle of the gardens with an umbrella table and chairs: I covered the area with large cardboard boxes, overlapped at the edges, then covered the cardboard with bark chips. I moved the outdoor furniture in place, added some containers packed with annual flowers for color, and in no time at all I was finished. I just had to sit back, relax, and eat flowers, herbs, and vegetables right from the garden.

Seeking Fieldstone

A lot of the stone that I used to pave my garden paths came from the ditches along the roads near my home. Each time the road department cleans the sides of a road, they use a scraper that takes away soil that might otherwise slide down onto the road. With each swipe of the blade, stone is also scraped away or exposed. Over time, the exposed stones usually fall down into the drainage ditches that run along both sides of the road.

Another place to find fieldstone is a fallow field where an old house, barn, or stone wall once stood. Of course, if you are thinking of harvesting stone from someone else's property, be sure to get permission first.

Being able to reach into each of the growing areas was critical. When planning a garden and the paths, keep that in mind so you don't have to step into the beds to get to the crops. Each time you step on the soil it becomes compacted, encouraging weeds and making life harder for the things you want to grow.

I wanted my paths to be just wide enough for one person to walk along them at a time. This would force visitors to the garden to take their time, read the tags, and stop to pick flowers and other treats. I believe that not everything should be done in social groups. My little paths were meant to encourage individuals to walk into the gardens one at a time and stay for a while.

The fieldstone paths in my little gardens were works of art in my eyes, and I enjoyed them more each year as flowers and herbs planted themselves between the stones.

When I installed those gardens, I used large cardboard boxes, used for shipping mattresses, on top of the sod. I topped these with peat moss, old hay, compost, and the contents of a cow barn to get the layers started. As the growing season progressed, I added inches of grass clippings, chopped leaves, and some soil from the road department when they cleaned the ditches.

Once the big 12 × 12-foot squares were made, I began adding paths in different configurations to access each section. It took all summer and most of the fall to collect enough stones and lay them to complete the paths.

MY BIG PATH PROJECT

When I moved to the farm, one of my first projects was the garden surrounding the front door. Neighbor Ed Wehner put up my signature green picket fence and installed a gate on either end of the side sections for easy access from the driveway and into the front garden. I planned the path.

It was my first stone path, and I was more interested in the design than where the stone was going to come from. I drew a meandering line from one gate, up to the front door, then to the other gate. I made the path the same width as the gate openings, widening it at the entrance to the house. Once I was satisfied with the configuration of the path, I defined it. Using two large gutter nails attached to each other with a piece of string the width of the path, I drew a line down both sides of the edge of the path.

I dug out the space between the lines to a depth of 4 inches and removed the soil. I refilled the 4-inch excavation with 3 inches of sand and began placing my stones in the sand. Building a fieldstone path in sand is like working a puzzle. The stones are placed depending on what looks and fits best. I ran out of stone long before I reached the front door.

As I worked, I documented the stone path saga in my newspaper garden column, lamenting the lack of stone. In no time, stones began arriving in the front yard. When I came down to get the paper, I would see several flat stones leaning against the fence. I wondered who was leaving them but figured it was a friend or someone who didn't want to be identified in my column. I kept filling in spaces with donated stone and thanked the anonymous donor in my column. (I later found it was a dear friend and neighbor, Lou Temple. This darling man was nearly 90 at the time and, like many mountain people, still able to live alone, drive, and do a day's work.)

Looking for roadside fieldstone in the mountain country of Sullivan County is easy. Any road will do. On Shandelee Mountain, all roads lead down, and all lead you to more country roads. My favorite road was one where the actual road cut across old stone walls. Every time the road crew came along to clean the ditches, they left behind parts of the old walls in the

---

Buying Stones

Order pallets of stone in just the right size and color for your project. A pallet costs $100 to $150, depending on the type of stone you choose. That's not a bad price, considering how long it took me to collect enough stone for the paths for four gardens. If cost is a factor, as it was with me, extra effort and time will get you all the stone you need for free.

---

ditches. As stone walls were now a part of the county road system, the stones were mine for the taking.

The plants in my gardens changed every year, but my favorite planting was the first one. The paths were bordered with short herbs and edible flowers, then other plants were added in graduated heights inside the borders. The borders were important to me for appearance and accessibility. After installing the borders, I used what space was left to grow taller vegetables and herbs.

Those gardens were where I showed off my great love of garden detail. The paths were installed first, and then the gardens were planted in the spaces that remained. That way I had access to every inch of the growing space. I could also walk around each garden on the grass paths that connected the gardens.

During those years my daughter Mickey lived at the other end of our 13 acres. It wasn't unusual to see her in the gardens, dressed for work, and eating her breakfast on the run. She once described her meal as a feast of small strawberries, tomatoes, different greens, peas, and beans. She would take her lunch in a baggie filled with small cucumbers, tiny squashes, tomatoes, and lettuces.

All through the growing season she would come home from work and go back to the garden for carrots, potatoes, beets, and beans for her supper. I used to watch her from the office window, where I would be writing, and remember the child who wouldn't eat anything green. Long after we had all left the table, after the dishes were done and some children were back at the table to do homework, she would still be there with a pile of peas on her plate.

(continued on page 110)

MY BACKDOOR GARDEN BEDS

Garden #1: I created four outer triangles by placing a diamond-shaped path inside the square. I get to a large central diamond from a single line of stones going across the middle. I planted four different thymes next to the outsides of the four triangles. Inside each of the triangles, I grow short herbs and edible flowers: curly parsley, spicy globe basil, tricolored sage, and winter savory. In this bed I grow four different dianthus in four different colors.

Garden #2: Four short paths lead to a central circle. In the center, a tomato cage supports early snow peas and, later, patio tomatoes. Around the edge of the circle, I planted golden sage. Each of the smaller beds has a different herb or short vegetable as a border and a different vegetable in back: Eggplant paired with bush wax beans; a lone squash plant shares with multiplying onions; a bush cucumber next to nasturtiums; and two or three Swiss chard plants with a border of spinach.

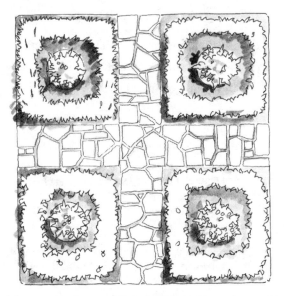

Garden #3: A path forms a simple cross. All the borders in this garden are either lavender or alpine strawberries. The beds are planted with four different tomatoes inside cages supported by tall stakes at three points.

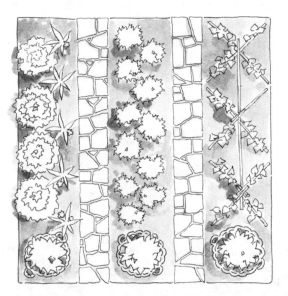

Garden #4 : Two parallel paths cut the square into three long beds. The outside bed has three bamboo tepees connected at the top with long bamboo stakes. Heritage pole beans grow on the tepees. Bottomless baskets grow potatoes, one at the end of each row. Italian parsley takes up the entire center row. The last row is given over to 'Red Russian' kale, interplanted with perennial Welsh onions.

A TURNING POINT

During the early days at the herb farm on Shandelee, I could often be found creating more gardens day in and day out. It was on one of those bright summer days when Steve, one of my neighbors, walked up the road with

Pick Your Own Salad

Summer dinner guests at the farm were usually surprised when I asked if they would like to go to the garden to pick our dinner salads. They would get a list of what was needed, a basket, and scissors for their harvest. Searching for and collecting salad ingredients was relaxing entertainment.

They harvested cut-and-come-again mixed salad greens, snow peas or slender young green beans, radishes, scallions, and red and yellow patio tomatoes. Last on the list were edible flowers. They were the jewels of the salad and deserved to be on top of the basket: chive blossoms, nasturtiums, scarlet runner bean flowers, and the tender tips of 'Purple Ruffles' basil flowers.

Gardens are for sharing. Those of us who have gardens sometimes forget that there are millions of people who do not. There are also millions who have never harvested a salad of fresh-from-the-garden fruits and vegetables. I have always enjoyed giving at least a few people the chance to get closer to the origins of the food they eat.

his weekend houseguest. They crossed the road and entered my gate. I welcomed the idea of some rest and stopped to lean on my rake and greet them. It was easy to tell Steve's guest was a gardener. She was enjoying my gardens way too much.

Steve Menges lived about 1 mile from my farm on Shandelee. His family had once owned a summer hotel called Menges Lakeside, located on the down side of North Shandelee Road. I had known Steve's grandmother, Anne Menges, who had started the hotel business. Steve lived part-time in a small house across from the old hotel. He would usually come up from the city on weekends and, in the summer, stop and see me in my gardens. This day he brought his houseguest, Cathy Wilkinson Barash.

Cathy was from Cold Spring Harbor, located on Long Island, New York, and a garden writer. She had had articles in many home and garden magazines and had published two books on tulips. Her new book on edible flowers was in the early stages of development, and Cathy was busy doing research and looking for opportunities and locations to take photographs for the book.

During the early days of our friendship, Cathy came to my farm to photograph and write about my gardens for her next two books. We spent hours in the kitchen, creating dishes from our recipes. I have listed some of my recipes that were used in Cathy's book.

HERBAL HINT

Upside-down tomato cages can become mini compost bins. Each time you clean the garden or harvest crops, deposit the trimmings and waste material into the cage. Use these easy-to-access cages to deposit kitchen wastes and make compost right where you need it.

All recipes appeared previously in *Edible Flowers: From Garden to Palate* by Cathy Wilkinson Barash.

Calendula Petal Rice

This recipe easily serves 8, but I make extra for the next day's lunch.

4 cups water	½ cup calendula petals, finely chopped
½ teaspoon salt	
½ cup onion, finely chopped	2 cups long-grain rice
2 chicken bouillon cubes	

In a medium saucepan bring water to a boil. Add salt, onion, bouillon cubes, calendula petals, and rice. Stir. Reduce heat to low, cover, and simmer for 18 minutes.

Burgundy Borage Punch

1 quart burgundy wine, chilled	Thin slices of orange (optional)
1 quart orange-flavored seltzer, chilled	Borage flowers

Mix burgundy and seltzer in a punch bowl. Add thin orange slices. Freeze borage flowers in ice cubes or in an ice ring to float in the punch. The brilliant hue of the flowers against the diluted red of the wine punch is perfectly beautiful.

Dilled Potato Salad with Dill Flowers

8 medium red potatoes, unpeeled	½ cup tender dill flowers, finely chopped
¼ cup onion, coarsely chopped	
1 cup celery, coarsely chopped	¼ cup fresh parsley, coarsely chopped
2 hard-boiled eggs, coarsely chopped	Salt and pepper
1 cup mayonnaise	Whole dill flowers
¼ cup brown mustard	

Dice potatoes into 1-inch cubes and boil until tender. Drain potatoes and toss with onion, celery, eggs, mayonnaise, mustard, chopped dill flowers, and parsley. Add salt and pepper to taste. Garnish with whole dill flowers.

Roast Chicken with Fresh Marjoram Flowers

¼ cup vegetable oil
Salt, pepper, and paprika
¼ cup all-purpose flour
1 frying chicken, cut into serving-size pieces

1¼ cups marjoram flowers, divided in half
1 cup white wine
1 chicken bouillon cube

Preheat oven to 375°F. Place a low-sided pan in the oven and add vegetable oil. Add salt, pepper, and paprika to flour in a plastic bag. Shake each piece of chicken in bag until coated. Place chicken pieces in hot oil in preheated pan. Bake for 45 minutes. Remove chicken to warm platter.

Place roasting pan on stovetop over medium heat. Add half of the marjoram flowers; slowly add 1 tablespoon of the remaining flour/seasoning mix to pan drippings and flowers. Stir continually for 5 minutes. Slowly add white wine and bouillon cube. If sauce gets too thick, thin with water.

Pour sauce over chicken and sprinkle with remaining marjoram flowers.

Macaroni Salad with Pea Flowers and Thyme Flowers

2 cups elbow macaroni, cooked until just tender, drained, and set aside
¼ cup each chopped red, green, and yellow bell peppers; celery; and onion
¼ cup peeled and grated carrot

¼ cup thinly sliced snow peas
½ cup pea blossoms
1 tablespoon thyme flowers
1 cup mayonnaise
¼ cup white vinegar
Salt and pepper

Place cooked and drained macaroni in a large bowl with peppers, celery, onion, carrot, peas, pea blossoms, and thyme flowers. In a separate bowl, mix mayonnaise with vinegar and whisk together to blend. Season macaroni mix with salt and pepper to taste. Add mayonnaise mix and blend thoroughly.

HERBAL HINT

Keep a garden journal. As your edible herbs begin to bloom, taste their flowers and jot down your reactions to each flavor. Later you can refer to your notes as you decide which flowers to use as edible garnish and in creating your own recipes.

My First Edible Flower Menu

During my quest for herbal knowledge, I made lots of discoveries. One was that the flowers of most herbs carry the flavor of the plant. By using the flowers, you add beauty and color with a subtle flavor to everyday foods. Once I knew what to look for, my own gardens contained all the edible flowers I needed.

Once you start growing and eating flowers, you may find yourself involved in a hobby that can have some pretty nice results. That's what happened to me. From the time Cathy Barash gave her first lecture and slide presentation to a group at my herb farm, I was hooked. I realized I had been missing out on something that was already a part of my gardens.

At that first lecture, we ended the evening with a small repast of dishes featuring edible flowers. Cathy urged me to use what I had in the garden in new and innovative ways. She even put on one of my aprons and helped with the preparation.

After a few phone calls to some of the ladies who attended that evening, and even to Cathy herself, I have put the menu together to share with you.

Menu

Biscuits with Thyme Flowers and Chive Flower Butter
Daylily Flowers with Nasturtium Flower Cream Cheese
Rose Cake with Rose Petal Frosting
Mint Tea with Mint Flower Crusted Lemons

Looking back, I can see it was a very simple offering, but the evening and the fun food sampling made an impression on the 20 women who attended. I remember the menu was planned based upon what was in the garden and in my refrigerator. Town—and the one grocery store—was 5 miles away, and I had made it a habit not to dash up and down the mountain, for a total of 10 miles, to get last-minute items.

How Edible Flowers Put My Herb Business on the Map

The evening was a success and the beginning of another phase of my new life in the garden. After that the schedule at the herb farm was full of groups who came by bus to tour the gardens, learn about lasagna gardening, and enjoy an herbal repast in the tearoom.

I added to the menu and in cooler months served a hot soup before the salad. And the salads got a boost by adding an old southern recipe for chicken salad that started with roasting the chickens with fresh tarragon. (Today we regularly serve the Southern Girl, a southern chicken salad served on a bed of greens with Red Delicious apples and walnut halves. In summer, it's garnished with edible flowers.)

And the gardens, well, it was the beginning of something wonderful. I planted with an eye on not just having flowers in the garden but also eating flowers from the gardens. With the list of "what's fit to eat and what's not" firmly planted in my mind, I grazed the gardens to see what was right to serve with what and what I needed to serve my guests.

I knew it was all going really well when more and more people could be seen taking pictures of their food before they ate. I took a few pictures also, and when I look back at those days, I see things I had forgotten.

THE FIRST BUSLOAD

When my first bus was due to arrive in a few weeks, my daughter Mickey came home from Washington and helped me put it all together. We cut small saplings and used them for curtain rods. We hung handwoven Austrian panels I had purchased in a box lot at a local auction. They looked marvelous and cost me one dollar for eight panels. I love a bargain!

Mickey also brought folding tables and chairs purchased at a chain store for very little. I had been too excited to think of seating for my little room. The only long wall held another long sapling, where I hung dried flowers and herbs from the gardens. From the small branches I hung hand-painted garden gloves, garden hats, tools, and little signs with sweet sayings.

Word gets around, and even though I thought I was retired, before I knew it I was as busy as I had ever been. Garden clubs, botanical gardens, and arboretums put together bus tours and visited the gardens. I began keeping a calendar to help me remember who was coming when. One thing led to another and the gardens—the main attraction—became the focus of my new business. Planting them each year to make them look different from the year before led me to make posterboard layouts with plant locations clearly noted.

Pat's A-List of Edible Flowers

In the café at the Potager, we love the way our customers admire the flowers garnishing the food. Folks love the flavor of our rice pudding, but it can look bland. The addition of a dash of cinnamon doesn't add color or ex-

HERBAL HINT

Even if you're not concerned about changing your gardens' appearance each year, it's still helpful to keep drawings of your garden designs along with your garden journal. Note the names and locations of the things you plant—and use pencil so you can note changes to your plan and substitutions in your plant lineup. These drawings will prove helpful when someone asks you what a particular plant is, when something disappears, or when something surprises you by being better than you expected and you want to go back to the nursery to get more.

Edible Flower Safety: What's Fit to Eat and What's Not!

There are some simple rules to follow when deciding what flowers to eat:

- Know what you're eating and know that it's safe.

- Enjoy the flowers you eat—if they don't taste good to you, don't bother.

- Eat only flowers grown without chemicals.

- Do not eat flowers that come from a florist or commercial nursery unless you are sure they have been grown organically.

- If you have asthma or allergies, eat flowers with caution—some types of flowers may trigger allergic reactions in sensitive individuals.

- Eat only the flower petals. Remove and discard the pistil and stamens.

citement, but a single Johnny-jump-up and a mint leaf or two atop a poof of whipped cream makes our rice pudding exciting.

What follows is a list of the edible flowers I consider to be the best and the easiest to use. I've put them in alphabetical order to make them easy to find and have included notes about how I like to use them. My ultrafavorites (because they are so easy) are marked with an asterisk (*). If you're just getting started with edible flowers, you might want to begin with the easiest ones.

ANISE HYSSOP
(*Agastache foeniculum*)

Anise hyssop is a member of the mint family and a tender perennial that grows to 4 feet in full sun to part shade. Every part of this plant has the scent of anise and the flowers, with help from bees, are a source of anise honey. Cut back the flower stalks to keep the plant flowering for a long time. This practice

> ### HERBAL HINT
>
> *If you're short on time, use anise hyssop flowers to give a homemade touch to "store-bought" refrigerator yeast rolls or cookie-dough-in-a-tub. Just add chopped flowers and bake.*

also keeps the plant from self-seeding. Start harvesting anise hyssop from the time flowers first come into bud. Add the flowers to salads and breads and use as a garnish.

Sprinkle anise hyssop flowers on the tops of yeast rolls, corn sticks, or sugar cookies before baking. Add candied fruits to yeast roll mix and chopped anise hyssop flowers, about a teaspoon to every six rolls, and discover the flavor of Italy.

*ARUGULA (*Eruca vesicaria* subsp. *sativa*)

An annual member of the mustard family, arugula is a cut-and-come-again green with a spicy, tangy flavor. This means you can cut plants to the ground and new greens will come to cut again. Once you let the plant go to flower, the leaves become a bit bitter, but if you like the spicy taste, the flowers still add excitement to a salad. I like the flavor of arugula in all stages but love the look and flavor of the flowers. The flowers are small and white with a spicy punch.

Dress a bunch of greens with a mild vinaigrette dressing, pile them in the center of the plate, and add strips of grilled chicken or pork to the top. Add crisp bacon and sprinkle a few arugula flowers on top for garnish and flavor.

*BASILS (*Ocimum basilicum* and other species and cultivars)

Basil is one of the most popular herbs; however, I think most basil flowers go unused. The flowers that are borne on stalks at the tip of each branch of a plant have as much flavor as the leaves and stems. By pinching back the flower stalks, you can keep basil bushy and producing leaves for a long time, but you have to stop pinching to get flowers to enjoy as well as leaves. I try to pinch the flowers off when they are small and tender. I use the entire flower, stem and all, in many ways, including basil flower butter, basil-flavored olive oil, basil vinegar, in tomato sauce, in oil and garlic for pasta, on salads, on pizza, in soups and stews, in flower pesto, and in yeast breads.

Purple basil flowers on the stem impart their special flavor and color to herb vinegars. Just drop a flower stem of any kind of basil into a bottle of white vinegar, and in about 1 to 3 weeks you'll have lovely basil vinegar. Use fresh basil at the end of cooking or just before serving. A few fresh basil flowers sprinkled on a salad, on pasta, or in soup impart intense flavor and add beautiful color.

HERBAL HINT

Basil needs full sun and good drainage, but not much else in the way of care. I sow basil seed directly in my garden in several successive plantings during spring and early summer. I cut one section for leaves and let one section go to flower.

*SCARLET RUNNER BEAN
(*Phaseolus coccineus*)

A tender perennial that's grown as an annual vine, scarlet runner bean is an attractive ornamental with the ability to quickly cover a trellis with vines. The brightly colored flowers taste like young green beans and look good on boiled new potatoes or sprinkled over salad greens. Any flowers you don't eat will produce beans that you can eat like green beans or by shelling out the beans after the pods have matured.

BEE BALM (*Monarda didyma*)

Scarlet bee balm is another member of the mint family and truly an American herb. Already favored by native Indians when the first settlers arrived, bee balm is a part of our heritage. We still use the flowers to make tea and in cookies and cakes. I love a cup of bee balm tea, but bee balm butter is my favorite way to enjoy the flavor of these flowers.

To use bee balm flowers, pull the curving, irregularly tubular petals from the central flower head, discard the head, and use the petals as a garnish or incorporate into soft butter. Sprinkle bee balm petals on salads, chicken, or fish. For hot tea, steep 4 teaspoons of fresh petals, or 2 teaspoons of dried petals, in 4 cups boiling water.

My experience with scarlet bee balm butter was a happy discovery that I could capture the flavor of certain flowers by incorporating them in butter, freezing the butter, and using it in the winter when I was hungry for the flavor of herbal flowers.

When my bee balm was at its best with early blooms, I harvested a basket of flowers. I washed the

HERBAL HINT

Bee balm can grow to be 3 feet tall, so I like to put it in the back of my herb garden, where it is less likely to shade out shorter plants. A member of the mint family, bee balm does have a tendency to spread and can take over a garden if you don't keep it in check. I dig up bee balm plants that have "walked" forward and use them to replace older plants.

flowers, then pulled the petals free. I measured ½ cup of petals and softened 1 pound of butter. I mashed the petals into the butter and divided it into 4 parts. I placed one part on a strip of plastic wrap and worked the butter into a roll about an inch thick, then I sealed the rolls of butter in the plastic wrap and put them in the freezer.

On hot breads, added to baked fish or chicken, and even on a broiled strip steak, the bee balm butter brought back memories of summer with each bite. The roll of red-flecked butter was pretty and made a lovely addition to my table when I set out a buffet for guests. Making scarlet bee balm butter was such a delightful experience that I experimented with other edible flowers mixed with butter. No matter how many I try, I still prefer the flavor and look of bee balm petals to any other flower butter.

TUBEROUS BEGONIA

(*Begonia* × *tuberhybrida*)

If you can bear to tear away the beautiful petals of tuberous begonia, you will be pleasantly surprised to find they have a tangy citrus flavor. The flavor is a perfect complement to fish or chicken.

BORAGE (*Borago officinalis*)

Borage is a rough-leaved, shaggy plant with beautiful blue star-shaped flowers. Borage can be a pest in the garden if you are a neat freak. I don't have that "neat" problem, and though I haven't planted seed for 6 years, I still have borage plants coming up each year. Some visitors to my garden find borage so attractive that they want to buy a plant right away, and I have to convince them to buy seed instead and have borage in abundance—in the future.

A hardy annual, borage is a handy herb to have. The more flowers you harvest, the more flowers you will have. I pick them to float in punch that we serve to groups visiting the Potager and for freezing in ice rings.

BROCCOLI (*Brassica oleracea*, Italica group)

How many times have I let the heads of broccoli go to flower by mistake? Too many to count. Now I don't care if some go to flower because I use the flowers on salads and in hot dishes. Once a broccoli plant's main head is harvested, smaller shoots form along the sides of the plant. If you can't get to all your large heads of broccoli, let them go to flower and cut the side shoots when you need broccoli for the table.

Here are a couple of ways that I like to use broccoli flowers:

- Fresh broccoli salad: Combine chopped broccoli; red, yellow, and orange peppers; and spring onions. Toss with oil-and-vinegar dressing and garnish with broccoli flowers.

■ Fresh broccoli and garlic with pasta: Stir-fry broccoli and garlic in olive oil, pour over pasta, and garnish with broccoli flowers.

*CALENDULA (*Calendula officinalis*)

Calendula is one of my favorite edible flowers—its bright yellow and orange blossoms add cheery color to almost any food. I received my first plants from a friend and master gardener, Bea Rexford, many years ago. By cultivating the seeds from the original plants, I have a bumper crop of calendulas each year.

Color alone keeps calendula on my list of favorites. When I have lots of flowers, I layer the orange and yellow petals with homegrown greens in a Cobb salad. Another favorite use for calendula is to add ½ cup of chopped petals to 4 cups of boiling water, 2 cups of rice, and 1 teaspoon of salt for a brilliantly colored side dish.

CHICORY (*Cichorium intybus*)

Chicory grows wild in the Northeast, and I like to pick a few stems for the bright blue flower petals and bitter taste. Rather than pick near the roadsides where the flowers may carry residues from exhaust and other pollutants, I pick in an unsprayed field or near my own gardens. There's nothing any prettier than a field of wild chicory and Queen-Anne's-lace growing together. In the South, chicory roots have long been used as an addition to coffee.

*CHIVES (*Allium schoenoprasum*)

Chives are probably the most-used edible flowers from my gardens, and they're so easy to grow. I can divide and divide, and then divide again. I can give away as many plants as friends and family will take and still have plenty of plants to sell at the Potager. Every little floret has the sweet flavor of a mild onion, and every part of the plant is edible. For a hint of onion flavor, pull individual flower petals from the central head, discard what's left, and use just the petals in salads or as an edible garnish. Steep whole flower heads in vinegar to give it a subtle onion flavor.

GARLIC CHIVES (*Allium tuberosum*)

Each part of the garlic chive plant, even the flowers, has a hint of garlic. When the flowers petals are added to salads and other light dishes, you are never overwhelmed with garlic flavor. You can keep garlic chive flowers coming all season if you cut the plant back to just above the ground after the first flowering.

CHRYSANTHEMUMS
(*Chrysanthemum* spp.)

That popular old standby for color in our fall gardens and Halloween displays is also a great way to add color and flavor to fall foods. Chrysanthemums come in a rainbow of colors and can be encouraged to winter over with a blanket of mulch.

Chrysanthemums have been cultivated in China since 500 B.C., both as a beautiful flower in the garden and as food.

*DAYLILIES (*Hemerocallis* spp. and cultivars)

I use the common tawny daylily (*Hemerocallis fulva*) that grows wild along the roadsides near my home in Westbrookville, New York. We live way off the beaten path with few cars on the road, so I'm not worried about exhaust fumes on the flowers. These cheery daylilies are so plentiful that I always have enough to use some fresh as well as buds to dry for later use.

After a good shaking to dislodge any insects, I wash the flowers, remove the stamens, and fill them with herbed cream cheese. The flowers are crunchy, with a pleasant, subtle flavor. Harvest the buds before they unfurl for thin slicing and stir-frying, or dry them to use in Asian-inspired recipes. I have so many of these flowers that I can also use them for centerpieces and food garnishes.

DIANTHUS (*Dianthus* spp. and cultivars)

No matter what you call them—clove pinks, pinks, carnations, or gillyflowers—you won't want to leave these charming blooms out of your gardens. Dianthus flowers have a sweet, clovelike fragrance that is pleasant

HERBAL HINT

Shake all flowers before eating them, especially tubular flowers like daylilies or squash blossoms. An insect may be hiding inside.

in the garden and in the kitchen. I sprinkle the pretty pinked petals of these sweet-smelling flowers in salads and on desserts. If you're diligent about removing the spent flowers from your dianthus, the plants will flower over most of the growing season, and even if you don't keep up with the deadheading, they will bloom in both late spring and fall.

*DILL (*Anethum graveolens*)

The entire dill plant is useful, but it's the flowers I use most often. I pick them when they are young, and even the stems are tender. They can be incorporated with cream cheese or chicken salad or just chopped into a bowl of salad greens. When cucumbers are in season, peel and slice them into a bowl and add chopped dill flowers and sour cream for a special taste treat. Later, when the blooms are closer to going to seed, I use them to make quick dill pickles or pickled green tomatoes and onions.

ELDERBERRY (*Sambucus nigra*)

Growing in the wet ditches and roadsides, elderberry bushes abound in the western end of Sullivan County, where I live. I have my favorite spots where I clip a few flower heads to make a cup of tea or just to experience the sweet taste of the flowers on my tongue. I come back when the berries are ripe to gather ingredients for elderberry and rhubarb jam.

ENGLISH DAISY (*Bellis perennis*)

Whether you add the petals to a salad of pale garden greens, use them to garnish newly dug potatoes, or sprinkle them over the frosting of a plain cake, English daisy petals are more than what the history of the flower promises. In England, these sweet little flowers are no more than pesky weeds, but for the flower eater they are a delightful treat.

*GARLIC (*Allium sativum*)

To enjoy garlic flowers, you need to grow garlic in your own garden or have access to a market that includes a local garlic grower. Garlic's round, green, and slightly sinuous flowerstalks are called scapes; these scapes should be cut before the flowers open and begin to set seed because this takes away energy from the main business of growing large cloves below the ground. The scapes have a pleasantly delicate garlic taste and are tasty when chopped up and added to salads or stir-fries. If you don't mind their strong fragrance, the tall, curvy scapes make interesting additions to flower arrangements.

HIBISCUS (*Hibiscus* spp.)

Hibiscus has a mild citrus flavor and an exotic look. Domestic hibiscus bushes can produce hundreds of flowers, but they have little flavor beyond a hint of citrus or cranberry. With such showy flowers, flavor is almost beside the point—it's their color and shape that is a great source of pleasure. Remove the stamens from hibiscus flowers and fill them with seafood or cream cheese–based foods. Garnish with extra flowers.

HYSSOP (*Hyssopus officinalis*)

Hyssop flowers are used as a flavoring for the liqueur Chartreuse and as edible flowers. Unlike many herbs, hyssop actually thrives in shade and average soil. Hyssop flowers have a bitter flavor but are used to flavor vinegars and in bread stuffing.

*JOHNNY-JUMP-UP (*Viola tricolor*)

With heart-shaped leaves like all of its violet family relatives and sweet, almost facelike flowers, little Johnny-jump-up is one of the most romantic flowers. In simpler times, lovers sent one another small bunches of the tricolored flowers to convey romantic thoughts, and Johnny-jump-up flowers are reputed to have been an ingredient in love potions. I find they candy well and look really good on salads and desserts.

LAVENDERS (*Lavandula* spp.)

Lavender has a long history of use in bath products and sachets that are used to scent linen closets. During the Middle Ages, lavender was one of the herbs used for strewing because of its clean, pungent aroma. Lavender is often included in potpourris and teas as a calming ingredient. Today many recipes call for lavender, and you can use the flowers as well as the leaves.

SWEET MARJORAM

(*Origanum majorana*)

A less hardy cousin of oregano, sweet marjoram produces copious quantities of pink to purple flowers that may be used to flavor vinegars, as a flavorful garnish for chicken or fish, and in salads. In addition, sweet marjoram flowers can be used fresh or dried in flower arrangements.

This is one of my favorite flowers to eat. I always have an abundant supply of the little purple flowers, so I can be very generous with them. Their flavor is somewhat like thyme and a bit like oregano. They're wonderful on roast chicken.

*MINTS (*Mentha* spp.)

Every part of the mint plant smells and tastes lovely, and because the plant is such a prolific spreader, you can use baskets of mint flowers and still have more left in the garden. For a lovely tea, add mint flowers to boiling water and steep. A sprinkling of mint flowers on chocolate ice cream, chocolate cake, or chocolate pie is very refreshing.

MUSTARD

(*Brassica hirta, B. juncea, B. nigra, B. rapa*)

Mustard is an important herb for its sharp, spicy flavor. The greens picked in the spring are truly wonderful after a winter of ho-hum flavors. Mustard flowers contain the same flavor and are pleasantly spicy. Like its cousin broccoli, the mustard greens in your garden may bolt—produce flowers—making the leaves undesirable at the table. That's when it's time to enjoy the flavor of the flowers. Add mustard flowers to olive oil and sauté fish or chicken in it, add the yellow flower petals to salads for a bitey taste, or sprinkle the flower petals over bland vegetables.

*NASTURTIUM (*Tropaeolum majus*)

If pressed to choose my favorite edible flower, I'd have to say nasturtium. I enjoy the look of every part of the plant, and its flavor is unequaled. At times I taste radish in the seed at the bottom of the flowers. Other times I taste pepper when I add the leaves and stems to green salads. When I stuff a flower with mild-flavored cheese, it complements the spicy flower.

I use nasturtium flowers, stems, and leaves in butters, on salads, and for a splash of vibrant color and flavor in almost anything that seems to need "something." To add a bit of peppery zip to foods, use chopped or whole flowers sprinkled on as garnish. One of my favorites is a mesclun salad mix with chopped nasturtium flowers, leaves, and stems mixed in and whole flowers garnishing the top. When I have lots of nasturtium flowers, I also like to use them to make pepper vodka.

Pepper Vodka

1   bottle of vodka (inexpensive vodka works fine)
2   cups nasturtiums per quart jar
    Wide-neck quart jars with lids

Funnel
Strainer
Decorative bottles

Fill each wide-neck quart jar with 2 cups washed nasturtiums. Pour vodka over flowers to cover; cap and place in a dark area for 2 to 3 weeks. Prepare decorative bottles and, using strainer and funnel, pour the flower-infused vodka into bottles and discard the old flowers. Float several new flowers, stems, and leaves in each bottle of flavored vodka and seal with a cork. Keep one bottle in the freezer.

ORANGE (*Citrus sinensis*)

If you're lucky enough to live in a place where orange trees grow and bloom, you can enjoy the flavor of the flowers long before the fruit is ready to pick. Orange flowers have a sweet, citrusy flavor and a fabulous fragrance. Add orange blossom petals to fruit salads or use them to make a delightful sorbet.

GREEK OREGANO (*Origanum vulgare* subsp. *hirtum*)

Delicate-looking white flowers reveal the identity of true Greek oregano. (If the blooms are pale pink or purple, the herb you're looking at is marjoram.) Even experienced herb gardeners and garden writers get it wrong sometimes, and less flavorful types of marjoram are often sold as oregano. Oregano's dainty white flowers have a delicate oregano flavor and may be used in the same ways as the leaves.

*PANSY (*Viola* × *wittrockiana*)

The little flower with the sweet face has a grassy flavor and lends wonderful color to every food you add it to. The same

HERBAL HINT

All the violas—pansies, Johnny-jump-ups, and violets—are edible and very pretty in salads, frozen in ice rings or cubes, or candied and used atop cakes. For the best effect, use only perfect flowers.

old green salad becomes an eye-opening experience when you add pansies to it. The more pansies you pick, the more flowers your plants will produce.

PEAS (*Pisum sativum* varieties)

The pretty white blossoms that appear on the pea vines in your garden have the same sweet, fresh flavor as the pods and peas they will eventually become—unless you eat the flowers. But the flowers are prettier, and you can enjoy them sooner than the pods and peas that follow them. Sprinkle the flowers of garden (also called English) peas, snow peas, or sugar peas over salads. Be sure to plant extra peas if you're going to eat pea flowers, or you won't get as many peas as you had planned.

RADISH (*Raphanus sativus*)

When you see radish flowers, it means you have left your radishes in the ground too long, and the roots are woody and inedible. But never mind—the petite white, pink, or yellow flowers have a refreshing, bitey flavor that can take the place of radishes in a salad. They are spicy, so use them sparingly—a little goes a long way.

HERBAL HINT

*The sweet peas (*Lathyrus odoratus*) in your flowerbed may look like the pea flowers in your vegetable garden, but this family resemblance is where the similarity ends. Sweet peas are poisonous and should not be eaten or used as a garnish on food.*

*ROSES (*Rosa* spp.)

The romance of the rose isn't lost when you eat its pretty petals. A sprinkling of rose petals adds color, flavor, and elegance to even the blandest of foods. Before you eat rose petals, pinch off the little white piece at the base of each one where it was attached to the flower head. Rose petals are a welcome addition to salads, and we often use them on salads at the Potager during the months when the roses are blooming. Using your favorite jam recipe, add the petals from unsprayed damask roses. These rose petals do not have the bitter white portion at the base. If you use other types of rose petals, you have to remove the white portion. You can also place rose petals on the bottom of a cake pan before pouring in the batter; the finished cake will have a delicate rose flavor and fragrance. Sugered rose petals are a pretty addition to desserts.

*ROSEMARY (*Rosmarinus officinalis*)

A taste treat wherever they're used, rosemary's pretty little blue flowers are less pungent than the herb's foliage. The delicate flavor of rosemary flowers stands out when they're used to season veal or chicken fillets. I love to add the flowers to olive oil that's used for dipping crusty bread. Rosemary flowers are also wonderful in butter-based bread spreads and in salads. They add a delicate rose-mary flavor to vinegar, which then makes an excellent dressing for a salad of greens and mixed flower petals.

*SAGE (*Salvia officinalis*)

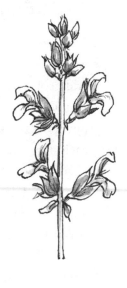

Sage is the one herb that has been a part of my life since childhood. It was the only seasoning I knew for a long time, and it was the first edible flower I ever ate. My daughter Mickey cooks at the Potager and her favorite edible flower is the sage flower. Each flower transports the flavor of sage to your palate.

I grow a lot of sage, so I don't mind picking the flowers from a few plants, but if my sage-growing space was limited, I might leave all the sage flowers for the bees and hummingbirds that love them. Because sage is one of my favorite flavors, I use it in many ways. Sage flowers in fried corn fritters takes only a few flowers, and a few sage flowers go a long way in adding flavor to a salad. Common sage blooms in May to June, so you have to be quick to use the flowers during this time. I make sage flower butter using only about ⅛ cup of flowers with enough finely chopped sage leaves to make ½ cup of sage, and add them to 1 pound of butter.

Pineapple sage (*Salvia elegans*) bears showy red flowers that have a hint of pineapple fragrance and flavor. This is another one of my favorite edible flowers. Pineapple sage flowers are delicious and look spectacular when added to green salads or mixed with fresh fruit.

HERBAL HINT

To gather sage seeds, leave the flower bracts intact until little black seeds form, usually by late fall. Cut the flowerstalks and put them into a brown paper bag to catch any seeds that fall out. Start the seeds indoors in late winter to early spring.

HERBAL HINT

Winter savory (S. montana) is from the mint family and for centuries was thought to have aphrodisiac qualities. I grow winter savory in little nooks and crannies of stone wall. The flowers appear on spikes in summer and have a hot, peppery taste.

SUMMER SAVORY (*Satureja hortensis*)

Best known as an herb for flavoring beans, summer savory is easy to grow from seed right in the garden and will reseed for years to come. The flowers of summer savory are showy and have the flavor of the whole plant. You can begin harvesting as soon as the plant begins flowering and still have lots of flowers in the garden.

You can dry summer savory flowers for use all year, and every kind of bean from green to lentil will benefit from the flavor. I tie the stems together with a rubber band and hang them from a wire coat hanger with a paper bag over the plant stems to protect them from light. Summer savory retains its flavor well when dried quickly.

Both summer and winter savories have wonderful flavor. Winter savory stays small until winter, when I use it to flavor soups and stews. I grow lots of annual summer savory to use during warm seasons.

SCENTED GERANIUMS (*Pelargonium* spp.)

Favored in Victorian times, scented geraniums remain popular and can easily become a modern-day gardener's obsession. Tender perennials that are usually grown as houseplants or "indoor/outdoor" container plants, scented geraniums come in an amazing array of aromas from apple and ginger to cinnamon and lime. Although their leaves are typically used for flavor and fragrance, scented geraniums' flowers are also edible and carry the same delicate character as the foliage. Lemon geranium flowers have a citrus flavor and may be used in desserts. Rose-scented geraniums are my favorite.

SUNFLOWER (*Helianthus annuus*)

Pick sunflowers in the bud stage, when they taste like artichokes. Prepare them by boiling the buds for 2 minutes in a pot of water. Remove the buds, discard the first water (throwing out the bitter taste), bring another pot of water to boil, add the buds, and continue boiling in clean water until tender. Drain. Add equal amounts butter and olive oil to a frying pan, sprinkle buds with seasoned bread crumbs, and, turning often, brown buds in the oil and butter mixture. If you're hoping to harvest sunflower seeds later in the season, plant extra sunflowers so you'll have some buds to eat and some to mature for a crop of crunchy seeds.

*THYME
(*Thymus vulgaris* and other species and cultivars)

If you have only ever used dried thyme, you may not know if you like thyme flowers. Their flavor is mild and refreshing. Add thyme flowers to salads and pasta, to fish and chicken, and to butter-based sauces.

*SWEET VIOLET (*Viola odorata*)

As you might expect, sweet violets have a sweet scent and go well with fruit, desserts, and in salads. They add so much to the appearance of the food they are combined with that it doesn't really matter that they have little flavor.

SWEET WOODRUFF

(*Galium odoratum*)

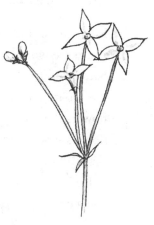

Sweet woodruff flowers have a nutty vanilla taste and are essential in May wine. They also have a sweet fragrance that makes them nice for adding to table arrangements.

HERBAL HINT

Growing up, I spent a lot of time at my Aunt Violet's house. (I know this is hard to believe—the name thing—but that was her name, and she was my mother's sister.) Aunt Violet always had time for the special things that made going to her house different and fun, and she often used her signature flowers, fresh or candied, to decorate the cakes she baked for family get-togethers and other occasions. After a wake or wedding, there, amid the baked beans, deviled eggs, and potato salad, would sit a platter of frosted fruit or a cake covered in 7-minute frosting and fresh flowers. Everyone knew what Aunt Violet had brought.

YUCCAS (*Yucca* spp.)

Yucca was a southwestern plant staple for Native Americans, who made their homes in places where the plants grew best and used all parts of this durable perennial plant. Yucca's large white flowers are crunchy and slightly sweet.

*ZUCCHINI (*Cucurbita pepo*)

If you are of Italian descent, your mom may have served you these wonderful flowers on crispy bread. Dipped in batter and fried with garlic in olive oil, zucchini flowers are an Italian tradition and probably one of the few flowers that most people have eaten. I also serve zucchini flowers whole and raw, stuffed with a seafood salad.

Here are a couple of very simple recipes for using edible flowers, to give you a chance to try them out without a lot of effort and kitchen work:

Confetti Cream Cheese

Add 1 part chopped edible flowers in lots of colors to 4 parts soft cream cheese. Mold into pleasing form and chill. Serve with a basket of crackers.

Flower Butter

Pick your favorite edible flower flavor and add 1 part chopped flowers to 4 parts soft butter. Use as a spread on bread, on hot vegetables, or in butter-based sauces.

Pass (Up) These Posies!

Although there are many lovely and pleasant-tasting flowers that you can eat, there are certainly many more equally lovely flowers that you *should never eat*. This is not an area for experimentation, either at home or when dining out—many common flowers are poisonous, and eating them can make you very sick or worse. I don't want to scare you away from eating flowers altogether, but it's important to be educated about what's on your plate. And because you can't be sure that every chef who tosses a flower onto a plate knows a daylily (safe and tasty) from a delphinium (pretty and toxic), it's best to know for yourself before you take a bite.

This list is far from complete, but it's a good start to knowing which of the flowers you may encounter in your own gardens should be enjoyed for their beauty but never added to the menu. Remember: If you ever wonder about the safety of a flower served to you in a restaurant—ask before you eat! And if you are considering eating a flower from your garden and you're not sure if it's safe, go to your library and look it up, search for more information online, or call your local Cooperative Extension office—before you sample even a petal. Eating flowers should be fun, and making yourself or your dinner guests sick—or worse—is not fun.

- Autumn crocus (*Colchicum speciosum*)
- Azaleas (*Rhododendron* spp.)
- Buttercups (*Ranunculus* spp.)
- Butterfly weed (*Asclepias tuberosa*)
- Calla lilies (*Zantedeschia* spp.)
- Castor bean (*Ricinus communis*)
- Clematis (*Clematis* spp.)
- Daffodils (*Narcissus* spp.)
- Delphiniums (*Delphinium* spp.)
- Foxgloves (*Digitalis* spp.)
- Goldenseal (*Hydrastis canadensis*)
- Hyacinths (*Hyacinthus* spp.)
- Hydrangeas (*Hydrangea* spp.)
- Irises (*Iris* spp.)
- Jasmines (*Jasminum* spp.)
- Lantanas (*Lantana* spp.)
- Leopard's bane (*Arnica montana*)
- Lily-of-the-valley (*Convallaria majalis*)

- Lobelias (*Lobelia* spp.)
- Mescal bean, Texas mountain laurel (*Sophora secundiflora*)
- Morning glories (*Ipomoea* spp.)
- Mountain laurel (*Kalmia latifolia*)
- Deadly nightshade (*Atropa belladonna*)
- Nightshades (*Solanum* spp.)
- Oleander (*Nerium oleander*)
- Periwinkle, vinca, myrtle (*Vinca minor, V. major*)
- Poison hemlock (*Conium maculata*)
- Potato (*Solanum tuberosum*)
- Rhododendrons (*Rhododendron* spp.)
- Sweet pea (*Lathyrus odoratus*)
- Tobaccos (*Nicotiana* spp.)
- Trumpet flowers (*Datura* spp.)
- Wisterias (*Wisteria* spp.)

༉

CHAPTER 4

Without food and drink I would have no (social) life: firehouse breakfasts, family

dinners, Sunday brunches, afternoon teas, and lunches with friends. Everything

that matters revolves around food, and there is nothing wrong with that. Part of

my business life is also about food. The café at the Potager is a favorite gathering

place, and good food is one of the reasons for its popularity. My daughter Mickey

is responsible for the good food, and the annual harvest from my gardens

surrounding the Potager adds to the flavor of those foods.

Recipes for Culinary Herbs and Edible Flowers

Food Is More Than Fuel

Have you ever picked up a fork full of food and, once you tasted it, remembered the person who first made this flavor for you? I have this experience with certain buttermilk biscuits: If they are not too big and have a light flavor and texture, I always remember my Grandmother Neal. It's the same with a relish called chowchow. She made cases of chowchow (a vegetable relish of cabbage, onions, and green peppers, packed in a sweet pickling brine like a bread-and-butter pickle) each year at the end of the summer season. She served this relish with pinto beans, and I remember my father loved the combination.

The way we feel about food is often a reflection of how we feel about family. We have warm fuzzy memories about meals and favorite dishes: Sunday dinner at Grandma's house, Mom's apple pie, Dad's homemade spaghetti sauce. The flavors and fragrances remind us of special times and special people in our lives.

My friends and I used to shake our heads and smile at older folks who would seem to talk endlessly about food: talking over breakfast about what they will have for lunch or what they had for dinner last night, how they feel about certain restaurants, and about the buffet that was served at cousin so-and-so's wedding. Now I am one of the older folk, and I am the one talking endlessly about food.

One of my nephews, Michael, is in the travel and tour business, and I remember him telling about one of his groups who were standing at the rim of the Grand Canyon complaining about breakfast, especially the lukewarm tea, too-brown toast, and overdone eggs.

The truth is, we all are interested in food, and as we grow older, it becomes more important because we have more time to think about it. When you do think about it, you have to admit that food is often the catalyst for our most memorable social activities, from first dates and engagement parties to supper clubs and neighborhood block parties.

Can you imagine how dull things would be without the food part of any occasion? A wedding without a meal, a birthday without the cake, a garden club meeting without tea?

Gardeners feed their souls on flowers, but they feed the family with fruits and vegetables. Herb gardeners do not live by wreaths and swags alone, but rather by the flavors the herbs bring to ordinary foods.

HERBS AND EDIBLE FLOWERS MAKE THE DIFFERENCE

When I became a serious herb gardener, I brought the flavor of the herbs I grew to the kitchen and to the foods I served. Cooking and eating the things you grow is the next level of pleasure for a beginner or experienced gardener. Over the years, I have introduced my friends and family to many herbal flavors they had not tried before.

The first time I roasted a chicken stuffed with tarragon sprigs, I watched as the aroma got the attention of my youngest child. A great cook herself, Liz appreciated the smell of anise and was surprised to see how I had simply stuffed two sprigs inside the bird and laid two sprigs on the outside at the junction of leg and breast. For me and my family, herbs have come a long way from that limp piece of parsley tossed on the plate by a diner cook.

Every garden surrounding the Potager has herbs growing within its borders, and some of the front gardens are planted with nothing but herbs and edible flowers. Mickey knows where every plant is and what it is used for, and she frequently can be found deadheading in the gardens to keep the harvest coming all season.

During the summer, I fill the planters that top the railing on either side of the entrance ramp with herbs and edible flowers especially for Mickey and the kitchen staff to harvest. The mixed greens that make up our salads are enhanced by the addition of pansies, nasturtiums, chive blossoms, and dianthus. The herbal flowers make our salads so pretty that our customers often may be seen photographing them before they eat them.

There are also special things we do for groups that come to spend the day at the Potager. We bake homemade herb bread in flower pots, serving each guest her own pot. Mickey places a penny over the hole in the bottom of each pot so the dough won't creep out during baking. After the dough rises, herbs—usually parsley, dill, or basil—are dusted over the top of each loaf. Mickey calls her creation "Penny Pot Bread."

Penny Pot Bread

You can make Penny Pot Bread using any basic bread recipe; the secret is in the preparation of the pots. We use new 4-inch terra-cotta pots. We spray them with cooking oil and bake them at 300°F for about 30 minutes. Then we spray them again, give them another 30 minutes in the oven, then let them cool before putting prepared bread dough in them to bake.

1	package active dry yeast (about 1 tablespoon)	1	tablespoon salt
½	cup warm water (about 110° to 115°F)	1½	tablespoons softened butter or vegetable spray
2	tablespoons sugar	1 to 2	tablespoons dried herbs
1½	cups plain yogurt	1	egg white, beaten with 2 tablespoons cold water (optional)
3¾ to 4	cups all-purpose flour		

HERBAL HINT

For faster penny pot herb bread, use frozen bread dough. Thaw the dough, cut 2 to 3 ounces from dough, and place in a prepared pot. Brush with egg-and-water mix and sprinkle with dried herbs; let the dough rise once in the pot. Bake and let cool on a rack before serving.

In a small bowl, add yeast to warm water along with sugar, and stir until yeast is dissolved and starts to bubble. Place yogurt in a large bowl. Stir in about 1½ cups of flour using a wooden spoon; add the yeast mixture, salt, and remaining flour, 1 cup at a time. You can use a mixer if you have a dough hook. If mixture is too dry to include all the flour, use some of it on a board, turn the dough out on the board, and knead flour in as you work it to a satiny stage that is no longer sticky.

Oil or butter a large bowl and place dough in, turning it to coat all sides with oil or butter. Cover the bowl with a clean dish towel and set aside to rise, about an hour, until the dough is doubled in size.

Deflate dough by punching it firmly in the middle 2 or 3 times and turn it out on the floured board again. Cut off 2 to 3 ounces of dough for each prepared flower pot. (Don't forget the penny.) Sprinkle the top of the dough with your favorite dried herb. Dill is my favorite, but parsley is a close second.

Let the dough rise in the pots to double the size, brush with egg-and-water mixture, and bake in a 400°F oven for 25 to 30 minutes or until each bread sounds hollow when you knock on it. Turn out on a rack to let cool before serving. Serve with your favorite herb butter.

HERB AND FLOWER BUTTERS

Preserving the flavor of fresh herbs and edible flowers in butter is one of the fun ways to take advantage of the harvest when it is at its peak. Butter keeps the flavors of herbs fresh long after the growing season has ended and offers a variety of options for using those herbal flavors—as a spread on breads or crackers, on cooked vegetables, in sauces or soups.

> ## HERBAL HINT
>
> *"Deadheading" is the removal of flowers that are past their prime. It's important to take the flower off behind where the seed is forming, rather than just pulling off the petals—a plant that has formed seeds has no reason to continue blooming.*

I'm responsible for making the herb butters at the Potager, and it's easy and fun to make them ahead and freeze them in shapes like roses, hearts, and stars. First, I set out several bowls and place a pound of butter in each bowl to soften. Once I have harvested the herbs or flowers, I remove any parts that aren't tasty and chop the remaining leaves or petals. To each pound of butter, I add ½ cup of chopped herbs or 1 cup of chopped flowers, mixing them thoroughly with the butter.

Nasturtium butter is really tasty and has just a bit of a bite to it. This is one of the prettiest herb butters, bright with bits of color from the chopped flowers. Add a couple of nasturtium butter shapes and a pot of dill bread to a bread plate, and you are sure to impress your guests.

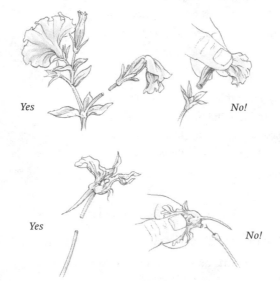

Yes *No!*

Yes *No!*

Deadheading encourages plants to produce side shoots, so they fill out and grow bushier rather than taller. It also promotes the production of more flowers.

HERBAL HINT

Before you start chopping and mixing, make sure there are no bugs hiding in the nasturtium flowers. Pick the flowers with long stems so you have something to hold while you give the flowers a good shake.

If you're not inclined to make butter shapes, simply roll the prepared butter into a log, using plastic wrap to shape it. Secure the ends of the wrap with freezer tape and freeze. It's easy to cut slices from the butter logs to use to flavor foods or as spreads.

In the Kitchen with My 10 Favorite Herbs

My history with culinary herbs started with simple additions to the everyday foods I cooked for my family. I graduated from one herbal flavor to another, making choices about what I would grow in my gardens based on what I needed to add to my pantry. Our life in the military brought us

Popular Herb and Flower Butters

Here's a list of some of the most popular butters made with herbs and edible flowers, along with ideas for ways to use them:

- Dill butter: Use on fish or chicken during cooking.

- Parsley butter: Use on vegetables, especially potatoes, and on pasta.

- Basil butter: Use on pasta, vegetables, and as a bread spread.

- Sage butter: Use to baste poultry, in stuffing, and as a spread.

- Thyme butter: Use to flavor soups, especially chowders.

- Bee balm flower butter: Use on vegetables and as a spread.

- Nasturtium butter: Use as a bread spread and on bland vegetables.

- Herb flower butters: Butters using just the flowers of sage, basil, summer savory, winter savory, chives, garlic, rosemary, oregano, dill, mint, and thyme have just as much flavor as the leaves of these herbs. Although the flavor of flower butter is a bit more subtle, the colors the flowers impart more than make up for any reduction in flavor.

HERBAL HINT

For a tasty and unusual appetizer, try fried sage flowers. Harvest whole stems of sage with flowers and leaves. Dip them in your favorite batter, and drop the batter-coated stems into hot vegetable oil.

in contact with people from all parts of the country and a few from other countries. These friends introduced me to the flavors of their different cultures, and I gradually added those flavors to the foods that I cooked.

Some herbs are acquired tastes, and not everyone enjoys herbal flavors to the same degree. An initial experience with too much of even a good thing can instill a lasting dislike of a particular flavor.

When I was new to the Northeast and eating foods that I had not tried before, I was overexposed to dried thyme. My husband's godfather would always be in charge of the Manhattan clam chowder, and he would always add way too much dried thyme to the pot. I've since grown many different varieties of thyme in my gardens, and I'm quite fond of the flavor of the fresh herb. But it took me a long time to overcome my distrust of thyme as an edible herb because of one cook's heavy hand with the seasoning.

To avoid overwhelming dinner guests with new or unusual herbal flavors, give them a chance to taste-test herbs in your garden or at the table, and let each person decide how much of an herb to add to the food on his plate. Taste-testing is an enjoyable way to become familiar with herbal flavors and to see which ones you want to add to your food.

By growing new herbs in my gardens and by sampling their leaves and flowers, I've become fond of a wide range of herbal flavors. On the following pages, you'll find recipes and tips for using 10 of my favorite herbs in your kitchen. Use these to stimu-

late your own creative ideas for enjoying the flavors of herbs in your meals. Once you get started, you'll find the possibilities almost endless.

IN THE KITCHEN WITH SAGE

For most of my young life, sage was the only culinary herb I knew, and it's the first perennial herb I plant when making a new garden. After all these years, sage is still one of my favorite herbs to grow and use. Common garden sage is not only a kitchen herb but also a part of my garden designs, and one I grow to cut and dry for my wreaths and garlands. It's also essential in the kitchen: Who would dare cook poultry without sage? Pork is flavorless without sage. And can you imagine stuffing without sage?

Sage can have a strong, bitter taste if not used in the right proportion. The best leaves are the small new leaves that appear at the very tip of the stalk. Dried sage is four times as strong as fresh sage and should be used with a light hand or it can overpower the dish you are preparing.

To cook whole poultry with a light sage flavor, try using whole leaves tucked under the skin of the bird. When using fresh sage leaves in stuffing, first chop the leaves into finely minced pieces. To dry sage leaves, cut whole stems and hang, either from an herb rack or in a paper bag, in the closet until dry. Once dry, you can crumble the leaves by hand or by using a rolling pin.

HERBAL HINT

Plant culinary herbs in little pots to use as table decorations. Place a pair of child's scissors at each place setting so guests can snip their own seasonings. Add pots of mint or parsley to the table after dinner. Both aid digestion and leave pleasant flavors in your mouth.

HERBAL HINT

I keep a basket nearby when I am stripping the dried leaves from herbs such as sage, rosemary, lavender, or thyme. Once the basket is full, I tie the twigs into bundles with garden twine. I keep the twig bundles handy in a basket near the fireplace or woodstove where they're ready to toss on the fire for a bit of romance and heavenly fragrance.

Chicken Breasts with Sage and Vegetable Sauce

4 boneless chicken breasts	1/2 cup each diced: celery, carrot, and onion
Salt and pepper	1 1/2 tablespoons finely chopped fresh sage
Olive oil	1/4 cup white wine

Rub chicken with salt and pepper. Cook chicken on a stovetop griddle in a small amount of oil on medium heat. Set aside. In a large frying pan, sauté vegetables and fresh sage in a small amount of oil over medium heat until vegetables are just tender. Add salt and pepper to taste. When almost finished, add 1/4 cup white wine and cook until liquid is reduced.

Treats from Tuscany

As one of the 25 million Andrea Bocelli fans, I appreciate how much we get from Tuscany, not just in music but in the form of food: olive oil, bread, fish, vegetables, and of course, wine. Tuscan-style food carries the flavors of the favorite herbs—rosemary and sage—of that region. I've found that you cannot follow a Tuscan recipe without having a ready supply of fresh sage, rosemary, and plenty of garlic.

One of the first off-premise weddings that Mickey and I catered from the Potager featured an entrée flavored with those herbs. The bride had some wonderful recipes with a Tuscan flavor, so we adapted her suggestions to our kitchen at the Potager and served 100 wedding guests a main dish of fresh grilled tuna on a bed of Tuscan-style white bean and vegetable salsa, flavored with sage, rosemary, and garlic.

Tuna, Anchovy, and White Bean Salad with Fresh Sage

1   6-ounce can solid white meat tuna packed in oil
2   rinsed anchovy fillets
1   cup olive oil
2   tablespoons red wine vinegar
½   cup chopped red onion

1   15-ounce can white beans, drained and rinsed
2   teaspoons chopped fresh sage leaves
2   tablespoons chopped fresh flat-leaf parsley
Salt and pepper

Drain oil from tuna and flake tuna in a medium mixing bowl. In small mixing bowl add anchovies and enough oil to make a paste. Add vinegar and more oil to make about ½ cup. Add red onion, beans, sage, and parsley to bowl with tuna and mix. Add oil and vinegar to tuna mixture; toss to coat. Add salt and pepper to taste.

White Beans and Tomatoes with Fresh Sage

4   slices bacon, chopped
1   cup chopped onion
3   cloves fresh garlic, crushed
1   teaspoon minced fresh sage

1   15-ounce can white beans, drained and rinsed
1   15-ounce can diced tomatoes in juice
1   cup chicken broth

Combine bacon, onion, and garlic in heavy saucepan. Cook until bacon is semi-crisp and onions are clear; stir constantly to keep garlic from sticking. Add sage, beans, and tomatoes, and stir in chicken broth. Serve over favorite pasta or as soup with crusty bread.

HERBAL HINT

Use sprigs of fresh herbs to garnish dishes that feature the flavor of that herb.

Country Ribs with Grilled Sausages, Rosemary, and Sage

This is a dish I developed by starting with a country rib dish my grandmother used to make. She boiled country pork ribs in water flavored with salt, pepper, and sage. She added potatoes and onions during the last 45 minutes of cooking time. The rib meat fell off the bone, and the potatoes helped create a flavorful sauce.

Here's my version of my grandmother's dish:

6 pounds of country-style pork ribs	1 tablespoon olive oil
1 tablespoon each minced fresh rosemary and sage	1 tablespoon minced fresh garlic
1 tablespoon salt	4 to 6 spicy or sweet Italian sausage links
1 teaspoon pepper	

Put country ribs on to boil in just enough water to cover. Add rosemary, sage, salt, and pepper to pot. In a heavy frying pan, heat olive oil and add garlic and sausage links. Cook on medium heat, turning to brown on all sides. Add to ribs to finish cooking.

IN THE KITCHEN WITH BASIL

Basil has a clovelike, anise flavor that is essential in many Italian recipes and tomato-based sauces. It's often used in egg dishes, with meat, in salads, and with vegetables; it's the main ingredient in pesto. In my opinion, eggplant and tomatoes are lacking something if basil is not used in preparing them.

I had never heard of basil until I married an Italian. He must have been appalled when I first cooked for him. (No, actually he loved what

'Napoletano'

'Purple Ruffles'

'Lemon'

'Genovese'

I cooked: southern fried chicken, mashed potatoes, milk gravy, buttermilk biscuits, and black-eyed peas with ham hock, with a pitcher of sweet tea.)

Not long after we were married, he took over some of the cooking: tomato sauce with lots of garlic, basil, and flat-leaf parsley. Did you ever experience heaven in a pot? I could eat half a loaf of bread, dipping it in the sauce to see if it was ready. Our Saturday sauce was just that: a special Saturday night dinner, and he made enough to last the week. (See "Lanza's Tomato and Herb Sauce" on page 4 for the recipe.)

As soon as he showed me the way, I began to grow and use more basil: basil, mozzarella cheese, and fresh tomatoes; basil pesto; basil with zucchini and onion; basil with arugula and radicchio salad. I graduated from plain, large-leaf basil to African blue basil, cinnamon basil, lemon basil, bush basil, Michael's basil, and basils that differed only minimally from my favorite, Napoletano curled leaf.

Basil Sauce for Beef

Here's one of my favorite cold beef recipes that you can make with deli beef, steak you cook and cool, or even with ground beef formed into patties. The secret is the sauce:

1¼	cups olive oil		¼	cup mint leaves
½	cup basil leaves		¼	cup lemon juice
6	tablespoons pine nuts or walnuts		4	large cloves fresh garlic
¼	cup flat-leaf parsley		2	level tablespoons Dijon mustard

Place ingredients in a food processor and blend to a coarse puree. You can prepare this a couple of days in advance and keep in refrigerator until ready to use. This is a topping for beef, and the best way I have ever had it was with thin slices of rare beef I cooked myself. I used top round and gave it a crust of tricolor crushed peppercorns, coarse salt, chopped Italian parsley, crushed garlic, and enough olive oil to bind it all together. I rubbed the mixture on all sides of the beef and wrapped bacon slices around it, holding them on with toothpicks, then I cooked the beef in a preheated oven at 400°F until the meat thermometer read "very rare." I took it out of the oven and let it sit for about 20 minutes before slicing it very thin. Piled on good bread and topped with a ladle of this sauce, it was absolutely wonderful!

IN THE KITCHEN WITH PARSLEY

Parsley has a delicate, celery-like flavor. We use it in just about every dish that comes out of our kitchens, but it is especially good in egg dishes, with fish and meats, in salads, sauces, soups, and stuffings. Just ahead is Nana's Secret Sauce, an essential part of my mother-in-law's culinary repertoire, featuring parsley as the main ingredient.

And where would we be without parsley? I used to think parsley was a dried bit of green packed in a jar. Later I learned it was a curly little poof of green on the side of your dinner plate. It wasn't until I began to grow herbs myself that I could discern the difference in parsleys. Now I can tell the difference between parsley that is grown from seed in its first year and the second year's growth before it goes to seed again. It's one of my favorite herbs to grow, and the flavor is so much more than that little poof of green on the side of my plate ever led me to believe.

Nana's Secret Sauce

1   cup flat-leaf parsley leaves
1   cup olive oil

6   large cloves fresh garlic

Place all ingredients in a food processor and pulse until just coarsely chopped. Keep in a closed jar in the refrigerator for up to 1 month. Use on hot pasta, on bread for toasting, and in other recipes that call for these ingredients.

HERBAL HINT

French-fried whole parsley stems are crisp and delicious. Simply drop clean, whole stems and leaves of parsley into a pan of hot cooking oil and fry until they're crisp and golden brown.

Easy Ways with Parsley

Don't leave this herb on the side of the plate! Parsley's fresh flavor earns it a bigger role in the kitchen than that of mere garnish. Try parsley in these quick and easy ways:

- Boiled potatoes with butter and fresh parsley: Drain cooked potatoes, place in a serving bowl, and pour melted butter over the top. Sprinkle with a generous amount of finely minced fresh parsley leaves; toss and serve.

- Pasta with oil, garlic, and fresh parsley: Drain cooked pasta and place in a serving bowl. Crush and chop four or more cloves of fresh garlic, and cook in olive oil until light brown. Add garlic and oil to pasta. Mince a generous amount of fresh parsley leaves and add to bowl, toss, and serve.

- Minced or coarsely chopped fresh parsley is the perfect addition to vegetables such as cauliflower, carrots, squash, and rutabagas.

- Keep parsley butter in the freezer so you can add the flavor of fresh parsley to any dish, even when your garden's buried in snow.

IN THE KITCHEN WITH GARLIC

I can't imagine how I cooked so many meals without fresh garlic. Those little cellophane-wrapped packages of small garlic cloves do not constitute fresh garlic, nor does that jar of chopped garlic in oil that you can buy off the shelf. Until you have grown and harvested your own garlic, you haven't ever tasted really fresh garlic. Have you ever smashed a clove of your own homegrown garlic? It's big, juicy, and pungent, and the flavor is big, hot, and very intense.

I don't know how anyone cooks without really fresh garlic, and it's so easy to grow you can have it even if all you have is a large container on the deck to grow in. Try it! You'll love it!

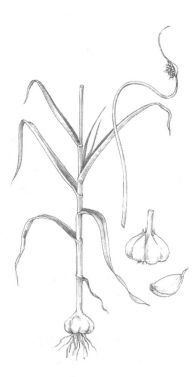

Fresh Green Beans with Fresh Garlic and Mushrooms

Blanch 1 pound fresh, trimmed green beans. In a large frying pan, add 3 table-spoons olive oil, 3 cloves crushed garlic, and 4 to 6 sliced fresh mushrooms. Toss until garlic is just crisp. Add blanched green beans and toss until beans are heated through. Season with salt and pepper to taste.

If you find the flavor of fresh garlic a bit too spicy for your tastes, you can enjoy a slightly less pungent garlic experience by roasting whole bulbs or individual cloves of garlic. Roasting garlic (see the recipe on page 61) gives it a sweet, mellow flavor that's wonderful on toasted bread, over hot pasta, or as a seasoning for vegetables.

The long stem that curls up from a growing garlic bulb is called a scape. The garlic flower forms at the top of the scape and carries a milder garlic flavor. I like to cut the scapes to keep the plant's energy going to the bulb, but I always let a few flowers form to use in recipes that call for edible flowers. Garlic butter made from these unusual flowers is delightful, and you can freeze the butter to use when the season is over.

IN THE KITCHEN WITH CHIVES

Chives have a delicate, onionlike flavor. We use chives in as many ways as parsley, and we should be using them even more, as they are one of the easiest herbs to grow. You can add chives to cottage cheese, cream soups, meatballs, poultry, sauces, or any kind of potatoes—especially scalloped potatoes. Chives enhance the flavor of fish, including canned fish. Last but not least, chive vinegar is one of the first herb vinegars I ever made and is still my favorite.

Simple Pleasures from Chives

If you think chives are just for snipping onto the sour cream on a baked potato, then you need to learn a few more uses for these tasty, easy-to-grow herbs. Here are some ideas to help you get started:

- Chive blossom vinegar
- Chive blossoms on salads
- Chive butter
- Chives with tomato soup
- Chives as edible ties for bundles of herbs or vegetables
- And, of course, snipped chives on sour cream for baked potatoes

Chive flowers can be added to anything I've listed above but are especially good in salads and cold sauces. I pull the individual florets from the base and sprinkle them on my food.

I must have been 25 years old before I discovered that chives didn't come in a little box kept in the freezer and brought out to sprinkle on sour cream when you were having baked potatoes. But what could you expect from a girl from rural Tennessee who left home before learning anything she might use in the outside world?

Once I discovered how easy chives were to grow and how many ways they could be used, I grew them like wildflowers. I let them reseed all through the gardens, I planted them as borders and in swaths that wound like streams of wavy green stems. When they came into bloom, I could have wept at their beauty.

HERBAL HINT

In early spring when chives are most tender, gather as much as you will need for winter. Using sharp scissors, snip the chives into tiny pieces and place in the freezer for winter use.

IN THE KITCHEN WITH ROSEMARY

Rosemary has a bittersweet, piney flavor and is something of a cultivated taste. Use it in meat or vegetable stews; with chicken, fish, or grilled meats; in soups; and especially with lamb, cabbage, or sweet potatoes.

For me, growing rosemary is like growing small fragrant trees. It's like a pine tree you can grow in a pot and bring into the house each winter to keep you company.

Rosemary is an elite herb—a little finicky and demanding, but with a whole lot of flavor and fragrance to make the effort worthwhile.

When I first became familiar with rosemary, I used it only with lamb, but it wasn't long before I was using it on chicken, pork, and some of my favorite vegetables. Rosemary-flavored olive oil has become a favorite of my family. We sit at the table, finishing our drinks or opening a bottle of wine, dipping hot, crusty bread into the delicately flavored oil.

Italian Sausage with Fresh Rosemary, Lentils, and Swiss Chard

1	quart water	¼	cup olive oil
1½	cups dried lentils	1	teaspoon chopped fresh rosemary
3	fresh garlic cloves, crushed		
8	ounces sausage, removed from casing and crumbled	1	pound fresh Swiss chard, ribs removed and leaves torn into pieces
½	cup each chopped carrot, celery, and onion		Salt and pepper

In a heavy pot, cook water and lentils on medium heat about 1 hour or until lentils are done. In frying pan, cook garlic, crumbled sausage, and chopped carrot, celery, and onion in 2 tablespoons olive until vegetables are tender. Add contents of frying pan to heavy pot with lentils and fresh rosemary, mix, and add Swiss chard to top and cover.

Add salt and pepper to taste and continue cooking until Swiss chard is wilted and tender and flavors are mingled.

Roast Leg of Lamb with Rosemary and Garlic

1	6- to 7-pound leg of lamb, trimmed of all fat	3	cloves fresh minced garlic
	Salt and pepper	2	whole carrots
2	tablespoons olive oil	2	large pieces of celery with leaves
2	tablespoons minced fresh rosemary leaves	2	parsnips
1	tablespoon grated lemon peel	1	large onion

Preheat oven to 350°F. Mix seasonings and herbs, and rub on lamb. Place lamb on rack over roasting pan with 1 cup water in bottom. Cut carrots, celery, parsnips, and onion into large pieces and place in water around lamb. Bake, basting with pan juices 2 or 3 times, for about 1½ hours or until meat thermometer reads 130°F or medium-rare. Let stand for 20 minutes before cutting.

Chicken and Sweet Potatoes with Fresh Rosemary

This is SO easy: boneless chicken breasts and slices of sweet potatoes cooked in olive oil with a stem of fresh rosemary. I live alone, and I cook myself a wonderful meal using one thinly sliced breast and one sweet potato cut into thin slices.

IN THE KITCHEN WITH THYME

Thyme has a sweet, pleasantly pungent flavor that not everyone takes to right away. Use it in chicken, egg, and fish dishes, and in sauces, soups, stews, and stuffings. Don't forget that it's the main flavor in Manhattan clam chowder.

I began growing different thymes at the farm on Shandelee: between field-stone paths, in rubble walls, in planters, and as a border plant. I fell madly in

love with woolly thyme cascading over a rock wall surrounding a pond in a garden I visited. Once I saw how it looked, I planted woolly thyme to cascade over all my miniwalls. The intriguing fragrance of caraway thyme is another pleasure you can enjoy just by rubbing your hand over the top of a planting. Caraway thyme also looks wonderful as it slowly creeps around natural fieldstone.

Once you begin growing an herb in the garden, it isn't long before it finds its way into your kitchen. An experience with too much dried thyme had left me cautious. At first I would pull just a few leaves and add them to a salad. Then I discovered how much I enjoyed the tender fresh leaves and began adding them to my favorite chicken dishes and fresh vegetables.

At the Potager, I grow thyme in a walkway that leads from the sidewalk to the middle of the property. Each year, I divide large clumps growing in other places and add to the thyme walk. Any thyme plants left over from summer plant sales also go into the walk.

Chicken Breasts in Thyme Oil

Boneless chicken breasts
1   cup water
½   cup seasoned bread crumbs

2   tablespoons thyme-infused olive oil
Thyme sprigs
Lemon slices

Dip chicken breasts in water, then into seasoned bread crumbs, pressing the crumbs into the meat. Pour seasoned oil into sauté pan and heat to medium, cook until both sides are brown and meat is firm. Garnish with thyme sprigs and lemon slices.

Fresh Corn Chowder

"When corn is in, you should eat it every day." This is one of my grandmother's sayings, and I couldn't agree more. There is no substitute for the flavor of fresh corn, and there is only about a 3-week window each summer for enjoying that flavor.

This is a quick dish; with corn muffins or crusty bread it can be a whole meal. It may seem like a lot, but trust me, none will go to waste.

8	ears fresh sweet corn	2	cups chicken or vegetable broth
2	tablespoons butter or margarine	3	tablespoons flour
1	cup finely chopped onion	2	cups milk
1	cup finely chopped celery	2	tablespoons fresh thyme, minced
1	large potato, peeled and cubed		Salt and pepper

Cut the kernels off the ears of corn, then, using the side of a knife, scrape the "milk" off the cobs into the bowl of kernels. Put butter or margarine in a large heavy-bottomed pot and add onion, celery, and potato; cook over medium heat for about 10 minutes, stirring constantly. Add corn and broth.

Combine flour and ½ cup milk in a small mixing bowl and stir until mixed thoroughly, then add to chowder pot and stir in remaining milk, thyme, and salt and pepper to taste. Optional: Top each bowl with seeded and chopped tomato or crumbled cooked bacon (or both) before serving.

IN THE KITCHEN WITH OREGANO

Oregano has a pungent, bittersweet flavor. Use it in Greek, Italian, and Mexican foods. Oregano goes well with pizza, pork, beef, and salads, and is essential with some seafood dishes, especially clams and mussels. Most of the dried oregano we buy is actually marjoram. Although the flavors are similar, once you have tasted true Greek oregano you will know the difference. One of the best ways to tell the difference is when the plants are in flower: Marjoram has purple-to-pink flowers and Greek oregano has white flowers.

Herbed Breadsticks

Cut one 12-ounce French bread loaf in half crosswise, and cut each piece in half horizontally. Brush 2 tablespoons garlic-infused olive oil over cut sides. Dip cut sides into a mixture of ⅛ teaspoon salt, 1 teaspoon each finely chopped Italian parsley, fresh oregano, and basil. Place bread on a baking sheet and bake at 300°F for 20 to 25 minutes or until crisp.

Italian Seasoning Blend

Harvest fresh herbs and hang to dry. Once dried, measure 1 part each oregano, parsley, basil, and marjoram. Blend together and store in small jars with tight-fitting lids. Label each jar.

IN THE KITCHEN WITH DILL

Dill has a sweet, caraway-like flavor. Surprised? As you become more familiar with the flavors of fresh herbs, you'll start to appreciate how complex and different each one tastes. Use dill in breads, on carrots, in chicken salad, in cream-based chowders, on cottage cheese, with cucumbers, in dips, on egg dishes, in fish sauces, in dressings, in soups, on sandwiches with fish, and with any yogurt-based dish.

At the Potager, we use fresh dill in many of our dishes: Vegetable and Herb Cream Cheese, Dilly Seafood Salad, Salmon Fillet in White Wine and Dill, Dilly Cucumber Salad, and my favorite, Dilly Confetti Pasta Salad.

Dilly Confetti Pasta Salad

Cook 2 cups small seashell macaroni according to package directions. Drain and set aside. In a large bowl, mix 1 cup yogurt, 1 tablespoon chopped dill, 1 cup frozen English peas (thawed), ½ cup each diced sweet yellow and red pepper, and ¾ cup ranch-style dressing. Add to pasta and toss to coat all ingredients with dressing.

Dilly Cukes in Zippy Sour Cream

Peel and slice 2 whole cucumbers into a bowl containing a mixture of 1½ cups sour cream and ½ cup mayonnaise, then add ¼ cup dill weed, crushed hot peppers, and salt and pepper to taste. I add a dash of Tabasco sauce, but adjust the heat to suit your own taste. Make ahead and chill for an hour before serving.

Mock Seafood Salad with Fresh Dill, Bacon, Lettuce, and Tomato on a Croissant

This is the most popular sandwich at the Potager.

Sealegs, thawed
Cooked shrimp
Minced dill leaf
Diced celery

Mayonnaise
Croissants, sliced for sandwiches
Bacon, cooked crisp
Sliced tomato and lettuce

Allow about 6 ounces of prepared sealegs and shrimp per person, then add fresh dill, celery, and mayonnaise to taste. Mix all ingredients together and pile on one side of a heated croissant; on the other side lay 3 slices of crisp bacon, 2 thin slices of tomato, and a large leaf of lettuce. It's messy but worth it. Serve with extra napkins and a fork to scoop up every last morsel that falls out.

HERBAL HINT

Dill is easy to dry. Hang whole stems from a hook or even the pot rack. When dry, strip the ferny leaves from their stems and store in an airtight container.

Seared Sea Scallops with Dill Weed

The combination of dill, lemon, and seafood is classic for good reason: Each complements the other, and both bring out the best flavor in almost anything the sea has to offer. Use this simple but effective combination on any seafood: dill, lemon, and butter.

12	large sea scallops		Juice of ½ lemon, seeded
	Salt and pepper to taste	1	teaspoon grated lemon peel
¼	stick butter	¼	stick chilled butter, cut in small pieces
¼	cup finely minced shallots		
½	cup dry white wine	2 to 4	sprigs fresh dill
1	tablespoon chopped fresh dill		Fresh lemon slices

Add salt and pepper to sea scallops. Melt 1 tablespoon butter in heavy skillet and bring to medium-high heat. Add scallops to skillet, cooking on each side until golden brown and just opaque in the center of each scallop. Transfer scallops to a heated plate and keep warm in oven set at 250°F.

In same skillet, add 1 tablespoon butter and shallots and sauté about 1 minute. Add wine and boil until reduced by half. Add dill, lemon juice, and lemon peel and cook for about 1 minute, then remove from heat. Add chilled butter pieces, a few at a time. Once the burner has cooled, place skillet back on low heat to melt butter. Taste and season with salt and pepper to taste. Pour over scallops and garnish with fresh lemon slices and whole dill sprigs.

IN THE KITCHEN WITH CILANTRO

Cilantro is the citrusy, peppery-flavored plant that adds a characteristic tang to foods from Mexico, southeast Asia, and the Middle East. It's a key ingredient in guacamole and salsas, as well as in seafood dishes. When cilantro grows up, its seeds change their name to coriander.

Mexican Burgers with Fresh Cilantro

Combine 1 pound ground beef, ¼ cup fresh minced cilantro leaves, 1 teaspoon fresh minced oregano, 1 teaspoon minced jalapeño pepper with seeds removed, 1 teaspoon chili powder, and salt and pepper to taste. Shape beef mixture into patties, coat grill with spray oil, and grill burgers on medium-high heat for about 6 minutes each side. Check for doneness. Grill buns just before burgers are ready. Place burgers on buns and give each one a teaspoon of sour cream, plus lettuce, tomatoes, and onion. Serve grated cheese on the side.

Papaya Salsa

This is so fast you can do it at the last minute. The addition of this salsa to chicken, fish, or vegetable dishes creates an unforgettable memory.

1 large papaya, peeled, seeded, and diced	*2 tablespoons lime juice*
½ cup chopped fresh cilantro leaves	*1 tablespoon rice wine or white vinegar*
1 tablespoon minced onion	*Salt and pepper to taste*

Mix all ingredients by gently tossing, then set aside for a few minutes before serving. Allow about ¼ cup per person.

Jicama Skillet Toss

Jicama is a potato-like vegetable that's available in most supermarkets. It adds a fresh crisp flavor to grilled meats. This dish is easy during the summer, and you can use the vegetables you like best as they mature in the garden.

To a large frying pan on medium heat, add 2 or 3 tablespoons olive oil, 2 cups peeled and finely chopped jicama, 1 cup finely chopped sweet pepper (green, yellow, or red), 1 cup corn kernels, ½ cup finely chopped onion, and 2 large cloves fresh garlic, minced. Toss as you sauté until vegetables are crisp-tender. Remove pan from heat and add ½ cup fresh minced cilantro leaves; toss and serve.

HERBAL HINT

Release the flavor from whole herbs by "bruising" the leaves before you add them to a recipe.

MINT MADNESS

If this were a listing of my 11 favorite herbs, I'd have mint on the list, too. Mint is something of a pest in the garden—it takes careful management to keep it from getting out of hand and into everything. But we make good use of our overabundance of mint at the Potager, and if I could bring myself to limit its rampant spread, I'd miss mint's cool, refreshing fragrance during the heat of the summer months.

Every day we snip sprigs of mint to garnish iced tea. Perfect mint leaves adorn every poof of whipped cream atop our desserts. Some English customers taught me how to make a delightful mint sauce, and our homemade chocolate mint sauce is a popular menu item, too. Yes, we use a lot of mint from the gardens surrounding the Potager, but we never run out.

Mint has taken over Herb Alley at the Potager. It started with a lasagna garden, built in the long, narrow corridor between the fence and the greenhouse. Stacked fieldstone frames a raised garden bed with the stockade fence as the backdrop. Once the stone was in place, creating a 1½-foot-high box, I covered the bottom of the box with card-

The Biggest Bully in Herb Alley

In a moment of madness, I planted some of the most aggressive herbs I could find in one long bed. The list included artemisia, oregano, chives, thyme, and mint. Calling them "herb bullies" and allowing them to duke it out for the available space, I watched what would happen in the years to come. For the first 2 years, most things held their own.

After the second year, the artemisia was pushed to the back of the bed, oregano and chives were still there but just in small spots, and thyme was clinging to a pocket of soil between the stones that held everything in place. Mint, however, was bigger and better than ever. And the winner is? Mint by 10 lengths.

board. The cardboard covered the natural grass and weeds that had been the old church lawn. Next I layered peat moss, grass clippings, and lots and lots of leaves to make a rich planting bed. That's when the madness took over, and I filled it with invasive plants. Now, 6 years later, it's all about mint—lots and lots of mint. Mint fills the planter and carpets the path.

Recipes from Friends and Family

Remember my mentioning that good biscuits always remind me of my grandmother? Food has a way of bringing back memories of important people in our lives, and cooking those memory-inducing foods helps to bind us together across generations and physical distance.

We often serve herbed biscuits at the Potager, and I make them for family get-togethers, too. They're such a simple pleasure and a comforting way to enjoy your favorite herbal flavors.

Herb-Flavored Biscuits

⅓ cup vegetable shortening, plus
    some for the pan
2 cups self-rising flour

1 cup buttermilk
   Finely chopped herbs, fresh or dried

Preheat oven to 400°F and coat biscuit pan with shortening. Place 2 cups self-rising flour in a large bowl, create a depression in the middle of the flour, add ⅓ cup shortening to the flour, and pour about 1 cup of buttermilk into the hole while mixing with your other hand to pull in more flour as you pour in the buttermilk. Mix finely chopped herbs into the dough as you combine the other ingredients. Chives, parsley, sage, rosemary, thyme, and oregano all add wonderful flavor and fragrance to the delights of homemade biscuits.

Don't overmix; add enough buttermilk to make the dough wet and turn out onto a board covered with flour. Turn the dough gently until it is a soft mound. Gently press dough into a rectangle using your hands. Once the dough is about 1 inch thick, cut out circles with a biscuit cutter or a glass dipped in flour. Place biscuits close together in greased pan. Bake for about 20 minutes or until brown.

The Potager and Mickey Lanza's Quick Sauce with Fresh Tomatoes, Garlic, Basil, and Italian Parsley

2 tablespoons olive oil
4 cloves garlic, chopped
8 plum tomatoes, diced
1 8-ounce can tomato puree

8 leaves fresh basil, chopped
4 sprigs fresh Italian parsley,
   chopped
   Salt and pepper to taste

Put olive oil in large frying pan and bring to medium heat, add garlic and tomatoes and heat through, then add tomato puree, and again bring to medium heat, stirring constantly. Add basil, parsley, and salt and pepper to taste. Serve over your favorite pasta, garnished with more fresh chopped parsley and basil.

As a member of the Garden Writer's Association, I've been fortunate to become friends with many kindred spirits. Among these are several friends who have added to my collection of herbal recipes.

Walter Chandoha's Whole Loin of Pork with Fresh Herb Crust

You won't find this recipe in Walter's new book. He came to Wurtsboro to teach Mickey how to prepare and cook the pork and stayed until it was finished so he could make the gravy.

 1   *whole loin of pork*

For the fresh herb crust:

 ¼   *cup olive oil*
 2   *tablespoons each chopped fresh sage, parsley, and rosemary*
 1   *teaspoon each salt and coarse-ground black pepper*
 3   *cloves fresh garlic, minced*

Preheat oven to 375°F. Score pork top and bottom by cutting across its surface with a sharp knife to create a diamond pattern only about ¼ inch deep. Combine remaining ingredients to make a paste. Cover pork loin with paste and place in a large roasting pan with about 1 cup water in bottom of pan. Cover pan with heavy-duty aluminum foil. Cook in oven until well done, about 1½ hours. The meat will continue cooking for 20 minutes after you remove from oven. Pork is best when it almost falls apart when sliced.

For the gravy:

 Pan juices
 ½   *cup red wine*
 ⅓   *cup butter*
 ½   *cup flour*
 Salt and pepper

To the pan juices, add ½ cup red wine. Continue cooking until wine is incorporated with pan juices. Mixture will be thin. In a medium-size pot melt ⅓ cup butter. Stir ¼ cup flour into the melted butter to make a paste. Cook for about 2 minutes, stirring the whole time. Mix pan juices into butter and flour paste, stirring constantly. Add salt and pepper to taste.

Courtesy of Walter Chandoha, author of *The Literary Gardener.*

Lemonade with 'Lemon' Basil Ice Cubes

Make a simple glass of lemonade extra-special with 'Lemon' basil ice cubes. Fill your ice cube trays and add a leaf or two of 'Lemon' basil to each compartment before freezing. Make your favorite recipe for lemonade, add ice cubes to individual glasses, and fill with lemonade.

This recipe appeared previously in *Basil, An Herb Lover's Guide* by Thomas DeBaggio and Susan Belsinger.

Cathy Wilkerson Barash's
Anise Hyssop Mushroom Pizza

This recipe is right out of Cathy's book, but I have actually eaten it at her house in Cold Spring Harbor on the north shore of Long Island.

5	cups all-purpose flour	1	cup lukewarm water
1	packet quick-rising yeast	1	tablespoon olive oil
1	teaspoon salt		

Preheat oven to 450°F. Mix 4 cups flour, yeast, and salt in a large bowl. Slowly stir in water and continue to stir. As mixture becomes doughy, add olive oil. Add more flour if needed. Knead until firm, adding flour if necessary to keep the dough from being sticky. Form dough into a ball, cover with a towel, and let rise in a warm place until doubled in size. Punch dough down and knead briefly. Roll dough out into a circle and place on a lightly oiled pizza pan. Bake in oven for 4 to 6 minutes to cook through but do not let it brown.

For the topping:

12	ounces mushrooms, sliced	½	cup Monterey Jack cheese, shredded
1	tablespoon olive oil		
½	cup anise hyssop florets, divided		

Preheat oven to 450°F. Sauté mushrooms in olive oil over medium heat until mushrooms are just cooked through but not browned. Toss in ¼ cup anise hyssop florets. Spoon mushrooms onto cooked pizza dough. Sprinkle with cheese. Bake 4 to 7 minutes, or until cheese begins to lightly brown. Remove from oven, sprinkle with remaining anise hyssop florets, and serve.

This recipe appeared previously in *Edible Flowers: From Garden to Palate* by Cathy Wilkinson Barash.

The Potager and Mickey Lanza's Stacked Chicken
Breasts with Fresh Oregano and Parsley

Allow one each of the chicken, cheese, ham, and onion per person:

	Olive oil	1	slice fresh onion
½	boned and skinned chicken breast	1	slice smoked ham
1	cup bread crumbs mixed with 1 teaspoon minced fresh oregano and 1 teaspoon minced fresh parsley	1	slice Swiss cheese
			Fresh oregano and parsley, for garnish

Preheat oven to 400°F. Using a large frying pan, heat enough oil to cook chicken. Dip chicken in water, then into herbed bread crumbs. Cook in oil until lightly browned, then turn and do other side. Place on a cookie sheet and set aside until all chicken is cooked.

In same pan, brown onion slices on both sides. Place onion on chicken, then slice of ham, and top with cheese. Place chicken stacks on baking sheet and place in oven. Bake until cheese melts. Garnish with sprigs of fresh oregano and parsley.

SATISFYING SOUPS FROM THE POTAGER

We tend to think of soup as a hot food eaten mostly during the colder months. That's true, but I have seen folks eating hot soups all year at the Potager. Fresh herb soups are easier to make during the growing season, but a trip to your freezer or the market will show you a good selection of fresh herbs available all year.

Sorrel Soup or Sauce

A hardy perennial, sorrel is an herb that will grow in the shade. The leaves have a sharp, lemony flavor and make a wonderful, fresh addition to salads. Once you try sorrel soup, you will have to have your own patch. Sorrel sauce is divine on fish, chicken, or vegetables such as cauliflower that need some zip.

2 tablespoons butter
3 tablespoons flour
2 cups liquid (milk, stock, or
   vegetable juice)

Salt and pepper
1 cup chopped sorrel
   leaves

Prepare a basic béchamel or white sauce: Melt butter in a heavy saucepan over medium heat. Add flour and stir until mixed thoroughly. Add liquid and whisk to combine. Add salt and pepper to taste.

For sorrel sauce, add 1 cup chopped sorrel to 2 cups white sauce.

For sorrel soup, add 1 cup chopped sorrel and thin basic sauce with 1½ cups milk.

HERBAL HINT

Pinch off seedstalks to keep tender sorrel leaves coming all summer.

Tuna, Apple, and Dill Sandwiches

Have this sandwich with a cup of soup for a true taste sensation. It's the most popular combo at the Potager, and it's almost too easy.

Combine your favorite canned tuna, drained and flaked, with 1 peeled and chopped 'Red Delicious' apple, ¼ cup chopped celery, and about ⅓ cup mayonnaise. Mix together, then add 1 tablespoon minced fresh dill. Serve on your favorite bread. Don't like tuna? Try canned white-meat chicken instead.

Cream of Lovage Soup

There is one fresh herb that is hard to find during winter: lovage. Lovage is a big herb in size, flavor, and fragrance. Growing 6 to 7 feet tall, lovage may not fit in your garden, but this dependable perennial carries the flavor of celery in every leaf and stem. If you love celery, you'll adore lovage. It is especially good in soups and can replace celery in any recipe, but cream of lovage soup is my favorite.

4 tablespoons butter	1 cup finely diced carrot
4 tablespoons flour	4 cups chicken broth
4 cups chopped lovage stalks	Salt and pepper
1 cup chopped lovage leaves	2 cups heavy cream
2 cups diced onion	1 cup minced chives

Melt butter in heavy soup pot. Add lovage stalks and leaves, onion, and carrot. Cook slowly so butter doesn't burn, stirring constantly until lovage is clear. Add flour and continue stirring until flour is cooked and incorporated into vegetables. Add chicken broth, salt and pepper to taste, and continue stirring. Turn heat to simmer, and cook until vegetables are tender. Remove from heat and add cream. Taste and add more salt and pepper if needed. Add chives and serve.

Crostini are "little crusts," small toasted slices of bread, made from Italian or French-style long breads, piled with small amounts of meats, vegetables, and cheese, and eaten as antipasta.

As soon as I had my first little crusted bread, I knew I loved crostini. For years I just ate the toasted bread with soups, but after having some interesting experiences with what you could pile on top of the small crusty breads, I experimented and sorted out my favorites.

Chicken Liver Crostini

¼ cup olive oil
1 small onion, finely minced
2 anchovy fillets, rinsed
1 clove fresh garlic
12 ounces chicken livers
1 cup chicken broth

¼ cup white wine
1 tablespoon finely minced fresh sage leaf
Salt and pepper
1 long bread sliced into 1-inch slices, toasted

In a large frying pan, bring oil to medium heat. Add onion, anchovies, and garlic and sauté until onion is clear and anchovies are smashed into a paste. Add chicken livers and cook until brown, about 4 to 5 minutes, stirring constantly. Add chicken broth, wine, and sage. Add salt and pepper to taste. When livers are just done but still tender, remove from heat and let cool for 2 or 3 minutes. Empty contents into food processor or onto a cutting board. Pulse quickly until contents are rough-cut. When cutting on board, cut with a long flat-blade knife until liver mixture is coarse—not a paste. Spread on toasted bread slices and serve before dinner.

HERBAL HINT

You can grow a lot of herbs for very little money and have an endless supply to dry or freeze. At the market, you'll pay about $2 for a few stems of an herb, but they are fresh, and you need only a few stems to make a soup. But growing your own means you know they are free of harmful chemicals.

The easy perennial herbs—oregano, mint, tarragon, chives, and sage—are always there for you to harvest and use. They require almost no effort, and each year they come back like old friends. Round out your supplies with annual and biennial herbs like dill and cilantro that will reseed themselves and return from year to year in the most interesting places.

Fresh Tomato Crostini

Cut fresh tomatoes into tiny cubes and flavor with salt, pepper, fresh basil, and olive oil. Pile on toasted bread slices and serve with chicken liver crostini (page 171).

Summer Vegetable and Fresh Herb Crostini

When the garden is in and vegetables are piling up on the back porch, it's time to make assorted vegetable and fresh herb crostini.

Fresh herbs, such as oregano, basil, chives, parsley, dill, and garlic
Olive oil
Balsamic vinegar
Garlic, crushed

Fresh vegetables, such as green and yellow squash, sliced thin; tomatoes, seeded and diced; cucumber, sliced thin; onion, sliced thin
Slices of toasted bread

Wash and chop the herbs and cloves of garlic and place in small individual dishes. Combine olive oil, balsamic vinegar, and crushed garlic to taste for the marinade. Dip vegetables in marinade, pile on toasted breads, and sprinkle herbs over vegetables. Or, grill vegetables before topping crostini.

CHAPTER 5

*A well-planned and well-executed garden of any sort is an investment
that pays off with delightfully satisfying results. Theme gardens can reflect
your special tastes and interests and, when carried out successfully, can bring
you years of pleasure. Creating a theme garden is easy—if you use
the lasagna gardening method—and lots of fun.*

Creating Lasagna Theme Gardens

What's in a Theme?

Theme gardens may be filled with plants that share similar characteristics or with plants that have special significance to you. The theme can be very obvious—like a garden of blue-flowered plants—or practical, like a garden filled with culinary herbs. You can even have a theme that's completely whimsical—a garden of plants with names beginning with "m," for example. You might choose plants with common features, such as fragrance, medicinal properties, or color. Or your theme might be much more personal, like plants that your grandmother grew in her gardens.

The idea is simply to enhance your gardening experience by making your gardens meaningful as well as beautiful and/or functional. Herbs lend themselves quite naturally to theme gardens because there are so many different uses for these practical and popular plants. One of the most popular herb gardens is a tea garden, in which all of the plants in the garden can be used to make tea.

I once met a woman who planted her entire garden with plants that had red flowers or foliage. Her plant palette included yarrows, globe amaranths, tulips, daylilies, bee balm, poppies, snapdragons, azaleas, and even red-leaved barberries and maples. It was a wonderful, happy place, and I fell in love with all the shades of red in her collection of bulbs, annuals, perennials, and shrubs. My eye is still drawn to red flowers, and I never peruse a garden catalog that has lots of red flowers without thinking of that woman and her unusual theme garden. I often play with the idea of planting a red garden for myself, but the truth is that I am a white garden person.

Finding Your Own Themes

Gardens can be magical places, and the garden that's built on a theme allows the visitor a rare glimpse into the mind and heart of the gardener. Themes usually evolve from a special interest of the gardener and can bring great pleasure to all who are invited to enjoy the garden. That said, my first themed garden didn't start with a careful plan for following a theme. Instead, it was the result of simple necessity: I needed a handy supply of the fresh herbs we used in the kitchen of our country inn, so I planted a garden of culinary herbs.

Nor was my first theme garden particularly aesthetic in its arrangement. The herbs were planted haphazardly outside the kitchen door. Many of the plants were given to me as gifts by gardening friends and neighbors, and as I obtained them, I simply plunked them in the ground closest to the kitchen. Eventually, I designed a more intentional garden of culinary herbs—my first real theme garden—based on the plants that grew in my "accidental" theme garden.

HERBAL HINT

I think one of the best parts of gardening is the person-to-person contact that results from a common interest. There are so many wonderful people I would never have met if we hadn't both been gardeners. Once I began to plant whole gardens full of herbs, I met even more people with similar interests.

Plants in My First Culinary Herb Garden

1. Common sage
2. Chives
3. Mother-of-thyme
4. Winter savory
5. Marjoram

6. Lavender
7. Variegated ginger mint
8. Rosemary (potted)
9. Basil (several types)
10. Parsley (flat-leaf and curly)

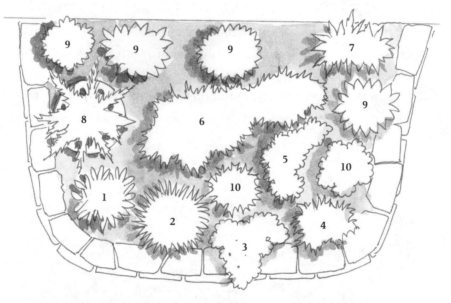

My first intentionally themed garden held culinary herbs that I used in the kitchen of the inn. The garden was planted on a gently sloping hill with a laid-up fieldstone retaining wall holding it all in place.

The White Garden That Happened

When I moved from the inn to the farm, I created lots of wonderful garden spaces with my easy lasagna garden method. Everything was a new challenge: gardens on a hay field, gardens on top of tree roots and around stumps, and gardens on top of packed soil where an old building had been. Each had its own challenging growing conditions.

I started my first white-themed garden where two trees had been removed, and the ground was full of roots and stumps. In addition, more than 60 years worth of pine needles had fallen on the ground under those trees, so the soil there was very acidic. Add layers of rocks, and you have the worst growing conditions you can imagine. All it needed was an application of lasagna gardening, and I planted the garden the first day after I started layering.

Of course, it didn't start out as a theme garden. While shopping for plants to go in the new space, I began to notice how I was drawn to white flowers and plants with white-variegated leaves. Over the years, I bought rhododendrons with huge white blooms, spirea with tiny white blooms, and groundcovers with white-splotched foliage. As the white garden grew, I took great pleasure in bringing home plants I had always wanted in my garden and realized the ones I liked best had white flowers.

Cardboard boxes and thin shipping cartons can be useful weed barriers in a lasagna garden. Cover the boxes with bricks for a day or two to flatten them, then add organic material to start building a bed of healthy soil.

That garden grew one jelly box at a time: Each time I got a delivery from the jelly company that furnished my gift shop with inventory, I flattened the boxes and laid them around the outside of the garden. I covered the boxes with layers of organic material, moved the border plants up on top of the boxes, and thus freed up space within the garden for new plants.

I loved that garden. The opportunity to make a garden filled with plants that spoke to me came at a time when I needed to do something just for myself. I bought the first white blooming plant as a gift to myself for my birthday. After that I celebrated all sorts of special days with new plants.

My white garden bloomed from early spring to late fall, from bulbs to fall asters and everything in between. I don't know if it was the beauty of that garden or my passion for it, but it brought others in to help. My friend

Preparing for Your Own Theme Garden

If you want your own theme garden, there are some steps to take before you actually begin to plant:

1. Pick a theme. If you already have a special interest, it's easy to choose. Let your special interest become the inspiration for your garden.

2. Research your theme, if necessary. If you're interested in creating a garden that reflects a particular time in history, for example, you'll want to find out what plants were used at that time, as well as which of those are suitable for your garden's growing conditions.

3. Pick a site. Most herbs prefer full sun (6 hours or more per day). It's easier to build a garden on a level area, but if your site is a hillside, plant a hillside garden. Allow room in your plan for your plants to grow or for changes to the plan.

4. Choose a design. Mark the design on the site, leaving room for paths.

5. Prepare to install a lasagna garden. Collect organic material to form the layers you will plant in.

6. Install a lasagna garden, following the steps described in Chapter 1.

7. Pull back the layered material to install your plants, setting them on top of the base layers of newspaper and then tucking the layers back around their roots. Press layered material around each plant to force out any air pockets around the roots, then water thoroughly.

Lou built a special arbor for the brilliant white clematis 'Henri' to grow on. Lou came and helped install the arbor, and when the first flowers opened, he was the one I invited to come and enjoy them with me. Though Lou is gone, he is still with me in my gardens. His arbor stands at the entrance to one of my herb gardens at the Potager, and my favorite old-fashioned climbing rose clambers over it.

Because I spent so much of my time in the white garden, it was naturally the place that took much of the overflow of herbs and perennials with white flowers and gray foliage that came through the garden center.

THEMES FROM HISTORY

Herb gardens often reflect historical themes that remind us of the important roles herbs played in centuries past. You might create a garden of herbs and plants mentioned in the writing of William Shakespeare, or a garden of medicinal plants from medieval times. Re-creating gardens like those grown hundreds of years ago really brings history to life—you can appreciate how resourceful people had to be when the herb garden was their main source of medicine.

Thanks to monks, who were among the few medieval people who could read and write, there are records and drawings of the gardens that were features of those ancient monasteries. The monastery garden was the forerunner of the potager, a garden filled with herbs, vegetables, and fruits. During medieval times, monasteries were islands of peace and culture. The monks were self-sufficient and located their gardens inside a wall that surrounded the property. Wells were also close to the monastery and the garden.

Monks and friars practiced healing arts, so the first potagers were filled with healing herbs. The herbs shared space with cabbages and other vegetables. Fruit trees were planted close to a wall and kept pruned to take up very little space. As you can imagine, it didn't take long for dill, chives, and parsley to end up in the cabbage soup or on boiled potatoes.

During the 17th and 18th centuries, France had some of the most beautiful herb gardens ever created. These were mostly formal gardens hedged by box-

To make new plants from boxwood cuttings, strip the lower leaves from a semi-softwood cutting that is about 6 inches long. Pour a teaspoonful of rooting hormone into a shallow cup. Dip the cutting into water, then into rooting hormone. Stick the cuttings in trays of moist sand or vermiculite and keep them in cool, humid conditions. Cuttings may take up to 6 months to form roots.

wood, but they also contained herbs, flowers, and food plants. Some of these gardens still survive today.

Boxwood as hedging for formal gardens became popular, and potagers, or kitchen gardens, abounded in every part of France. It wasn't long before the use of boxwood as a hedging plant spread to other European countries. Later, in America's colonial gardens, formal plantings were created with boxwood. You can still see what these gardens were like in restored historical villages such as Colonial Williamsburg, Virginia.

Boxwood is still a favorite small hedging plant in today's gardens. Much to my delight, I found old plantings of boxwood on the property where my daughter and I make our home in Westbrookville, New York. Cuttings from these hardy shrubs have provided me with the beginnings of the hedge that surrounds a new herb garden. This garden has a planting of old roses and is located in front of the 1890 building that houses the Potager.

Themed Herb Garden Plans and Plant Lists

I love theme gardens! Themes keep you focused and give you a solid sense of direction. And theme gardens are so wonderfully pleasing. When you decide on a theme, it's usually something you already have an interest in.

Take butterflies, for instance. If you love butterflies and want to attract them to your yard, the logical herb garden to make would be one filled with plants that attract butterflies. You can even design a butterfly garden shaped like a butterfly and filled with plants that attract butterflies and caterpillars. The butterfly shape should include paths so you can access all parts of the garden to maintain order.

My first butterfly garden at the farm was filled with plants recommended by the Federated Garden Clubs of New York State. Most of these plants were perennial flowers, not herbs. The location was in one of the first lasagna beds I created at the farm and was on the site of an old hay field. At first the beds were unframed, but because of a slight tilt toward the next property, I boxed them in. It was a demonstration of what to plant to get the most butterfly action.

Beware! This could be addictive! You might get so involved in your butterfly garden that you decide to build more than one. You might collect a small library of books that teach you about butterflies and gardening. Or you might meet an equally enthusiastic butterfly gardener. Between the gardening and reading you might find your passion—if you are lucky.

A GARDEN FOR BUTTERFLIES

In mid- to late summer, butterfly activity reaches its peak in the garden, and almost anything that's blooming is likely to be visited by these elegant insects. Still, there are some flowers that are preferred over others, and if you want to be assured of butterfly sightings, it helps to think like a butterfly! Planting favored flowers like yarrow and bee balm is a step in the

---

HERBAL HINT

When framing garden beds, try to keep the measurements simple: One 4 × 8-foot garden requires three 8-foot boards (two 8-foot lengths for the sides and two 4-foot lengths for the ends). If you don't have tools to cut the one board in half, ask the lumberyard to do it for you. In addition, most cars, vans, and trucks can handle 8-foot lengths of lumber.

Plant List for a Butterfly Garden

1. Yarrow (*Achillea* sp.)
2. Pinks (*Dianthus* sp.)
3. Lantana (*Lantana camara* cultivars)
4. Trumpet honeysuckle (*Lonicera sempervirens*)
5. Bee balm (*Monarda didyma*)
6. Parsley
7. Rosemary
8. Sage
9. Goldenrod (*Solidago* sp.)
10. Thyme
11. Mexican sunflower (*Tithonia rotundifolia*)
12. 'Velvet Queen' sunflower (*Helianthus* 'Velvet Queen')

right direction—compound flower heads composed of lots of small flowers are popular butterfly stops. It also helps to include food for caterpillars because these less-desired garden visitors are the beautiful butterflies of the future. My first butterfly garden included parsley for that purpose; it's the preferred caterpillar food for parsleyworms, which mature into swallowtail butterflies.

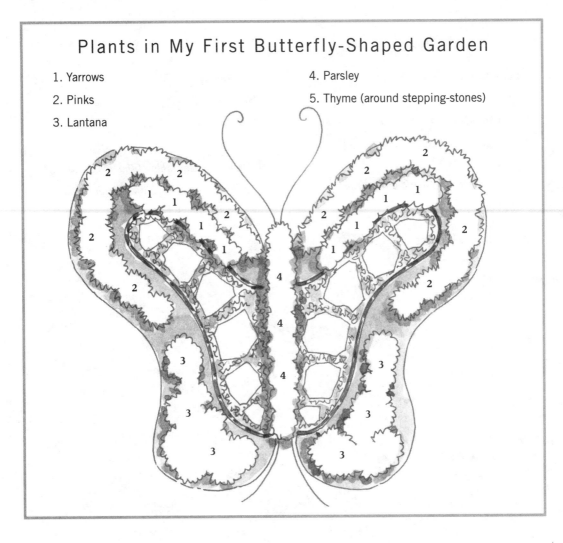

Plants in My First Butterfly-Shaped Garden

1. Yarrows
2. Pinks
3. Lantana
4. Parsley
5. Thyme (around stepping-stones)

A BUTTERFLY-SHAPED GARDEN

Later I got more creative and built a butterfly-shaped garden, with paths accessing all the wider areas. This garden required no outer framing because it was built on a level area. I planted this garden with butterfly-attracting plants so that real butterflies would come to visit my floral one.

A WHITE GARDEN

When you have been gardening as long as I have, you know what plants and colors you want. I never knew how pleasing a white-themed garden would be to me until I planted one. I began with annuals with white flowers. As my interest and knowledge grew, so did my plant list.

Finances were a deciding factor back in those days. I was on a budget that didn't allow a lot of luxuries. Each time there was something to celebrate, I bought a plant for my white garden. I also chose plants that reminded me of favorite relatives: snowball viburnum for Etta, bridal wreath spirea for Della, and Lady Banks roses for Deborah. Remembering my mother's birthday sent me to the garden center for unusual hostas, and I came back with an array of white-striped and white-edged selections.

That first white garden also had lots of herbs that fit the theme: artemisias, thymes, Greek oregano, garlic chives, feverfew, and horehound. These herbs had either white flowers or silvery gray foliage.

From the time I planted my first white garden at the farm on Shandelee, I had a tremendous desire to plant a white-flowering herb garden. It helps

Plant List for a White-Flowering Herb Garden

White-flowering bee balm (*Monarda* 'Snowmaiden' and 'Snowqueen'): Plant near the back of the border.

Garlic chives (*Allium tuberosum*): Put this in the middle of the border.

Feverfew (*Tanacetum parthenium*): White flowers appear on bushy plants.

Horehound (*Marrubium vulgare*): This plant has clusters of tiny white flowers above fuzzy light gray leaves

White-flowering Jacob's ladder (*Polemonium caeruleum* 'Alba'): Plant in the middle of the border where taller background plants give a little shade.

White-flowering lavender (*Lavandula angustifolia* 'Nana Alba'): A dwarf variety, so plant near the front of the border in full sun; needs good drainage.

Pansies (*Viola* × *wittrockiana* 'Majestic Giant White' and 'Delta'): Both have large, edible flowers.

Silver thyme (*T.* × *citriodorus* 'Argenteus'): These are small plants with silver-edged leaves and a subtle lemon fragrance.

White-flowering thymes (*Thymus serpyllum albus* and *T. serpyllum* 'Snowdrift'): Plant near the path in full sun or as a groundcover.

White violas (*Viola* hybrids 'Sorbet Coconut' and 'Velour White'): Both have edible flowers and enjoy part shade; plant them toward the front of the border.

if you know what your best color is, and I know that mine is white. I like to surround myself in the color that brings me a measure of peace and calm. The white garden on Shandelee gave me tremendous pleasure and a sense of peace, and each time I worked in it I enjoyed a spiritual experience that restored my soul.

You know you got it right when what you have done continues to please you. It's 10 years later, and I'm still planting that white-flowering herb garden. If not for my limited space, this theme garden could have gotten out of control. I couldn't stop adding plants—old favorites and new discoveries.

Plant List for an Aromatherapy Garden

1. Lavender
2. Rosemary (in pots)
3. Basil
4. Bee balm
5. Fennel
6. Sweet marjoram
7. Thyme
8. Juniper (*Juniperis* sp.)
9. Chamomile
10. Lemon balm

Garden could also include:

- Catmint
- Roses
- Scented geraniums

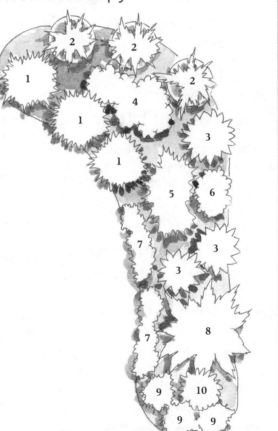

A Fragrant Mood

Need a lift? Try the herbs listed below to lighten your mood.

Antidepressant: lemon balm

Calming: sweet marjoram

Concentration: basil

Invigorating: rosemary

Relaxing: chamomile, fennel

Soothing: chamomile, lavender, catmint, scented geraniums, rose, thyme

Stimulant: juniper, thyme

Uplifting: bee balm

AN AROMATHERAPY HERB GARDEN

Fragrances have powerful abilities to awaken our memories and affect our moods. Herbal aromas are widely used to impart benefits through aromatherapy, and it's fun to plant a garden filled with these special scents. The herbs I've chosen for my aromatherapy garden are common and easy to find. They are also easy to grow and maintain.

A SALAD AND HERB GARDEN

When I plant my salad and herb garden each year, I try some new varieties of salad greens, but my perennial salad herbs are already in place. Basil, rosemary, and parsley are planted fresh each year, and I always find new basils to try.

This is such a beautiful garden with all the colorful lettuce, edible flowers, and salad herbs, so I keep it close to the door. Even when I'm not making salad, I can enjoy it. Each year I find new ways to plant different

HERBAL HINT

If you are planning a garden using lots of plants, look for a grower who sells flats wholesale, ask your garden center for a discount on large orders, or grow them yourself. One package of thyme seed will grow several flats of plants, or you can sow the seeds directly in the place they will grow.

Plant List for a Salad and Herb Garden

- 'Caesar' basil
- 'Magical Michael' basil
- 'Purple Ruffles' basil
- 'Sweet Genova' basil
- Borage
- Calendula
- Chicory
- Chives
- Garlic chives
- 'Patio Pickle' bush cucumbers
- 'Bouquet' dill
- 'Ducat' dill
- Garlic
- Johnny jump-ups
- 'Buttercrunch' lettuce
- 'Raisa' lettuce
- 'Red Fire' lettuce
- 'Red Salad Bowl' lettuce
- 'Tango' lettuce
- 'Victoria' lettuce
- Nasturtiums
- Imperial Series pansies
- Italian parsley
- Salad burnet
- Salad rocket
- French tarragon
- Lemon thyme
- 'Supersweet 100' cherry tomatoes

colors of lettuce. One year I may plant red-leaf lettuce with lime green bibb in a lattice design; the next year I find something new and try new designs.

This may be one of the most fun gardens in my long list of gardens at the Potager. When choosing herbs for this garden, keep in mind the flavor of each herb's individual flowers and how they will look in the garden and taste in your salads.

A DRYER'S GARDEN

The drying garden is a place where decorating dreams begin. Wreaths, bouquets, swags, rings, and bunches of herbs all hanging in a row—oh, my! If you are a gardener/crafter, you will know what I mean when I say that growing your material is the first step toward year-round pleasure from the garden. From early spring to late winter, the fruits of your harvest will give you oodles of pleasure and allow your imagination to come to life with little cost or effort.

From one package of seeds you can grow enough strawflowers to keep you busy for months or years. Your garden can be a wonder to behold and provide enough dried material for hundreds of projects. Yellows, reds, blues, and pinks are just the beginning of a wide range of colors to choose from.

The simplest way to use and enjoy dried plant material is in a bouquet. My grandmother always had a bouquet of dried hydrangea blooms in a vase in the dining room. On her one and only trip out of Tennessee to Jacksonville Beach, Florida, she brought back a bundle of sea oats, and from then on they were displayed in another vase in the dining room.

My mother kept dried flowers all around the house, although it wasn't entirely intentional. They started off as fresh flowers in water and later became dried flower arrangements as the water evaporated and they dried naturally. Each year she brought in fall leaves and carefully placed them where everyone who visited could enjoy them. They were beautiful in her collection of white stoneware pitchers, but you guessed it: They stayed too long and were brittle by the time she replaced them with holiday greens.

Dried herbs and flowers are a part of my own life. There are giant purple/green hydrangea blossoms in some of my mother's white stoneware pitchers on the living room mantle, and dried herbs hang from a rod in the kitchen. Homemade herbal potpourri fills my grandmother's Depression-glass bowl in the bathroom, and a giant dried herb and flower wreath hangs over my bed.

Every year my gardens hold many plants that lend themselves to drying and using in crafts, but the list changes from one season to the next, depending on what caught my fancy at planting time and what was left unsold from the garden center. There are a few plants, however, that I'm sure to always have because they form the foundations of many of my projects. These are artemisias, yarrows, love-in-a-mist (*Nigella damascena*), and sage. I also gather some of my drying materials from the roadsides, including wild yarrow, pearly everlasting (*Anaphalis margaritacea*), wild rose hips, and Queen-Anne's-lace.

Plant List for a Pizza Garden

1. Greek oregano
2. Italian parsley
3. 'Greek' basil
4. Garlic
5. Garden thyme
6. Garlic chives

7. 'Tumbler Hybrid' tomatoes
8. 'Southport Bunching' onions
9. 'Cherry Pick' pepper
10. 'Tri-Fetti' hot pepper
11. 'Kermit' or 'Ichiban' eggplant

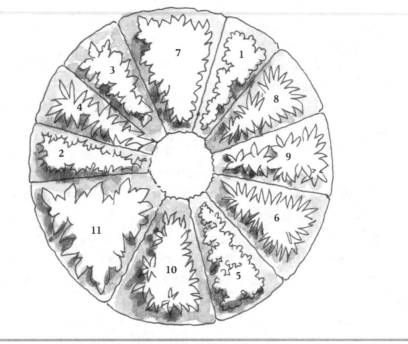

A WHEEL OR PIZZA HERB GARDEN

The sheer fact that it's fun is reason enough to plant herbs, tomatoes, and other vegetables in a wheel design so that they resemble a giant pizza. Each opening between "spokes" can contain one herb that would be used on pizza or in the tomato sauce. Imagine the delight of visiting children or grandchildren at being able to pick the herbs and vegetables that give pizza its special flavors from a pizza-shaped garden.

A DYER'S GARDEN

Want to know what it was like to live in the old days when nothing was easy and putting a little color in your life was a trip down a road that seemed to never end? Natural dyeing was a long and labor-intensive process. Back then, the promise of color in an otherwise drab fashion world would justify any amount of work and effort.

Plants for the dyer's garden include familiar herbs like comfrey, chamomile, goldenrod, marigold, and tansy. All of these plants will produce some shade of yellow. To make other colors, you must expand your garden to include elder for green; meadowsweet for black; nettle for grayish green; St.-John's-wort for red, green, or brown; sorrel for beige/pink; and woad for blue.

Many of these plants were traditionally harvested from the wild, but that practice is no longer recommended except in cases of clear and verifiable overabundance, such as an entire field filled with goldenrod. Even then, it's important to get permission from the property owner before you begin gathering plants.

Before the 19th century, nearly all dyes were natural and derived from plants. Leaves, flowers, and roots were gathered and boiled. Natural fibers—wool, silk, linen, and cotton—were dipped in the boiling hot liquid, then stirred while the brew boiled until the cloth reached the desired color. Dyes were uneven and splotchy until people began to strain the liquid. This reduced the splotchy look but did not eliminate it.

Natural dyes were not permanent until the use of mordants, compounds that fixed the dye. Without a mordant, the dyes ran and the color quickly faded. The most widely used mordants are alum, iron, copper, and

HERBAL HINT

When harvesting plants for dyeing, it's best to pick flowers just as they are coming out and when leaves are young. Dig roots in fall and cut them into pieces well before you are ready to use them.

chrome. (Today's mordants can be purchased at drug stores, high-end craft stores, or dye supply houses).

The wool dyeing process consists of several steps: preparation of the material, preparation of the mordant, preparation of the dye, and the dyeing process. That sounds like a lot of preparation, and it is. It's also messy, although the actual dyeing process is quite simple.

THE HERB AND EDIBLE FLOWER GARDEN

A garden of edible flowers and herbs can provide a growing season of delight for the eyes as well as the palate. Whether you group plants to create a pattern of colors and textures or mix them into a riotous multicolored display, this is an easy garden to enjoy. Use any or all of nasturtiums; pansies; pinks; scarlet runner beans; violas, Johnny-jump-ups, and old-fashioned violets; 'Lemon Gem' marigolds; and basil, dill, lavender, and chives.

THE SHADY HERB GARDEN

Yes, there are herbs that will grow in the shade, or in partial shade, at least. Although most herbs thrive in sunny sites, a garden of herbs in less than full sun is possible. Your best bets are to be found among the mint family herbs—those vigorous growers that can become invasive, particularly in moist, rich soil. Still, you can enjoy a lovely selection of herbal teas using the herbs that tolerate shade: mints, lemon balm, bee balm, and catnip.

Just be sure to keep a close eye on these shady characters so they don't overrun the rest of your gardens. Any of them may be planted in an open-

---

HERBAL HINT

Need just a bit more sun? Lop off a tree branch or shape a shrub to admit more light into your garden.

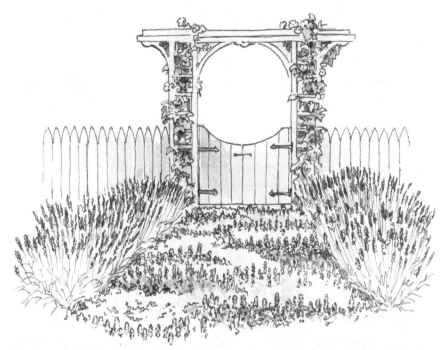

My thyme walk at the Potager is bordered with lavender and includes the following kinds of thyme: woolly, creeping, oregano, lemon, silver, and caraway.

bottom pot or bucket set into the soil to limit the run of their roots. You can also mow around the perimeter of such a garden and easily cut back any escaping shoots.

THE THYME GARDEN

I became intrigued with thymes while visiting Well-Sweep Herb Farm in New Jersey. The folks there grow 300 different thymes, and they have many areas where thyme is used in very inventive ways. Once established, it needs little care, and it's one of those rare plants that's tough enough to tolerate foot traffic at the front of a border or between paving stones.

Just last summer, I decided to create a thyme walk leading from the public sidewalk to the greenhouse. I had lots of plants, and the space was already marked. I planted the thymes and let the rest of the installation rest for the winter. In the fall I had my helper, Charlie, clear the leaf debris from the side gardens, including the thyme path. He did such a great job he raked most of the surviving thymes out of the path—aarrggh!

In the spring I saw that the few thyme plants that had survived the winter—and Charlie's rake—had filled in the path beautifully. That fall, I again planted leftover thyme in the path and, in addition, bordered the walk on both sides with lavender.

THE TEA GARDEN

Tea is perhaps the most popular and widely accepted way of using herbs. The first herbal teas were medicines, of course, and were among the easiest ways of preparing and administering treatments. Whether an herbal tea actually worked medicinally or not, just drinking the hot tea often made the patient feel better. It's much the same today: When we want to feel better, we make a cup of hot tea, herbal or otherwise.

Making a proper pot of tea is a matter of accumulating the right components and putting them together in the proper and time-tested way.

1. Use a china, crockery, or other nonmetal pot.
2. Bring water to a rolling boil.
3. Rinse the pot in some of the boiling water to heat the pot.
4. Add tea/herbs to pot. Use loose tea leaves (bark, twigs, seeds, pods, etc.), allowing 2 tablespoons fresh tea leaves (1 tablespoon dried tea leaves) for each cup of water. Add an extra tablespoon of tea leaves for the pot.
5. Fill pot with boiling water and cover.
6. Allow 5 minutes for tea to steep before pouring.
7. Strain herbs from tea as you pour into cup.
8. Serve with a selection of honey, lemon or orange slices, warm milk or cream, and sugar.

Tips for Teas

Here are a few more tips for enjoying your herbs in homemade teas:

- Once tea has brewed at least 5 minutes or until desired strength is reached, strain it and discard leaves and herbs.

- Sage tea is good for colds and fever.

- Rosemary tea is used to alleviate headaches.

- Lemon herbs can replace the slice of fresh lemon in tea.

- Chamomile tea is said to improve one's disposition.

- Once tea is brewed, keep the pot covered with a tea cozy to keep tea hot.

- Taking tea at the same time every day keeps your body on schedule.

- Always use a lid when infusing tea so the "good chemicals" don't escape.

- Suit your own tastes when deciding what herbs to use to make tea. It should taste good.

- Not all herbs are suited to making teas, and some plants are dangerous to ingest. You should know about the plants you plan to use as tea.

- Never use the directions from one of the ancient herbalists to make tea (or any kind of medicine). They are dead.

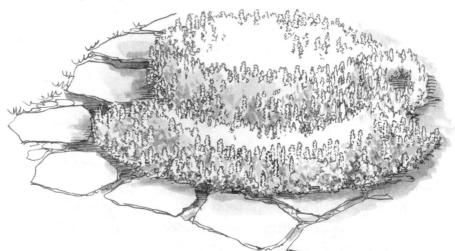

A garden planted in the shape of a teacup is a fun way to display your tea herbs. You can even create a whole "set" of such teacups, each featuring a different herb. Use different varieties, or different herbs, to create the appearance of tea in the cup and to separate the cup and saucer. Good herbs to use in this kind of planting include sage, chamomile, lemon thyme, lemon balm, rose, apple mint, horehound, hyssop, rosemary, savory, marjoram, and anise.

Tea Herb Combinations

A garden of tea herbs may prove to be one of the most rewarding gardens you ever make. You probably already have some potential tea plants growing in your garden and can start right away to create herbal tea blends. Here is a list of herbs that combine into tasty teas:

- Rose petals and rose hips
- Fruit leaves: blueberry leaf, strawberry leaf, raspberry leaf, and scented geranium
- Mint, lemon verbena, and lemon balm
- Angelica, orange peel, and blueberry leaf

- Thyme and lemon leaf
- Peppermint, ginger mint, and chamomile
- Apple mint, chamomile, and valerian
- Sage and lemon leaf
- Lemon thyme, lemon grass, and lemon verbena
- Horehound and chamomile
- Anise hyssop and borage
- Bee balm and blueberry leaf
- Rosemary and rose hips

A MEDICINAL GARDEN

Herbs were the original medicines, and a garden of medicinal herbs is a fascinating way to bring history to life. Although I have a tremendous interest in the history of medicinal herbs, I don't use them as medicines and never advise anyone else to use them that way. I am not a doctor or a trained herbalist. There are plenty of people who are qualified to give such advice, and many excellent books on the subject exist. If your interest in medicinal herbs runs in that direction, please consult an expert before treating yourself with herbs. My medicinal gardens are strictly decorative, and I plant them for their historical interest.

Plants for a Historical Medicinal Garden

Horehound: The leaves are used to flavor horehound candy for relief of cold symptoms and coughs.

Chamomile: The flowers have been used as a sedative by making them into tea. They are also used in hair rinse for blondes.

Echinacea: The dark pink flowers with prominent cones are beautiful, but it's the roots that have the medicinal power and are used as an anti-infective.

Feverfew: The yellow-and-white daisylike flowers have a sedative quality when brewed into tea.

Lobelia: Some species of lobelia have been used in teas to treat asthma and also dried and used as a tobacco substitute.

Foxglove: The leaves have been used to treat dropsy and heart ailments. All parts of this plant are poisonous.

CHAPTER 6

As I got into the habit of planting herbs to enhance the flavors of food, I began to appreciate the beauty of living herbs at my doorstep. When winter threatened to erase them from the landscape, I harvested them and brought them indoors to dry. I hung bunches of herbs from beams, and they repaid me with drifts of fragrance and memories of summer. From there it was natural to begin using them in aromatic and decorative crafts around my home.

Decorative Uses for Herbs

From Herb Gardener to Herb Crafter

I often tell folks, particularly those who have never had an herb garden, that it doesn't matter whether you use the herb plants; they are just wonderful to have in the garden. They smell good and look fabulous. However, if you plant an herb garden, it's more than likely that you'll eventually find yourself making wreaths, potpourris, and other fragrant and decorative embellishments for the home. It's irresistible!

When I was an innkeeper and had my own herb gardens, I harvested huge bundles of fragrant herbs and hung them from the beams in the main dining room. The room was 30 feet wide by 60 feet long, and the main support beam spanned the length of the ceiling. It wasn't attractive in its original state, so anything I did to decorate it was an improvement.

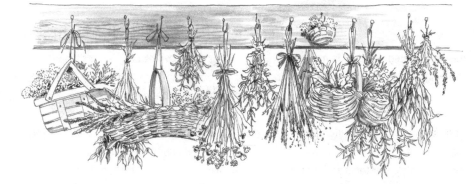

In the beginning, I had no desire to craft anything from my herb garden. All I wanted was fresh herbs for the inn kitchen. My gardens were so prolific that they produced much more than the cooks would ever need, and my thoughts naturally turned to ways in which I could use the overflow. The bare beams in the dining room beckoned.

Once my herb harvests were hung on the beam, I needed something more. Between the bunches of herbs, I hung baskets I had collected over the years. The whole dining room began to look cozier, and customers remarked on the herbal decorations. From time to time I would be asked to sell bunches of herbs or baskets, and for years I just said "No" to these requests.

After we had been at the Inn on Shandelee for about 8 years, I increased my harvest from the herb garden to be able to add to my little gift shop. Also, instead of hanging my private collection of baskets, which included my grandmother's sewing basket, my parents' first picnic basket, and my uncle's old fishing creel (everyone wanted to buy them, and I didn't want to sell these heirlooms), I bought new baskets that I didn't mind parting with and sold them.

HERBAL HINT

When cutting herbs for drying and crafting, wait until afternoon so any moisture on them has dried. If you are cutting herb flowers, cut them before they are fully open.

Tool Totes and Disposable Drop Cloths

Working with dried material is messy. No matter what you do or how careful you are, there is always fallout, sometimes with the best pieces ending up on the floor.

In a perfect world we would each have a whole room set aside to work on herb arrangements and crafts. Our tools and craft supplies would all have a place, and everything could be stored away. Our room would have a door, and we could walk away in the middle of a project, close the door, and return to find everything just where we left it.

Alas, there is no such thing as a perfect world. When most of us want to do a project, we have to find a place to work, set up, and take down once the project is finished.

The answer to an easier cleanup is just an inexpensive drop cloth away. I buy the clear plastic kind and cut them into pieces that fit under my kitchen table and chair where I work. They cost from $1 to $3 each. Anything that falls on the floor lands on the drop cloth. When the job is finished, I just fold up the plastic with the droppings still in it and throw it away, scraps and all.

Because I have no special room for my numerous projects, I keep my basic herb-crafting tools in a large plastic tote. I have several tool totes: one for painting tools, one for woodworking tools, and one with small garden tools. They are just the right size to fit in the space under the kitchen sink.

My retail business at the inn included bunches of dried herbs, baskets, and a Hoosier cupboard full of jellies, jams, herbal vinegars, and herb jellies. It wasn't long before some guests at the inn asked me to make up a gift basket that included a selection of the homemade products we had for sale. The finishing touch in that first gift basket was an antique jam pot, and it was quite a hit. I began going to local auctions and yard sales to look for small antiques to add to the inn's decor and to my inventory. What had begun as a way to add to the herbs I needed in the kitchen was now truly one of the ways I entertained myself.

The Herbal Home

Once you start your herb garden, you will begin to use herbs in more ways than just as teas or herb bundles to hang from the ceiling. Herbs have all kinds of uses in the home and can help you with cleaning as well as keeping your home smelling nice.

Scenting the home with herbs is as old as history. Ancient civilizations used herbs as incense, burning the most fragrant herbs in religious ceremonies. At the same time, the burning herbs helped freshen the air inside the dwelling.

Later, castle dwellers—and people who lived in humbler homes—strewed herbs on the floor to keep the air fresh and deter disease. When they got old, these strewing herbs were swept away and replaced with new ones. The strewing herbs not only smelled good but also looked nice because they included wildflowers. Somewhat more recently, herbs were used to freshen linen presses and clothes chests. As dressers and clothes closets came into fashion, so did sachets. The Victorians made herbal pillows to dream on.

Today we call those little pillows "dream pillows," and different combinations of herbs are used to induce different dreams. Jim Long of Long Creek Herbs in Missouri is an expert on herbal dream pillows and has a book filled with their history and directions for making your own.

Dream Pillow Herb Mixture

Combine 1 ounce each dried mugwort, lemon verbena, chamomile, peppermint, rose petals, and hops. Place in an open bowl near your bed, or sew them into a small muslin bag that you can place inside your pillowcase.

Many different plants became known as household herbs for their uses in the home. Teasel heads were used to loosen the nap when preparing wool, lavender was used to prepare a furniture polish, and horsetails were used to do the polishing. Herbs were used as fabric dyes, and gardens routinely contained dye plants such as indigo, woad, madder, and pokeweed.

POMANDERS, POTPOURRIS, AND POCKETS

Although the custom of strewing herbs on the floor has fallen out of practice, we still use fragrant herbs in traditional ways such as potpourris, pomanders, and pocket pillows to scent our homes. I use many of the herbs I grow to make potpourris that scent the rooms of my home with pleasantly subtle fragrances.

Herb Pomanders

For this project you need a pair of sharp scissors, a ball of floral foam, and a supply of herbs. Suggested herbs to use are rose-mary, sage, marjoram, or thyme—it's important that they have woody stems to pierce the floral foam.

A trio of herb pomanders makes a great centerpiece. Use the point of the scissors to poke holes in the foam balls, then insert short sprigs of herbs in decorative patterns.

Pomanders were traditionally made from fruits studded with cloves. The holidays wouldn't be the same without a bowl full of these spiky and spicy reminders of Christmases past. I still make some fruit pomanders each year, but most of the new pomanders I make are balls of floral foam studded with herb twigs. These herbed pomanders are decorative and easy to make, and they last much longer than their fruit-based forebears.

Potpourri from the Herb Garden

Potpourri is one of the easiest home fragrance products you can make from your garden. Even in a small garden space, I have more than enough room to grow enough herbs to make lots of potpourri every year. I take my sharp scissors and a basket to the garden and start cutting.

I make decisions about ingredients based on what I have available in the garden and what smells nice. One of my favorite combinations is lavender stems and flowers, dianthus petals, and marjoram flowers. To this I might add some gray-green poppy heads, brown spiky coneflower centers, and bee balm petals. Then I "dress up" the mixture with seasonal additions, such as small pinecones, dried eucalyptus leaves, or seashells. Or I might find some pieces of decorative bark and add those to the potpourri blend to give it a rustic, woodsy appearance.

Pat's Pleasing Potpourris

Growing and mixing your own potpourri is one of the easiest ways to start enjoying your garden herbs inside your home. If your fondness for potpourri comes from a familiarity with commercial blends, you may be disappointed initially by the appearance of your homegrown mixtures: Homemade potpourri bears little resemblance to what is sold commercially. You'll quickly come to realize, however, that homemade potpourri is subtle where store-bought is "in your face" (and up your nose). Your homegrown mixes will have muted colors and gentle fragrances; what they won't have is the overpowering and even irritating aromas typical of most commercial potpourris.

Most of the herbs and flowers you grow in your own garden can be used in potpourri, as well as bits of bark, seedpods, and pinecones from your landscape. There's no need to plant a separate garden for potpourri ingredients because nearly everything from your herb garden is fair game for use in potpourri. Experiment with all your herbs and see what dries best and what keeps its fragrance. You don't need

a recipe to make potpourri, but here are some of the successful blends I have made to help you get started.

Rose potpourri: Use dried rose petals and whole rose blossoms; add rose essential oil. Rose petals tend to lose their natural fragrance very quickly.

Lavender potpourri: Combine equal amounts of dried lavender flower petals and any "filler" material you choose—moss, dried ferns, small pinecones, etc. Lavender holds its fragrance longer than any other herb, and it may be years before you need to add a few drops of lavender essential oil to refresh this potpourri.

Sage potpourri: If you like the smell of sage, this is the easiest blend to make. All parts of the sage plant—leaves, flowers, and stems—have the unique sage smell.

Drying is easy: Simply cut large stems and tie them together with a rubber band. Hang in a well-ventilated location out of direct sun, and everything will be dry within a week. Crumble or cut all the stems and leaves into chunky pieces and pile in a bowl or basket.

Bowls and baskets filled with fragrant garden potpourri are an easy way to administer aromatherapy to yourself, your friends, or your whole family. It's also a way to bring the garden into your home.

Herb Pockets

One of the projects that impressed our inn guests was the addition of herb pockets to their rooms. An herb pocket is an opening in a pillow or a small bag hanging from the bed skirt. Into these pockets I placed little sachets filled with herbs. I also tucked the sachets in drawers. In the lobby, I kept a basket full of sachets and different herb pockets for sale. Many times when I was out of one or the other, guests would come down with the different products I had left in their room and buy those.

Herbal Wreaths and Swags

Wreaths and swags are especially nice when they are handmade and the material comes from your garden. Your creations will greet your friends at the door as evidence of your special interest. When making an herb wreath, the first consideration is what to use for a base: foam, straw, wire, grapevine, woody herb branches, or other materials. You can purchase a variety of wreath bases, but some are easy to make:

- Bend coat hangers or other strong, flexible wire into sturdy wire wreath bases.
- New growth from 'Silver Queen' or 'Silver King' artemisia can be shaped into pretty herbal bases that look good enough to hang unadorned.

■ Grapevines can be shaped into attractive wreaths that stand alone without any other embellishments. They are easier to make when the vines are still green and pliable. (You may read about soaking grapevines in the bathtub, but it isn't necessary.) Even when the vines are old, I still cut them and make them into wreaths without any soaking. Cutting off the larger pieces of vine and the pieces that won't bend makes this job easier.

With an abundance of wild grapevine in my area, I can't pass up free material for my herb wreaths. I make lots of different-size vine wreaths, then decorate them with bunches of herbs as they come into season. Most years I have wreath bases left over. These go over an upended tomato cage to become decorative pieces for the garden.

From the smallest 4-inch wreath base, I can create herbal embellishments for every room. These little wreaths look particularly nice in

One year, I used one of the grapevine wreath–covered tomato cages as a Christmas tree. It was so attractive I needed only to add tiny white lights to transform it into a holiday decoration.

HERBAL HINT

Cut grapevines to use in wreathmaking and take them to a large, outdoor, open space away from bushes, hedges, or other vegetation. I use the space in front of my garage so I can stretch the vines out before I begin making my circles.

bathrooms, bedrooms, or kitchens. I also like to hang these mini wreaths from corners of furniture such as dressers or hall coatracks. Attached to wide decorative ribbon, they can be hung over mirrors for an unusual decoration.

Use 12- to 14-inch-long pieces of slender grapevine to make small wreaths. One is never enough, so it's okay to get carried away when you start making these little wreaths. You can use them individually or in groups—the more you make, the more you will use.

Herb Wreath How-To

1. Choose a base for your wreath and gather the herbs you plan to use.

2. Using sharp garden shears, snip the herbs into 3- to 4-inch lengths and gather them into small bundles, using fine-gauge floral wire to fasten each bundle.

3. Once you have assembled a good quantity of herb bundles, use a continuous strand of wire to wrap around each bundle and then around the wreath, repeating until the wreath is covered. As you attach the bundles, pull them alternately to the right and left to cover the base completely.

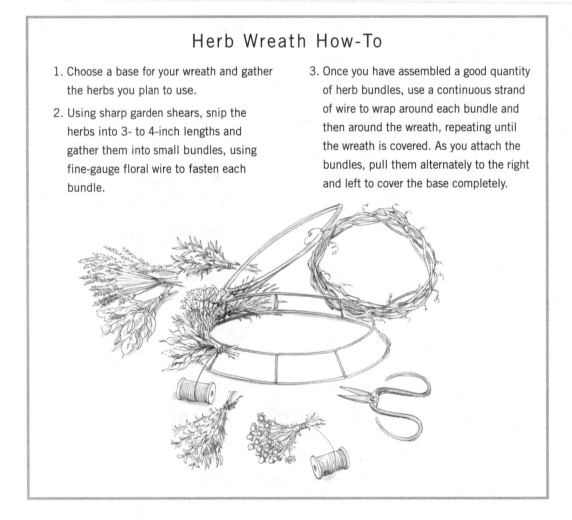

HERBAL HINT

If you use fresh herbs and flowers to cover your wreath bases, be prepared to fill in the gaps that will develop as the materials dry.

Making Herb Swags

Garden twine, strengthened with medium-gauge wire, is the base for my herb swags. You'll also need floral wire, green floral tape, sharp wire snips, and small pruners or garden shears, as well as the herbs and flowers you want to use.

1. Cut a piece of twine and a piece of medium-gauge wire the desired length of your finished swag plus 6 inches.

2. Tie herbs and flowers into small bundles, fastening them with floral wire.

3. Using the floral wire from its spool without cutting it, wrap it around a bunch of herbs and then around the twine and wire, then around another herb bundle and back around the twine, repeating until you've covered the twine and wire base or run out of bundles of herbs and flowers.

4. Use floral tape to secure and wrap the ends of the herb and flower bundles.

Simple Herbal Ornaments

Decorating with things from the garden is a trend that isn't going away. Whether you bring favorite garden pots inside to create a tablescape or use an old birdbath for a side table, you can't go wrong. I loved looking at some of my garden things so much that it was only reasonable to use them year-round. Instead of piling everything in the garden shed, I bring in a rustic bench, a galvanized watering can, a birdbath, a few old rakes, and my garden hats.

There are loads of quick and clever things you can do with herbs to create home decorations or gifts. My favorites are the ones that require little time or skill but produce good-looking results—who doesn't love those kinds of projects? For example: Fill a decorative terra-cotta pot with a round piece of floral foam and stick small pieces of your favorite herb into the foam to create a green sphere with lots of texture. Carry the theme a little further and wrap some herb leaves or stems around the base of a candle. Tie them in place with a piece of decorative twine or raffia.

DECORATING YOUR TABLE WITH HERBS

Whether you're hosting an herb-themed luncheon or tea, celebrating a special occasion, or just having some friends over for coffee, it's fun to dress up your table with some simple herb crafts. Many of the projects that follow are so simple that they barely qualify as projects, but your guests will be impressed far beyond the small effort you spend in the crafting. And you'll be amazed at how easy it is to make good-looking herbal centerpieces, favors, and place-setting decorations.

HERBAL HINT

A simple glue-gun stand will save you from spilled glue and burned tabletops. Mine has also saved me from burning myself with hot glue.

Getting Started

There are some basic materials that you'll need to get started on some of the projects from your herb garden. They are things many gardeners and crafters already have in their potting sheds or in rooms devoted to crafts and flower arranging. I started with just a few of these things, but my collection of supplies has grown gradually along with my repertoire of herb crafts.

- A glue gun is a must, and they are simple and inexpensive.

- Don't forget to keep an ample supply of glue sticks on hand. Few things are as annoying as being in the middle of a project and running out of glue sticks.

- Floral foam comes in blocks and is sold by the block or by the case. I never buy fewer than six blocks of it, and around the holidays I try to have a case on hand. When working with fresh herbs and flowers, soak the foam thoroughly before inserting fresh material.

- Reel wire comes in many different sizes, and I usually have a thin one and one a bit thicker. This is sometimes called paddle wire.

- Floral tape is a stretchy green tape that is perfect for holding bundles of herbs together and for wrapping stems.

- Floral scissors are short, sharp blades with large grips. You may need several different kinds of scissors, snips, or pruners. I also keep a sharp knife for cutting stems and foam.

- Raffia comes in large braids or in smaller bundles, and if you never buy a piece of ribbon, you can get by using raffia for all sorts of decorative tying.

- Garden or jute twine has dozens of uses in the garden, in the craft room, and in the house. It comes in brown or green, and I keep both on hand.

- Floral stub wires in different gauge, from fine to heavy, will answer many needs from wiring large stems to wiring together bunches of herbs and flowers and making hairpins for fastening large leaves to your projects.

- Wire-ring or single-wire wreath bases

- Chicken wire

- Rack for air-drying herbs and flowers

- Rubber bands

- Terra-cotta pots

- Decorative ribbon

- Storage boxes, jars, and tissue paper

- Silica gel for drying flowers and other thicker plant materials

- Jute rope in different sizes

Transform plain pots and balls of floral foam into unusual herbal accents by gluing large leaves over them in overlapping patterns. The large leaves of lemon trees, bay, sage, and lamb's-ears work especially well for this purpose.

Leaf-Covered Pots and Spheres

The leaves of some herbs make attractive coverings for pots and picture frames. I have also used these very textured leaves to cover round balls to pile in a basket. Bay or lemon leaves look good, but try fuzzy lamb's-ears for a unique look. Large-leaf cultivars of sage also lend themselves to this simple project.

Start with a clean pot—clay or plastic—a supply of large leaves, and a glue gun, and you'll soon have a pretty leaf-covered pot. Overlap the leaves to create a fish-scale effect, or vary their direction from row to row to make interesting patterns. A basketful of leaf-covered floral foam balls also makes a unique accent; use straight pins to hold the leaves in place while the glue dries.

An "Instant" Herb Basket Centerpiece

This project is practically foolproof, but the results are guaranteed to attract attention. You can use this basket as a centerpiece or on a table near an entryway. Be sure to put it where visitors can brush the herbs to release their fragrance.

Take a large basket with a handle and line it with a plastic bag or aluminum foil. Arrange several small pots of herbs inside to fill the basket and disguise their tops with sheet moss. A variation of the instant herb basket

A layer of moss that hides the pots inside it makes this basket look like a miniature herb garden. You can dress up a plain basket by covering the outside with stems of herbs cut to similar lengths. Secure the herbs around the sides of the basket with a rubber band, then hide the rubber band with a wide, decorative ribbon.

is to fill small pots with floral foam and stick sprigs of herbs into the pots, using a sheet of moss to hide the pots and foam.

There are some really pretty little wire baskets on the market now, and they make great containers for herbs. Fill them with a piece of floral foam, stick stems of herbs into the foam, and disguise the foam with moss. Or simply tuck a potted herb plant into a basket and add a ribbon or raffia bow. Use two or three of these little baskets as a centerpiece, and add napkin rings made from sheer ribbon and herbs.

To create herbed napkin rings, cut wide, sheer ribbon into 6-inch lengths, lay herb leaves and flowers on it, and fold the ribbon over them lengthwise, gluing the edge closed. Then form the ribbon into a circle and glue the ends together.

Herb Topiary

This decorative sculptural piece uses what is handy and lasts a long time. You'll need an aged terra-cotta pot, some plaster of paris mix, a sturdy and fairly straight branch (or a wooden dowel), a foam sphere, some gravel or decorative stones, and enough herb material to cover the sphere.

Fill the pot with mixed plaster of paris and set the branch in place. When the plaster is set, secure the foam sphere onto the top of the branch, which is now the "trunk" of your topiary. Cover the sphere with the herb of your choice. Hide the plaster of paris with decorative gravel.

HERB CANDLES

Candles are a popular feature in home decorating, and when you use them in combination with herbs, the effect is more than pleasing. Here are some of my favorite herb candles. All are easy to make using herbs from your garden. Trust me: Anyone can glue pressed herbs and flowers to store-bought candles.

Candle Pots

Use soaked floral foam to fill a terra-cotta pot. Insert a special candleholder designed for use with floral foam, or use three small pieces of bamboo and some floral tape to create a tripod to hold a candle. Once the candle is in place, cover the remaining floral foam with your favorite herb.

I take a tour of the garden to see what will look and smell nice in my candle pots. During the summer I use scented geranium leaves to create a ruffled effect.

Herb-Wrapped Candles

This technique is so simple you will use it again and again. Start with any size pillar candle, and cut enough herbs to cover the bottom half. Place the herbs vertically against the sides of the candle until it's completely wrapped, then use a rubber band to hold the herbs in place. If you intend to burn the candle, make sure the tops of the herb stems are well below the top of the candle. Trim the ends of the herbs even with the bottom of the candle so it will sit securely. Once the herbs are arranged to your satisfaction and trimmed neatly, disguise the rubber band with raffia, ribbon, or decorative twine.

Stems of rosemary, sage, lavender, or thyme work well for this simple project, and the resulting candles look fantastic!

HERBAL WALL HANGINGS

For the last 25 years, I've been making wall hangings for my kitchen. I use most of the herbs, garlic, and peppers each year and get the pleasure of making a new wall hanging with the next year's harvest.

Garlic, Herb, and Raffia Braid

For these really easy hangings, I use a purchased raffia braid as the base. The braid is sold as a craft item and is usually pulled apart to use the individual strands. All you have to do is tuck garlic bulbs and herbs into the braid and hang it on the wall. Some years I use mostly garlic with a few sprigs of rosemary, sage, and thyme tucked around them. In other years, the mix is different, depending on what is growing in abundance in my gardens.

Chile Pepper and Herb Wall Hanging

If you like chile peppers and grow your own, here's the hanging for you. This calls for some flexible wire that you can use like thread. Tie a knot in one end of the wire so the peppers won't fall off. Wearing disposable rubber gloves, push about five or six red peppers on the wire before you add an herb bundle. The herb bundles can be made from all one kind of herb or a mix of several different herbs. Continue threading peppers and herbs until you have the length you want. Tie a knot in the other end and hang it on the wall.

Herb Sack Wall Hanging

Choose a fabric that goes well with your kitchen, bedroom, or bath, and cut it into 6 × 10-inch rectangles. Fold each rectangle in half to make a 6 × 5-inch sack and sew up the sides, leaving the top open. Fill with your favorite herb mix, and tie the top shut with a decorative ribbon. Make several of these little herb sacks and hang them from a strip of burlap ribbon.

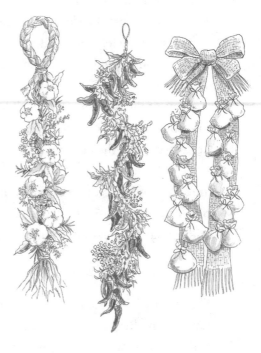

Herb Twig Bundles

I've already described using bundles of herb twigs in the fireplace to release their fragrance while burning firewood, but it's such a treat that I think it's worth mentioning it again. Working with herbs is a pleasure

HERBAL HINT

You can sew herb sacks by machine or by hand.
If sewing's not your thing, close the side seams with fabric glue
or fusible tape. Use the same fabric sacks to make herb sachets
for drawers and linen closets.

from beginning to end, and at the end of a project, what's left on the floor of the craft room is a supply of twigs.

After a project was finished, I used to clean the floor and take all the trimmings out to the trash. One day, I was in the middle of a cleanup and on the phone with one of my children at the same time. Afterward, I noticed that I had broken all the herb twigs into similar lengths and just without thinking lined them up in a neat bundle. With a piece of leftover garden twine, I tied the bundle at the middle and stacked several bundles like miniature firewood. They looked nice stacked, so I transferred them to a basket. And they smelled delicious even without burning.

Since then I have tied several bundles to a burlap ribbon to hang on the wall, tucked them in gift baskets with a note on how to use them, and filled countless baskets with them. This was a case where I truly made something out of nothing.

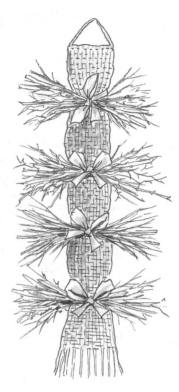

Gifts from the Herb Garden

Everything you make from your herb garden has the potential to become a gift. Knowing your family's and friends' tastes will help inspire you. The fact that you have grown the herbs, then made them into gifts, pretty much ensures they will be a success. Practice makes perfect, and after you have made some of your favorite craft projects a few times, each one will start to look good enough to give as gifts.

HERB-EMBELLISHED HATS

Hats make wonderful gifts for gardeners or for anyone who wants to be outside and keep the sun off her face. If you are buying a hat for someone else, make sure you buy from a store that will make exchanges or refunds. If you are embellishing a purchased hat as a gift, be prepared to see the hat used as a decoration in the recipient's home rather than as a piece of clothing.

For this project to work, the hat itself is everything. It must be the kind of hat that fits most heads well and makes whoever wears it look fabulous. First choose the hat; then choose the embellishments. This could be a combination of dried herbs and flowers and a pretty ribbon. It could also be just a simple ribbon and one kind of herb.

In addition to the basic herb crafting tools, you will need a hat form that allows you to hold the hat off the table and to turn it in a complete circle. These forms are easy to find and can be purchased at wig stores, gift shops, or even hair-product outlets.

Knowing your hat style is important. Once you know that, you can buy the same style again and again, decorating it in a different way each year without ever wearing the same look two years in a row.

I still have my old hat that I wore in my photo on the back cover of *Lasagna Gardening*, but by the time *Lasagna Gardening for Small Spaces* was written, I was ready for a new picture. I had moved on to another hat and another style. I really wear my hats both in and out of the garden. My collection of hats has grown, but to some of my children they all look alike. It's because I know my style.

FOR THE LOVE OF FLOWERS

I met Patricia Yelle at one of my Victorian teas. All the ladies came in fancy hats and some in special dresses. If they thought I was going to let them get away without showing them what I could grow without digging or tilling, they were mistaken.

Someone took a picture of the group—not inside at the darling little tables dressed in Battenburg lace cloths and centerpieces of fresh herbs, but out in the garden clustered around the potato bed.

I don't remember Pat remarking on the garden method or being curious about how big my potatoes were. I do remember her looking at my wildflower field and walking around the production beds filled with herbs and flowers for cutting. I also remember thinking at the time that she must be an artist.

We didn't see one another often, but I enjoyed being in her company. One day I saw her at a craft fair where she had some of her work displayed. There were beautiful pictures and lovely dried and pressed-flower art. I remember thinking she must have such patience to do this delicate work.

Pat got her start pressing flowers when she tucked some slightly droopy tulips into her phone book to save them and found them well preserved and still quite colorful a week or so later. It wasn't long before her husband couldn't open the phone book without finding pages of pressed flowers. Pat began to bring home everyone's old phone books, and once they were filled with flowers, she would stack them in a closet.

Pat's pressed-flower art was admired by everyone who saw it, and soon she was making gifts for friends and family. Her first big project was invitations for her daughter's wedding. It was a short segue from making gifts and decorations for her own home to offering her unique gifts for sale. Pat purchased space at craft fairs, and the popularity of her products kept her busy in her spare time.

Pat still presses her flowers in old phone books, but she has a storage system that is compact and easy to catalog. Her rolling carts are stacked drawers in different sizes that hold packages of flowers in different colors and textures. The dried and pressed flowers are placed in old-fashioned waxed bags by color and variety.

One of the things that drew me to Pat and Jack Yelle was the way they were preparing for their retirement. They would never be members of the "What are we going to do today?" club. These were two people who would always have another project, so when morning came they would leap out of bed to get the day started.

A Flower Crafter's Rules to Live By

- Never pick the last flower. Leave some to go to seed.

- Never pick anything on the endangered plant list. Get a copy of the list from your local Cooperative Extension office.

- Don't get greedy. Leave some for others to enjoy.

- Don't pick more flowers than you can press in one day. If you take too many flowers at once and you can't process them, they will deteriorate and not be pretty enough to press.

- When picking fall flowers and seeds, leave lots of seeds to reseed the area, assuring next year's bloom.

Pat Yelle's Easy Pressed-Flower Candle

Tall pillar candle
Mod Podge

Alcohol
Dried and pressed herbs and wildflowers

Your purchased candle should be at least 6 inches tall to be able to accommodate large flowers. Using a rag or paper towel, wipe the candle with alcohol to remove any residue that would keep the flowers from adhering. Spread a thin layer of Mod Podge or any other decoupage product on a section of candle where you want to stick the pressed flowers. After all the flowers are in place, apply a thin coat of Mod Podge. Let dry and apply another coat. You may need at least three coats.

This is a great project for kids, and Pat Yelle has taught it to both boys and girls in groups like 4-H and Scouts. One of the by-products of doing a project like this with children is it teaches them patience.

Potpourri 101

A child can make a small dish of potpourri with just a little help from you. Take a bowl or basket (or even a brown paper bag) to the garden and fill it with little snips of fragrant herbs. Pick bright flowers that will dry well and show how simple it is to toss them around. They can dry in the paper bag, and the child can shake up the herbs each day to keep them from packing down. Be sure they have a special container to display their potpourri in, and put it in their room.

CHILDREN'S HERBAL PROJECTS

It's a wonderful thing if you can interest your children in joining you in the garden. It's just a small step from the garden to the craft room, where they can really unleash their creativity. If you allow them to be a part of what you are making from your herbs, they may get involved and share your interest. You can only try.

My first examples of container herb and flower gardens meant to inspire my kids are also the ones I still like best today. Those wonderful rectangular window boxes make equally wonderful herb gardens. The kids can fill, plant, and water their own gardens. If your kids are like mine, they will make a contest of the whole thing.

HERBAL HINT

It's never too early to expose children to the wonders of the herb world. Allow them to garden with you, smell and taste the herbs, and to harvest and make things with the harvest. These early lessons will stay with them all their life.

Pat's Lemon Herb Topiary

In order to spend time with my grandchildren, I go to their houses so I can visit with them without making them leave their busy lives, but I still like to take along all the components to make fun herbal crafts like this topiary.

Lemon- or lime-scented geranium plant   *Small scissors*
Wire coat hanger   *Pliers*
Raffia   *Decorative pot with drip saucer*

Choose a plant that has a relatively straight stem. Use pliers to straighten the curved top of the coat hanger. Make a circle or diamond out of the larger part of the coat hanger. Repot plant into decorative pot. Insert a small straight piece of the hanger into the soil near the base of the plant. Tie stem to one side of the hanger and gently train it around the wire frame. Trim any small stems that are going the wrong way. Cover the exposed soil with a mulch of moss, small stones, or other decorative material to retain moisture around plant's roots. Fill drip saucer with stones and set pot on top. Water from bottom.

CHAPTER 7

The very act of getting in touch with the earth is satisfying in many ways, not the least of which is the way it renews your spirit. I have used herb gardening to quiet my troubled soul and to bring calm to a volatile situation. By having several herb plantings around all my properties, I can, at any given time, brush by a plant that makes me feel good. And isn't feeling good what it's all about? Nothing lifts my spirits like time spent in my gardens among the herbs.

Renewing Your Spirit with Herbs

Overwhelmed? Go to the Garden

Whether you are feeling just a little down or your world seems to be coming apart, go to the garden. If this sounds too simple, remember the simple way is many times the best. I would like to think that everyone knows the garden is the place to get it all back together.

Unfortunately, that's not the case. Traditional gardening is too hard for some—and too unappealing for others—but it's what we first think of when the garden beckons. If your memories of gardening were sown by a gardening parent or grandparent, you probably think that traditional gardening methods, based on the hard work of agriculture, are the only way to grow. The traditional, labor-intensive method is also what many experts and garden writers still advocate.

In an age of advanced communication, where we are bombarded with information on any subject we desire, much of what is said about gardening is still about traditional methods. Change is hard for some, but when new ideas refute what has been accepted as the only way, change will come—albeit slowly. (When people hear about lasagna gardening, they think it's a new idea, but it's really been around for many years. I've merely updated it to make it practical and appealing for busy, modern gardeners.)

The person who needs to go to the garden most is usually already overwhelmed by life. The last thing he or she needs is something that is too hard, and directions like these are very hard.

Traditional Gardening Directions: Select a site, lift (dig) the sod, dig or till the area to a depth of 18 to 24 inches, incorporate (another word for dig) soil amendments into the soil.

Just reading these directions makes me tired.

Lasagna Gardening Makes It Possible

It's been said that the concept of lasagna gardening has inspired lots of folks to get into the garden. Lasagna gardening is friendly, not only to the gardener but also to nature. When you create a lasagna garden, using natural materials that are often free for the taking, you are recycling and feeding the earth. At the same time, you are keeping tons of vegetation out of the landfill by using what you used to put on the curb.

When I needed a way to stay in the garden that did not tax my strength or add to the decline of aging back muscles, I found a way in an accelerated version of Mother Nature's very own recipe.

Lasagna gardening is about making garden spaces with great soil. It's about easy planting and easy maintenance. It's also about being able to find the pleasures of gardening without stressing your body with hard physical labor. Growing herbs is truly a joy. I want to share some of my favorite parts of being an herb gardener. I hope they will inspire you to plant your own herb garden, lasagna-style.

There are plenty of qualified herbalists who can tell you how to use herbs to heal a wide variety of physical ailments. I am not one of those people.

HERBAL HINT

Feeling low? Go to the herb garden but don't wear gloves! *Spend time cleaning favorite herb plants of dead stems and leaves. Harvest a few culinary herbs for dinner or to hang from a peg so you can continue to enjoy their fragrance inside. After a few minutes in the garden, smell your hands. It's instant aromatherapy!*

For me, healing with herbs is an extension of healing with gardening, and it's something I've discovered over a lifetime of gardening by simply recognizing that I was happier outside puttering around the garden. When sorrow and sadness came into my life, gardening was the way I renewed my spirit and the way I returned to my normal routine. Nothing lifts my spirits like time spent in my gardens among the herbs.

When I first began to garden, I just focused on growing food to feed my family. It was enough to be able to bring fresh vegetables to the table to nourish my children. Some of the best moments for me were when I prepared and served an entire dinner from the garden, and the children ate and enjoyed what I served.

The way I gardened in those early days as a wife and mother required lots of energy. I was lucky to have the energy and strength that enabled me to do all that was required of a parent, wife, homemaker, and gardener. The whole family became involved with the vegetable garden: My husband tilled, I planted, and we all weeded, watered, and harvested.

There was lots of grumbling among the children about their share of work in the garden. I felt rather strongly about everyone doing their share to maintain a home (and garden), and for the most part they would get to it, knowing they couldn't play until the work was done. When they were really young, they wanted to be where everyone else was, doing whatever we were doing. As they got older, they felt obliged to squabble and argue about anything that had the connotation of work.

After a little practice, the garden began to take less time and energy. With a little spare time, I remembered how my grandmother bordered her garden with flowers. I decided to do the same, and during preparation for new plantings, I left room for flower seeds in the border and plants within the garden. I followed my instincts and planted easy annuals that grew well in the hot Georgia sun.

It was about this time that I also added herbs to the gardens. A friend gave me some divisions of her plants and told me where to plant them: parsley as a border plant, basil and chives with tomatoes, and sage throughout the garden. My interest in herbs was piqued. As soon as I needed more basil, I moved on to growing from seeds. When I saw the wide

Growing Herbs from Seed

If there is one aspect of gardening that can get you away from being too self-centered, it's growing from seed. I grew hundreds of plants from seed in the unfinished great room of my old farmhouse. There wasn't enough light, water had to be carried to the plants from my make-do kitchen, and dust covered the leaves as construction work continued. It didn't matter. During that first spring after leaving the inn, I gained a new sense of self.

It's been more than 12 years since then, and I still buy a large bag of special seed-starting mix and plant as many flats as the bag will fill.

To get started you will need:

- Seed-starting mix
- Clean pots
- Seeds
- Watering can with a fine spray

Follow instructions for each individual plant. Keep seeds evenly moist using a fine spray. Wait until two true leaves (not the first leaves, but the ones that look like the mature plant's leaves) emerge before transplanting. Thin by cutting away the least hardy plants. If the light comes in only one direction, turn the trays from time to time to keep seedlings growing straight.

range of plants that could be grown from seeds, a passion was born, and a new world of flavors began to unfurl for me and my family.

By incorporating herbs and flowers in and around the garden, I found a different kind of happiness. I can remember experiencing the unusual feeling of leisure. As I cut herbs for the kitchen and flowers for my home, I knew it was something that had been lacking in my busy life—this feeling that I could take time to do something just for the fun of it. As backdoor herbs and flowers from my gardens found their way into our home, my family shared in my newfound happiness.

TAKE TIME TO PLAY

My grandmother must have known this feeling as she picked flowers from her 2-foot border and placed them in a homely mason jar before sharing them with her family at mealtime. The old mountain woman who was my grandmother is never far from my mind and heart. She helped to instill an overzealous work ethic in me, but somewhere I had forgotten how to play. Was it possible my grandmother was still looking over me and giving me a gentle nudge, pushing me toward the lighter side of life?

Gardening provided me with an outlet for excess energy, and through it I cultivated a passion. I couldn't wait to go to the garden, and all my other work flew by so I could do just that. Herbs and flowers became my happy plants. Vegetables were still the main crop and my daily focus, but they represented the working part of gardening, an extension of my daily housework. Growing herbs and flowers represented time away from work. I was

Time Out

The garden became important to us in many ways. It was more than just a food factory. We enjoyed just walking through the rows or looking at it from the lawn. It was all such fun, and frequently my husband and I would take our evening drinks out to the garden, where we had a couple of chairs. I loved the idea of watching the beans grow (it was a source of humor, too). It was a time-out from the busy world.

in the middle of a life change, and it was the perfect time to get excited about a hobby. I acknowledged the need for leisure and play time and made them a part of my daily routine.

I can't remember when I moved the herbs out of the vegetable garden and into a separate space. It sort of evolved as my interest in herbs grew. I found gardening with herbs wonderfully fulfilling and spent more and more time working among my ever-increasing herb plants. I loved the different fragrances, interesting textures, and, especially, the history of certain plants. I also loved the paths that allowed access to each plant without walking on the soil.

During that time I also began to collect herb books to learn more about the plants that were becoming a big part of my gardening efforts. In each book would be some interesting tidbit about a certain herb. It was like dangling a carrot before a horse. The more I learned, the more I wanted to learn. One book led me to another and then another. Each bit of herbal history sparked my growing interest.

I used to spend lots of energy in the garden. I saw gardening as a way to put food on the table and to get outside more. However, it wasn't until I became an herb gardener that my personal hobby took hold. Once I became a serious herb gardener, I had something to look forward to that was all mine. During the time I spent in the garden, I was developing a hobby that would eventually evolve into a lifelong interest.

You Can Be a Gardener

My philosophy is that anyone can be a gardener. It requires no higher education, no experience, and no title like "Head Gardener," "Master Gardener," or "Head Poobah Gardener." One day you say, "I am a gardener," and you are one. Gardening is something you never stop learning about. It's a lifetime of continuing education.

Great satisfaction comes from the act of gardening no matter what, how, or where you garden. Some of the best gardeners never put a spade in the earth, but rather plunge a discarded tablespoon into a pot. One person's prize dahlia is another person's ripe tomato. One gardener's backyard plot is another gardener's container collection. Gardening is the act of growing or, rather, assisting in the process of growth. The day someone asks what you do as a hobby and you answer, "I'm a gardener," you are one.

> ## HERBAL HINT
>
> *One thing you need to be a gardener is patience. Waiting is what gardeners do—waiting for spring, waiting for seeds to sprout, waiting for plants to arrive, waiting for flowers to appear, even waiting for trees to grow, flower, and produce fruit.*

I didn't really think of myself as a gardener until I had spent 10 years at the inn. One day I was invited to participate in a Master Gardener course through our local Cooperative Extension office. Only experienced gardeners were asked to attend that first class, and I was in a group that included some very experienced people. I felt privileged to be a part of it. I made lifelong friends in the group and gained a wide respect for the Master Gardener program.

Finding Inspiration in the Herb Garden

Following my grandmother's lead, I found myself turning to the garden time and time again. I would give up gardening when things were difficult—not enough space, too hot, too hard—dozens of excuses. But it was almost like a forgotten friend was tapping me on the shoulder, telling me she's still here and I should go to the garden.

Grandmother was the first person to inspire me to be more than I was. The hardships she knew and how she rose above them were guiding lights for me. As I watched her in her gardens, she unknowingly planted the seeds of the gardener I would become.

My grandmother's pantry inspired me to grow more food than we could eat during the season. As a child I would stand in her neat pantry filled with shelves; I loved to look at the filled jars—soups, vegetables, and even sausage preserved for winter meals.

As an adult, I canned my own harvest and displayed it on cupboard shelves. It didn't matter that I really had no time for canning and wasn't very good at it. I wanted my own children to see what it was like to grow, harvest, and preserve food. Even though I had no real pantry, my cupboard was filled, and I did have a large freezer where we stored most of the harvest. Many times I would see one of the children looking inside at the bags of food we had put aside.

I suspect, with my life filled with children and the disarray that is natural with so many little people, I craved order. The garden was a perfect place to obtain order. With all the rows and paths running in straight, orderly lines, it was my haven. Later, my herb gardens brought more order because they were arranged in blocks, beds, and boxes with neat border plants. For a long time, the garden was the only order in my life.

Gardening Is Better Than Running Away

When you have seven children and all the confusion that goes with them, there are times you want to run away from home. When I couldn't really run away, I could go to the garden. There's something magical that happens when you are mucking about. On the worst days, when weather kept me out of the garden, I could go to the greenhouse. I could dabble with seeds and cuttings until things righted.

One activity leads to another in the garden: Taking a walk leads to pruning, and pruning provides cuttings for rooting. Cutting an edge around beds leads to closer inspection of plants, and decisions are made to move crowded plants. That means you need to create more planting space or pot some plants.

Going Organic

When I found an old pamphlet written by J. I. Rodale that extolled the advantages of growing organically, I was inspired to follow his methods. Everything he said made sense, except the work involved. I began growing organically at about the same time that I needed to become independent of power tools. I was searching for a way to stay in the garden and live alone.

After 36 years of marriage, I was embarking on a life without a partner. I would no longer have someone to lift the other end of the sofa or to till or dig the garden in spring. Many things were no longer an option, but if I could find a way, I could stay in the garden. J. I. Rodale's pamphlet wasn't a part of my original garden plan, but I was ready to be more earth-friendly.

Soon after reading that pamphlet, I subscribed to *Organic Gardening* magazine. Robert Rodale was the editor then, and his magazine struck a chord with me. I became inspired to become a serious composter under the magazine's influence.

We owned the inn and a 200-seat restaurant back then. I managed the kitchen waste, nagging cooks and dishwashers to take the separated waste to a giant composter behind the inn. I thought I was doing the

right thing until the waste became too heavy to turn. It was lots of work, and I remembered that when I moved to the farm and began a smaller system.

Learning from my first mistake, I constructed a neat system using smaller containers. I had one of the first four-bin composting systems on Shandelee Mountain. I managed the waste from my property and from the kitchen, never wasting a thing.

Many times my inspiration has come from books and magazines. In the beginning, I subscribed to *Early American Life* because it had articles on living in America and also on the first early herb gardens. Later I subscribed to many newsletters. *The Herb Companion* magazine continues to add greatly to my knowledge of herbs and has helped me know many of today's best-known herb gardeners.

CREATING SPECIAL PLACES FOR RESTING

I know I am a workaholic. A large part of that behavior results in a sort of maniacal gardening fever. I've created my own 12-step recovery program to what I call being a "gardenaholic." Unfortunately, gardening fever still hits every spring, and I fall off the program on a regular basis. All this work—that, by the way, makes me very happy—also makes me tired.

Now that I am in my third quarter of life, I can finally admit to needing rest. I admit that I do get tired. I also admit to needing places to go where I can find not only quiet but also peace.

I need, even crave, time and opportunity to sit and listen to nature. It's one of the reasons I place seats in and around the garden. Growing older has tempered my work habits, and I feel the need to sit more frequently. I listen to my body, and when it tells me to rest, sometimes I do. One of the best parts of resting in your own garden is you get another view of the plants and insect life that live there.

The quiet time allows me to enjoy what I have created, and I have trained myself not to see the garden's imperfections as more work to be done.

When I was first alone, I felt I might have to move away from all that had been in order to find a new life. However, I resisted moving, and instead of going out into the unknown, I stayed put and found a wonderful new life in my gardens.

For whatever the reasons, my life took on a new familiarity; I took my first cup of coffee at dawn in the gardens. I watched bees come awake, I saw how the dewdrops glistened like cut stones as the first rays of light touched them, and I watched birds fly from their nests in search of food. I found my own spirit in the quiet of morning.

RENEWING YOUR SPIRIT IN THE HERB GARDEN

A garden provides us with a place to grow—and not just plants. When I was a child, I grew up watching my grandmother work in the garden. I understood she was providing food for us with the planting, harvesting, and putting by. What wasn't obvious was that she was also helping me grow a work ethic by her example.

As a young mother, I took my children to the garden to experience a growing process that would stay with them always. When they were babies, they were planted in a playpen near where I worked. As they grew to toddlers, I took them into the garden and let them help. During their growing years, we planted herbs and vegetables for our food and grass and flowers for the comfort and beauty they brought.

As the children grew into teenagers, I had to set and enforce garden rules: Everyone weeds, everyone picks, and everyone helps prepare for canning or freezing, so everyone can eat. It wasn't easy to keep them down on the farm when their friends were at the mall, but I'm happy to say we persevered, and they turned out pretty well. (Actually, they turned out great.)

Many years later, I would see the results of our time in the garden together. Some became good gardeners, and some took their own children to the garden.

MOVING, PHYSICALLY AND MENTALLY

Some of our possessions are like dear old friends. Getting settled in a new place is usually hard, but it's easier if you can fit some of your old things into your new space. It's like bringing along old friends.

My move to Wurtsboro from Shandelee was more than a move from one piece of real estate to another. It was a move from one way of life to another. It required transporting some old plant friends to mingle with the new to help me make the change. Before I could begin the move, I covered all the grassy areas with wet newspaper and covered the paper with an inch of peat moss.

HERBAL HINT

To move plants with as little stress as possible, move them with large rootballs in baskets and buckets lined with wet newspaper. Leave the wet paper around the roots when you put the plants in the ground. The paper decomposes, but before it does it will provide a nesting place for the rootball.

Back at the farm, I divided plants and harvested seeds to bring the flavor of my old gardens to the new location. Plants from my old gardens were dug with a ball of soil attached and each carried in its own basket. The baskets were first lined with layers of wet paper to keep the rootball moist and intact during the move.

At the new site, I set the plant, ball of soil, and paper basket liner on top of the 1-inch layer of peat moss over the paper that covered the old grassy lawn. Each plant got a thick blanket of mulch around its rootball. I have to admit that first year the garden looked lumpy, but by the time winter came I had put down enough layers of shredded leaves and chipped bark to level it all out. The move was a success, and all the plants survived.

It's now our eighth winter in Wurtsboro. The temperatures read in the single digits after a warm spell. Snow is piled several feet high where the snowplow has pushed it aside to open the driveway, and I am snuggled in my old Irish fisherman's sweater, sitting at the whitewashed desk in my house on the side of the hill.

The plants in gardens at the Potager are also snuggled in their beds, covered with what we call "poor man's fertilizer," or snow. I have no fear of them freezing and pushing out of the ground; the freeze is deep and here to stay awhile. When the snow begins to melt, I will walk the gardens, checking for plants that have been heaved out of the ground by thawing and freezing.

Looking back, it seems I have been following my grandmother's lead: following her into the garden, following as she worked from early morning to dark, following her as she foraged for herbs, bark, and twigs to keep us both healthy. She led me down a path that is still unwinding before me—a path I still set my feet on every day and that has led me in the right direction, most of the time.

Recently I have wondered if she is still looking over me, for my life seems charmed at times. As I do my work at the Potager, travel the road to see my children and grandchildren, and invest time in my friends, I thank God and my grandmother for their care of me.

Living an Herbal Life

How do you go from a cup of herbal tea to living the herbal life? It kind of sneaks up on you. One day you plant a few basil plants to provide you with enough fresh basil to make pesto. The next thing you know you are planting 10 or 20 different basils and have become known as the neighborhood basil expert.

It was like that for me. At first I just wanted to have a few fresh herbs for the inn. In a few years I had expanded my herb garden from a small space beside the kitchen steps to a 40 × 40-foot lasagna garden on the only flat space on the property. It was the first time I had planned and executed an entire no-dig, no-till, layered garden from the original concept. Implementing that first lasagna garden was fast, easy, and economical, leaving me with enough time, energy, and money to buy and plant more than 25 different herbs.

Using lasagna gardening methods and illustrations of early herb gardens in books and magazines as inspiration, I was able to create similar designs in my own gardens. With my easy method of gardening, I could see a design one day and have it re-created in my garden the next.

The winter season was the time I spent reading. I read about the history of herbs and all the ways they had been used in the old days. I also read the work of new herb growers and of the ways they were using herbs today. There were flaws in much of the information, and I thought common sense would eventually sort it out.

One such bit of bad (but common) advice is that herbs will grow well in poor soil and difficult growing conditions. With just a couple of exceptions, herbs will thrive in good soil just like other plants. Yarrow really does do well in poor soil. The stems stand up straight, and even though the flowers are small, they too hold their heads up. However, some of the yarrow hybrids produce bigger blooms with more flowers to a plant in good soil. They grow so well the stems get huge and fall over with the size of the blooms.

Herbs in the Bath

Once I had my house and gardens in order, I began to experiment with ways to use the herbs I was growing at such an alarming rate (all that good soil, you know). The first place I used them was in the bath. With a package of cheesecloth from the grocery store and some good rubber bands, I was ready to make some herbal bath bags.

It took a bit of research, but soon I had sorted out the herbs I had in my garden that would make my bath a delightful herbal experience.

> ## HERBAL HINT
>
> *You can buy muslin bags or make bags from muslin yard goods or even from thin washcloths. I prefer to use cheesecloth cut into squares, filled with herbs, and tied with a good-size rubber band. I toss these bags once I've used them and never feel extravagant. I've found that the herbs cling to the cloth, regardless of what kind you use, and it's not easy to reuse them.*

Herbs to Use in the Bath

Here are some of my favorite combinations of herbs for the bath. There are many other herbs you can use, but these are herbs I grew in my own gardens, and I think they are simple plants you might also grow. I always add Borax and an emollient such as oatmeal, cornmeal, honey, glycerin, or comfrey (1 part herbs to 1 part Borax and 1 part emollient).

- For a relaxing bath: chamomile, comfrey, lavender, lemon verbena, or thyme.
- For a soothing bath: calendula, catnip, comfrey, hyssop, rose, sage, tansy, or yarrow. Sometimes I combine the different herbs and sometimes I use just one.
- For a stimulating bath: hops, lemon balm, marjoram, peppermint, rosemary, savory, or yarrow.

Using 4- to 6-inch squares of cheesecloth, place 1 part herbs to 1 part emollient in the middle. Use 2 or 3 tablespoons herbs in each bag. Pull up the sides and wrap with a rubber band. Hang the bag over the faucet by the rubber band, or drop the bag into the bath water.

Herbal Lawns, Big and Small

Installing, maintaining, and mowing lawns may be the most popular outdoor pastime, but it's not for everyone. There are some of us who get that glazed look in our eyes when someone begins sharing their views on grass lawns. I guess I'll never get it about all that grass: gobbling up water, taking hours to cut, and using more fertilizer than whole gardens.

Installing a New Herbal Lawn

If you decide to make a change to your old-fashioned, high-maintenance, chemically treated lawn, do it in stages. It's like being on drugs (your lawn has been on drugs): You have to come off gradually. First, don't put any chemicals down for a season. Keep the lawn watered, but don't cut too close. Try not to get riled up over a few dandelions.

Aerate the entire lawn and, if you can spare the time, put down a thin layer of sifted compost or sifted mushroom compost, health food for your lawn. Either in early spring or fall, begin sowing your new seed mixture. Keep it watered, and if your old lawn wasn't too good to begin with or if it's a new lawn, put down straw to hold the moisture in while the seeds get started.

If you live where the winters are cold and the summers mild, here are alternatives to water-gobbling, chemical-dependent, high-maintenance grass lawns. How about an herbal lawn? Not an all-herb lawn, but a combination of natural grasses, low-growing wildflowers, and herbs. This kind of mixed lawn is inexpensive to install, easy to maintain, and, if kept mowed (I know, it still needs mowing), will look neat and green. With a lot less mowing, you can have a truly lovely (in my eyes) lawn that will bloom and have such wonderful smells you won't believe it.

Another kind of herbal lawn would be one with only one kind of herb: thyme, Roman chamomile, pennyroyal, or mint. I recommend this only for small spaces because it's a bit expensive to get started and a bit difficult to manage.

HERBAL HINT

While living on the farm, I had an herbal lawn. One summer I allowed the plants to grow quite high, mowing only when I was sure the seedheads were set. This assured me of another year of the great selection of self-seeding annuals and biennials growing and blooming in the grass. Another thing I did one year was to cut everything except a special, kidney-shaped area that I let grow until it flowered and set seed. During blooming time, it was a magical place where children romped and butterflies flourished.

When we moved to Sullivan County, the property surrounding the inn was overgrown with hardhack and blueberries growing right up to the barn. Lucky for me, my husband liked to mow grass. He began mowing in wider and wider circles until by the second year he had mowed all the way to the pond.

Before we had been there 5 years, he had mowed the area so many times that all the natural grass came back and provided soft and sometimes fragrant seating for several thousand who came to enjoy open-air concerts.

There were lots of surprises in our new lawn: patches of mint growing down by the pond, wild thyme growing in the middle of the field, and a stand of scarlet bee balm that surfaced one summer by the barn. The natural grass was the biggest surprise of all. With mowing and without water or chemicals, the grass was amazing in its green beauty.

The best surprise was yet to come. When I moved across the road to the farmhouse and started mowing my own lawns, I could let patches or whole fields grow up. That's when I would see the beautiful wildflowers growing among the grasses. And that's when I got the idea to plant seed mixtures to see how they would look and perform.

My latest test is the thyme lawn at the Potager. I'm using plants instead of seed because I have plants left over from the garden center each year. I'm 2 years into the project, and this year (the second summer) will be the year when all the different thymes will finally cover the space. The thyme lawn isn't complete, but I have started an experiment in an adjoining space where I planted plain grass seed.

I planted the grass seed late in the season just a couple of weeks before killing frost and snow. Under the protective cover of straw, I could see the grass was sprouting. Later, under a cover of several feet of snow, the grass was still green. The test is to see how green and lush my new grass will be without using any chemical fertilizer. I plan to let part of it grow without anything, and in another section I will use organic fertilizer and see what happens.

HERBS FOR THE LAWN

There are many ways to have an herbal lawn. If your space is large, combine herbs and grass throughout for a mixed lawn. If you have a small space, you can leave the grass out and combine herbs or plant just one kind of herb. Some of the herbs that make great additions to grass or stand on their own are listed below.

Chamomile (*Chamaemelum nobile*)

When most people think of an herbal lawn, chamomile is the herb they often think of. But chamomile has some drawbacks as a stand-alone groundcover.

Chamomile lawns can tolerate winter lows of –20°F, but a chamomile lawn will die out in extended summer highs in the 90s. To plant a chamomile lawn with plants that cost between $2 and $3 per plant, you will need about 200 plants for a 5 × 8-foot space. That is a lot of dough.

Of course, you can grow your own plants from seed. Packets contain about 100 seeds and cost about $3 each. You'll probably yield about 50 plants per seed packet. Growing chamomile plants from seed can take up to a year before you can walk on the lawn. To

grow plants for transplanting to the lawn, you need to start the process in January or February and pot up twice. Growing seed directly on the lawn also can be tricky. If you do succeed, you'll need to hire someone to help you care for it.

A chamomile lawn is a living green carpet that blooms. Tiny yellow-and-white daisy flowers dot the deep green leaves with a fragrance of fresh-cut apples. The spongy turf is soft to the touch and wonderful to walk on. Roman chamomile is a hardy spreading perennial that will keep a small lawn covered if the climate is right. It may be difficult to find true Roman chamomile. Many times it is listed as *Anthemis nobilis* or by some other name. The upright-growing German chamomile (*Matricaria recutita*) grows too tall and would need frequent mowing. The problem is knowing the difference when the tag just says "chamomile." Instead of all this struggling, plant a very small chamomile lawn in a large pot or as a seat. You could also do a path, spaces between stones in a path, or just a manageable square within your grass lawn.

Mother-of-Thyme (*Thymus serpyllum*)

This is an easy lawn and is as close as a package of seed. You can raise plants and transplant into the lawn or sow seed directly. Each plant will create a low mat of nearly evergreen leaves and produce tiny pink flowers. Thyme has very few needs and, if encouraged, can fill in large spaces in a very short time and last for years. Mother-of-thyme (also called creeping thyme) can be used in recipes just like any other thyme.

HERBAL HINT

When buying seed for a thyme lawn, look for either creeping thyme or mother-of-thyme. They are the same and are the least expensive.

In the hamlet of Willowemoc on a property owned by friends, I found a patch of mother-of-thyme growing in a field. On closer inspection, I found the old foundation where a farmhouse had stood. I could only suppose that farmer's wife had thyme growing in a kitchen garden. The house must have been gone for more than 40 years, and the thyme was still there.

Speedwell, or Veronica (*Veronica* spp.)

This herb can make the difference between a nice lawn and a spectacular herb lawn. The creeping habit keeps the plant low, and the gray-green leaves on this hardy perennial look good in any garden situation. This European import is used in a variety of plantings and also used for a variety of ailments. If you can let it grow and keep from mowing until it blooms, you will enjoy the amazing electric blue flowers. After the flowers is time enough to mow.

Wild Strawberry (*Fragaria vesca*)

Hardy perennials, wild strawberries are easy to grow from seed, spread quickly by runners, and grow low to the ground. The lawn stays low without mowing. In addition, they produce a crop of berries that have a flavor unequaled by any other berry. The leaves are a glossy green all summer and turn purplish in fall. Wild strawberry leaves are used in teas and for medicinal purposes.

When I was very small, my grandmother would ask me to pick wild strawberries in a teacup. When the cup was full and I had eaten my fill, we would take the cup full of berries home, and she would mix them with sugar. In the evening, she would split a buttermilk biscuit and layer half the berries on each one. Just before we ate them, she would pour on some heavy cream. Just the thought of this memory makes my mouth water for that flavor.

Sweet Violets (*Viola odorata*)

A lawn of sweet violets is almost too easy if you have the right conditions. These tiny plants have pretty heart-shaped, ever-green leaves that bear tiny purple flowers in early spring and again in fall. They will self-seed and cover an area in part shade in very little time. I like to see them growing in a lawn sown with a thin cover of grass seed. However, if you have a lawn with just sweet violets, you never have to mow.

Woolly Yarrow
(*Achillea tomentosa*)

Pretty, fuzzy gray leaves form a lush lawn that never needs mowing until after the big yellow flowers have faded. It grows best when planted in full sun in average, sandy soil with good drainage. Flowers are the same size as plants that grow to 2 feet tall and can be used in all the ways the taller flowers can, except they have really short stems.

No Land? No Problem!
A Container Garden for Every Porch

Herbs and containers just seem to be made for each other. You would have to live in an enclosed, windowless apartment (and even then I would suggest grow lights) to think you had no way to grow herbs.

We live in a container world. There has never been a better time to be a container gardener. We have many choices in size, material, and finish. In order for the industry to be able to show what they have to offer, garden centers have added on to their display space to hold an ever-growing inventory of containers. There's something for everyone.

CONTAINERS BRING THE HERB GARDEN INDOORS

When you live in the colder regions of the country, bringing part of your garden inside during winter can mean the difference between a good winter and a bad winter. In these temperate regions, some tender perennial herbs are necessarily grown in containers: lemongrass, pineapple sage, lemon verbena, and rosemary.

Pineapple Sage (*Salvia elegans*)

My first experience with pineapple sage was a memorable experience. The delicate pineapple fragrance, the fruity taste of the leaves, and the look of the leaves and flowers made it a delightful encounter. I decided it would be a good thing to grow this lovely, tender perennial plant and find ways to enjoy it in my kitchen.

Having a plant of your own can lead you to try it in more ways than usual. I added a sprig to my iced tea and to a frosty pina colada and put the intensely red flowers in whipped cream cheese that I spread on crackers or in the throat of a daylily for an entirely edible flower.

In my daughter Debbie's Atlanta garden, pineapple sage overwinters. She cuts it back hard, and it resprouts in spring, growing to a height of 5 feet before summer ends. Many times she will get two flowerings during one season. In my New York garden, I grow one plant in a large pot that stays outside all summer and comes in for winter. I can't resist taking a nibble each time I pass the plant on my way to other parts of the garden. My plant rarely reaches 2 feet tall, partly because I use so much of it.

To propagate pineapple sage, take stem cuttings and root in a sterile potting soil or a mixture of sand and peat moss. If you grow your plant in the garden and you live in a colder region, take several cuttings to bring in for winter and let the one in the garden go.

Lemon Verbena (*Aloysia triphylla*)

After my introduction to a larger-than-life potted plant at Gilbertie's Herb Farm, I was determined to grow lemon verbena myself. In the cold climate of my New York home, I had no choice but to grow it in a pot—and not even a big pot—because I had limited space.

Regardless of what you have heard about the finicky nature of lemon verbena, there are just a few things you need to know to succeed: good drainage, good drainage, good drainage. If your verbena is allowed to sit in water, the roots will rot. Verbena needs to go dormant during winter and be fed with fish emulsion in spring and all during the growing season. In cold regions your plant can be kept in full sun, but in warmer regions it responds to part shade or cooler areas.

Because verbena loves pruning, it's a perfect herb to make into topiary. Changes in temperatures may cause its leaves to drop, but don't worry; they will grow back quickly. Gather the dried leaves and use them in potpourri,

---

HERBAL HINT

When planting in half-barrels or any container, make sure there are enough drainage holes. Place the container on top of several bricks or clay "pot feet" for even better drainage and less moisture buildup beneath the container.

where they will retain their lemon scent for years. Tea made from the leaves is one of the most delicious of the lemon-flavored teas. A cup of hot lemon verbena tea can act as a gentle sedative and can calm an upset stomach. Take stem cuttings to root for additional plants.

TAKING TO THE AIR: HANGING HERB BASKETS

When we think of hanging baskets of herbs, most of us think of lush foliage that seems to be growing without anything supporting the roots. The foliage is so thick and lush it completely covers the container. In reality, we usually end up with baskets that are all too visible and thin stems of foliage looking straggly and less than lush. Many times it's because we have chosen the wrong plants, or even the wrong pot for the wrong plant.

Plants that naturally creep and cascade are more likely to look at home in a hanging basket—creeping thyme, cascading rosemary, catmint, peppermint, oregano, thyme, silver thyme, and golden oregano. Combine any of these plants or grow just one variety, and you will be surprised at the outstanding results.

There are other considerations involved in making sure the display is a success. The method you use to plant the hanging herb basket and the location of the basket for display is as important as the plant you choose. Where the basket will be hung is critical. It must hang from a sturdy support as the watered basket will be quite heavy. Watering also means dripping onto the area underneath the basket for as much as an hour after. How much light the area receives is directly related to what plants you have in mind for your hanging containers.

HERBAL HINT

Pinch and prune your herbs, and they will respond with more lush growth. The oils left on your fingers after pinching will impart the individual fragrance of the herb to your skin, and that isn't bad either.

Directions for Hanging Baskets of Herbs

- Choose a wire basket large enough to hold several (three to five) plants.

- Choose a liner for your basket that is attractive underneath and sturdy enough to hold soil and plant roots without falling apart. You may want to place loose sphagnum peat around the pot, then place the solid peat or cocoa fiber mat on the outside.

- Use lightweight potting soil that won't pack down.

- Mix water-retaining granulars (Soil Moist, for example) into potting soil before placing in pot. Read directions for correct amounts, and do not use more than is recommended.

- Attach a hook to a sturdy beam in a place where the pot will drain over the lawn or another area that water will not harm.

- Hang pot only to a height you can comfortably maintain yourself. If pots are too high, you will be less likely to water and groom when it's needed.

- Choose plants based on their light requirements: thyme and oregano in full sun, catmint or peppermint in part shade, rosemary in part sun.

- Purchase enough plants to plant around the top and bottom of the entire basket—not just on the top.

- Purchase plants that appear healthy (bright green foliage, no sign of insects, and not potbound).

- Water potting soil and liner until they are as moist as a squeezed-out sponge.

- After planting, cover the exposed soil with a light organic mulch: buckwheat hulls, cocoa hulls, moss, or other very lightweight material.

CHAPTER 8

Growing herbs is easy and very satisfying. Long before I began writing about

gardens and gardening, I grew herbs. They usually hugged the back door so I could

pick what I needed from a precarious perch on the last step. It was a simple

planting, meant to provide fresh flavors for the foods I prepared for my family. I

never gave a minute of thought to insect or disease problems, and looking back, I

don't think there were any—at least none I can remember. If my basil died, it was

probably the result of too-cold night temperatures, which merely meant that it was

time for the basil to call it quits for the season anyway.

Solving Garden Problems Organically

Herbs Have Few Problems

Ask anyone who grows herbs to tell you about the problems they have in their gardens, and they will usually have to take a few minutes to think about it. Generally speaking, herb plants have few problems, and when problems do arise, they usually can be controlled with commonsense solutions.

It's not that herbs aren't susceptible to pests and disease, and they certainly aren't immune; they just have far fewer problems than most other plants. In fact, many seasoned gardeners make use of herbs' trouble-free natures by planting them among their flowers and vegetables to help protect more susceptible plants from pests. Known as companion planting, this practice takes advantage of the insect-repelling properties of some fragrant herbs, while other herbs help the garden by attracting beneficial insects that prey on pests.

I find it difficult to offer anything but positive encouragement to new gardeners. I think there's plenty of evidence to support the switch from traditional gardening methods—like back-straining double-digging—to the no-dig approach of lasagna gardening, and building the soil is a good way to head off a lot of problems. If you talk to enough gardeners, you'll find that there are as many opinions on how to garden as there are gardeners. You'll also encounter those gardeners who will talk endlessly about all the problems that could occur.

If you listen to all the things that *could* go wrong and all the problems that you *might* have, you might become too discouraged to plant a garden. For example, insects and other pests, such as aphids, weevils, whiteflies, spittlebugs, spider mites, scale, beetles, earwigs, leaf miners, and mealy bugs, might infest your garden.

If the number of bad bugs doesn't scare you, how about caterpillars, stem borers, or nematodes? What about diseases like powdery mildew, rust, an-

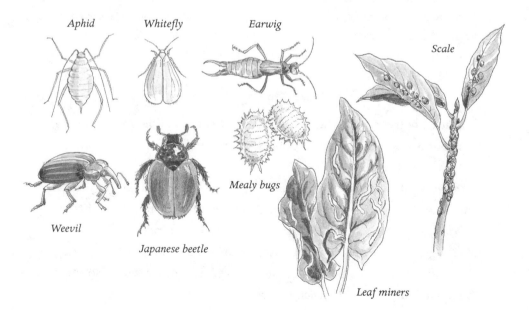

Aphid *Whitefly* *Earwig*

Scale

Mealy bugs

Weevil

Japanese beetle

Leaf miners

Groomed to (Not Quite) Perfection

It was the summer of 1991, and I was ready for my first group to arrive from the Brooklyn Botanic Garden. It had been just over a year since I had begun to establish my display gardens at the farm, but they were all in full fruit and flower and groomed to perfection. I had plucked every unsightly leaf, staked every wobbly stem, and even fluffed the soil. What had been a neglected hayfield was now a showplace of plants, all growing in rich soil created by my lasagna method. The perennial herbs were well established—bushy and blooming—summer vegetables were producing ample harvests, and plantings of annuals filled the gardens with big bursts of color. All was right with my world.

By 5:00 A.M. on the day of the arrival of the first group of visitors from the respected botanic garden, I was sitting on my back step with my first cup of coffee, surveying the results of my labors. I felt confident that everything was in order and that my visitors would be impressed by the sight of so much beauty created by so little traditional garden work.

I had just enough time to give the property another walk-through—just for the fun of it. I filled my cup and started at the entrance to the front garden. I couldn't resist leaning on the gate to see what my guests would see: The flagstone path was filled with creeping thyme, softening the edges of the stones, and bordered with tufts of blooming dianthus and nasturtiums. Clumps of poppies and bearded iris bloomed in front of the evergreen border, and the gray foliage of 'Powis Castle' artemisia provided a soft background.

As I entered the gate and made my way toward the opposite side of the front door, I could hardly believe my success at the huge bed of 'Russell Mixed' lupines. Their soft yellow, deep pink, purple, and white blooms were huge and had filled the opened gate as if they were escaping.

It was my last chance to get photos before the group arrived, and I started for the door to

thracnose, botrytis, bacterial wilt, blight, leaf spot, and damping-off? Not to mention slugs, snails, grasshoppers, cutworms, and all manner of diseases that cause rot.

Do you still want to plant an herb garden—or a garden of any kind? After hearing about all the bad things that *might* happen to your plants, it's easy to have second thoughts. My advice is to go on, take a chance, and make a garden. Use this formula: lasagna gardening, companion planting, soap and water, and a lot of common sense. And don't worry so much about what might happen when you go on instinct.

pick up my camera when something caught my eye. I walked back to the lupines and looked more closely at the stems.

I couldn't believe my eyes. The stems were covered with aphids. I felt sick: The nasty little bugs were sucking the life from my flowers, and there was no time to do anything about it. How could I face my visitors when they saw so many insects? I didn't know what to do.

I rushed to the kitchen sink and surveyed the contents in the cupboard beneath it: liquid dish detergent, dishwasher liquid, furniture polish, silver polish, copper polish, and Murphy's Oil Soap.

I would normally prepare a spray bottle with dish detergent and water, but this called for extra measures. I reached for the Murphy's Oil Soap and prepared four spray bottles with a mix of 1 part Murphy's to 12 parts water. I sprayed all the lupines with the mixture and ran to hook up the water hose. I sprayed the stems with the hardest spray possible, hoping to knock the aphids off the stems. The oil in the Murphy's would have made it impossible for the insects to hang on, and the force of the spray would wash them to the ground.

After going over the planting several times with the hard spray, I felt I had done all I could and put all my supplies away. By this time, the sun was way up, and it was getting very warm. I could only pray the sun wouldn't bake the flowers, which were now covered with what amounted to cooking oil.

Making my way to the backyard and my forgotten cup of coffee, I felt distressed by the chink in the armor of my perfect garden. With all the attention I had given to every aspect of the gardens, nature had still found a weakness to attack.

Even knowing so much about gardening and all the problems that could happen had not protected me from an invasion of insects. The ending of the story was happy: The guests didn't know about the aphids, the plants didn't suffer from the spraying, and I came away from the experience wiser and not so complacent. Nature is a force to be reckoned with, and I was determined to stay on the offense to keep troublesome garden problems at bay.

HERBAL HINT

Dish soap and water is one of my favorite treatments for many garden ills. When plain soap isn't enough, try Murphy's Oil Soap (mixed with water) or a premixed insecticidal soap. In general, my approach to problems is this: Ignore all the bad stuff that might happen and most of what does happen, and deal with nearly everything else with good old soap and water.

Preventing Problems

Of course, there are some fundamentals that apply to any type of gardening. Observing these basic plant needs goes a long way toward heading off problems. A successful garden starts with good, improved soil with good drainage, at least 6 hours of sun per day, no competition from too-close trees and shrubs or grass and weeds, paths that allow access without compacting the soil, and a source of water.

These are not difficult rules to live with. A lasagna garden is composed of nothing but organic soil amendments, and it has the best drainage because you have not invaded the hard-packed clay and rock but have built up on top of newspaper. The underlying newspaper keeps grass and weeds from invading your garden and competing for nutrients the herbs need to grow. Pruning a few branches allows sunlight into even the shadiest areas,

A Healthy Soil Foundation

One of the surest ways to have a problem-free garden is to make sure you have healthy soil for your plants to grow in. With the lasagna method, it doesn't take a lot of work to supply this condition:

- Don't lift the sod, don't weed, and don't take out the rocks.

- Do mark off the area you want to use for your garden; do lay down thick pads of wet newspaper to cover the marked-off area.

- Do cover the paper with peat moss or compost.

- Do layer organic soil amendments to a depth equal to the roots of the herbs you want to plant, or to a depth of 4 to 6 inches if you're planting seeds.

- Do water gently as you layer, so the bed is as wet as a squeezed-out sponge.

Once you have the required number of inches of soil amendments layered on top of paper, all you have to do is pull the layers back to (but not through) the paper, set a plant on top of the paper, and pull the layers of soil amendments back around its roots.

It's that easy to create the right growing conditions for plants or seeds. This method applies to any kind of plants and any kind of garden. When you provide the right growing conditions, the plants grow strong and healthy, helping them to resist disease and the effects of insect infestations.

and simple paths give you access to all parts of the garden to harvest your herbs. Building a path is really easy when you use either thick pads of newspaper or cardboard as the bottom layer and cover it with wood chips.

Add companion planting to great growing conditions, and you take another step toward trouble-free gardening. Don't let down your guard—keep a sharp lookout for trouble, and nip it in the bud before it has a chance to get established. Watch for insects and knock them from your plants with a strong spray from your hose, or douse them with a soap-and-water mixture. Watch for wilting or spotted leaves and investigate their cause so you can either treat the problem or remove the plant before it spreads to the whole garden. As the old saying goes, "The best defense is a good offense."

In the last quarter-century, I have made lots of gardens. For more than 15 of those years, I have used the lasagna gardening method. As soon as I gave up chemicals, began layering instead of digging, and used only organic soil amendments for my growing layers, I noticed my plants were healthier. I'm sure this was because the soil was healthier, and my plants never became dependent on chemicals.

DON'T SHOP FOR TROUBLE

Once you've created that good, healthy garden for your herbs, the last thing you want to do is to bring home problems from the garden center. No matter how caught up I get in shopping for plants, I always try to make sure that every plant I buy is free of pests and diseases before I bring it home. I'm firmly convinced that most problems come home with the plant rather than the plant getting sick once you bring it into your garden. Give every plant purchase a thorough examination before you buy it.

Buying plants is an emotional experience. The best-laid plans can go right out the window when you see a greenhouse full of spring color. It's easy to get worked up into a buying frenzy and forget that you are supposed to check each plant for insects or disease. After a long winter away from the garden, a greenhouse full of color is a magical place. Suddenly, it's all about the bloom and nothing but the bloom—your shopping cart seems too small, and you wonder if you need to visit the ATM machine. It's a feast, and your

HERBAL HINT

Check each plant you are thinking of buying for pests and diseases. Look closely for whiteflies, mealy bugs, and scale, small pests that can easily hide under leaves and on stems. Also look for discolored leaves, black or brown spots, and holes in the leaves. If the growing medium is dry, plants may not have been given the best care and may be stressed, making them more susceptible to other problems. Carefully slip a plant from its pot to see if the roots look healthy— light-colored to white and firm—and not too crowded. A plant that seems to fill its entire pot with roots is likely to have a hard time getting established in your garden.

eyes are always bigger than your stomach. Every gardener has this experience from time to time (maybe even every spring); the key is to enjoy the occasional plant-shopping frenzy without undermining the healthy conditions you've created for those new plants to thrive in.

DON'T BE AFRAID TO ASK

Most gardeners are friendly folks, and nearly all of them take some pleasure in sharing their know-how with others. That's why the greatest way to learn the answers to your questions is to ask another gardener. Even if you're reading this book for guidance, that's what you're doing. And if I don't address your particular questions here, try a gardening friend or neighbor—you'll be amazed at what you can learn over the garden fence!

During tours and teaching sessions at the Potager, my visitors often ask me about problems they're having with a particular herb in their garden. As I listen to each gardener describe this or that "horrible" bug or disease, I find myself thinking that everything is relative. How horrible can it really be?

Most times my answer to these problems is "patience." Give Nature a chance to correct what is wrong, or if you need to do something, look to the space under the kitchen sink for a simple solution: soap and water.

Through my involvement with the Garden Writers Association, I have had the good fortune to meet many of the best herb gardeners in the country. Even though I've been gardening for many years now, I still have things to learn. I like to ask my fellow gardeners questions, too.

To gather more information about potential problems in the herb garden, I checked in with Jim Long of Longcreek Herbs in Oak Grove, Arkansas. Jim is an herbalist who has achieved amazing results on his modest but productive piece of land in the Ozarks. Consider him an expert on all aspects of growing and using herbs.

I asked Jim what kind of problems he had encountered when growing herbs and how he solved any problems he had. There was silence as he mulled my question. He had to think about it because nothing jumped out at him. Finally he replied that nothing stunning came to mind right away, but he would get back to me. When I heard from him again, he shared a couple of concerns that his customers often ask him about.

Q Why won't my sage keep growing for more than a couple of years?

A The standard garden sage (*Salvia officinalis*), as well as the variegated varieties and even 'Bergarten' sage, all benefit from an annual pruning. If left to their own habits, sage plants get tall and lanky and fall over, causing the woody center of the plant to die out.

However, it's easy to prevent that. Simply prune the entire plant back to about 6 inches tall each spring before the new leaves begin to grow. Then, about every second year, let one limb grow out the side. When it is long enough, put a brick on it to weight it down. In a short while, the branch will develop roots, and you will have a new plant.

> ## HERBAL HINT
>
> *Most woody perennial herbs respond to a good hard pruning in spring.*

Q Why can't I grow cilantro?

A Lots of people swear they can't grow cilantro (*Coriandrum sativum*). They buy a plant or two in spring, when nurseries have marigolds and petunias on display, take it home, and plant it, whereupon it immediately bolts into flowering, sets seed, and promptly dies.

Cilantro is a cool-season plant, like dill, poppies, larkspur, and bachelor's buttons. That means that it does best when planted in late fall or winter, or even as late as February to early March in northern areas. The cilantro will come up very early, unbothered by frost or even late-winter snows, and will reseed itself, just like dill. Typically it will produce two crops, one in very early spring and one in early fall. Save the seed, which is the seasoning herb coriander, and use it for cooking.

You can repeat plantings of cilantro so that you have a continuous supply until hot weather hits; then no matter what you do, it will bloom, set seed, and die. Some selections, such as 'Slow Bolt' and 'Longstanding', will delay going to seed longer than other varieties. But all are reliant on cooler weather, and once the hot season starts, the plant loses its flavor and goes to seed.

For a reliable supply of summer cilantro for making salsas and other dishes, grow Mexican cilantro (*Eryngium foetidum*) or Vietnamese cilantro (*Polygonum odoratum*), both of which thrive in summer heat.

Once you understand the normal life cycle of this popular herb, you may never buy cilantro plants again. It makes more sense to propagate some herbs from seeds, and cilantro is one of them. It makes no difference if you garden in the ground or in a pot; the plant will respond the same way. I like to make successive sowings to assure myself that I will have a constant supply of cilantro leaves and seeds.

I haven't planted cilantro in 4 years in my friend's Roscoe, New York, garden. I planted one package of seed in an 8-foot row early one spring. The row provided more cilantro than I needed, then I let the plants go to seed and harvested one small bag of coriander seeds. The remaining seeds were left to sow the next year's crop of cilantro.

> ### HERBAL HINT
>
> *Learn to recognize herb seedlings. Some herbs, such as dill, can become a bit weedy, self-sowing and springing up all over your garden. These seedlings will grow into full-size plants if you don't weed them out, and that's an advantage only if you want more of a particular herb. It doesn't pay to be soft-hearted about "volunteer" herb seedlings that you don't need or want—weed them out before they reach flowering size, or they'll take up space you intended for other things this season while sowing still more seeds for the season ahead.*

Each spring since then, there is cilantro coming up everywhere. I harvest what I need from plants that are in my way, then remove those plants, leaving enough to go to seed. Now, 4 years later, I may sow another row, although I don't really need to. One thing I have learned is to wait until the coriander seeds are mature, then remove them and sow them back in the same row. Doing this prevents so many random plants coming up in the path where everyone walks.

Grow What You Know; Know What You Grow

From reading my books, you may have figured out that I write about only what I know about from my experiences either in my own gardens or gardens I've visited. Most of the plants I describe reside in my extensive border gardens that I've created in the last 15 years. I've become fond of these herbs and flowers and plant them over and over again. I always say, "When the formula works, don't mess with it."

Because I have such a fondness for certain plants, I have assured myself of an unending supply by learning how to propagate each one. For daylilies and yarrow, division is the way I increase my supply. Rooted stem cuttings are the answer for rosemary, tarragon, and lavender. And even though it takes a long time, stem cuttings are also the way I have learned to increase my boxwood supply.

WORTH THE EFFORT

As I've already said, most herbs are fairly trouble-free, and some herbs come to be favorites because they're so easygoing. Others, of course, become favorites because they're beautiful or have a particularly lovely fragrance or flavor; these we may love in spite of the grief they cause us in the garden. Following are my own observations about some of my favorite herbs and flowers. You may grow these same plants in your gardens and never have a moment's worry because region-specific growing conditions are at the root of some problems. These are simply my experiences with these plants, in hopes that they'll provide you with useful guidance in your own garden.

Daylilies (*Hemerocallis* spp.)

I grow many kinds and colors of daylilies throughout my gardens for their beauty and ease of care. I also grow them for the edible flowers we use at the Potager. Daylilies are durable plants that have few problems, but from time to time I see the effects that slugs have on the leaves. When this happens, I put down a collar of wood ashes or sandpaper at the base of the plants. Anything abrasive to the slugs' soft, slimy bodies will deter them from climbing the leaves to dine.

Lavender (*Lavandula angustifolia*)

Someone asked me this question about lavender, and I didn't know the answer, having never had this problem: What do you do when spittlebugs attack your lavender? I passed the question to Jim Long, who recommended removing the bubble masses—ugh—and cleaning up the garden. By this, he explained, he meant clearing out any weedy or overgrown areas (where spittlebugs might hide) and dividing your lavender if the plants are crowded together.

Rosemary (*Rosmarinus officinalis*)

Remember the saying, "A dry rosemary is a dead rosemary"? It may have been referring to potted rosemary, but it's also true about rosemary growing in the garden. Keeping rosemary evenly moist is a challenge, but it's necessary to preserve the plant's health.

To help keep the soil moist, add some organic material when you are planting rosemary (a lasagna garden is all organic matter). As soon as you are finished planting and have given the plant a good watering, add a couple of sheets of wet newspaper over the top of the soil, then cover the paper with a pretty mulch. All this care will keep water from evaporating from the soil surface, and the organic matter will keep the roots cool and just moist enough. Besides moisture problems, I have seen infestations of whiteflies on rosemary that was grown in a greenhouse, but rarely on plants in open air.

HERBAL HINT

A month before you plan to bring a rosemary plant inside, and before digging the plant, cut side roots by using a sharp shovel pushed straight down around the plant's perimeter. This cuts the side roots, making the plant easier to move, but gives it time to recover from that shock. Water well and keep evenly moist until ready to pot. About 2 weeks before the first frost, lift the plant, pot it up in a container big enough to support the root system, and bring to the porch. Keep the plant on the porch until it recovers from the stress of being moved from the garden. Once you bring the plant inside, keep it away from direct heat. Place the pot on a drip dish filled with small stones. Keep water in the dish and let the plant drink from the bottom while the wet stones provide humidity. Spray with a mister to further humidify the air around it.

Tarragon (*Artemisia dracunculus*)

It pays to check your tarragon plants occasionally for root rot. This occurs when we get too much rain and the growing area doesn't get a chance to dry out. My tarragon plant (singular) is right at home in a section of the white garden where the drainage is very good. The sandy soil and close planting of ornamental grasses nearby keep my one and only plant happy. I cut tarragon to use fresh in the kitchen and to dry for use in winter, and each year I cut stems for rooting plants for gifts to friends. This much cutting keeps the plant in good shape for years.

Herbs Make Good Plant "Buddies"

In all my gardens I have combined herbs, hardy perennials, and edible flowers. It's a fun way to garden, and by combining plants that have different blooming times, different textures, and different colors, I avoid being bored with what I have created. I strive for a long period of bloom in each garden, and the diversity of plant material helps me accomplish that goal. A less visible but equally important benefit is that the plants protect one another from many problems.

GOOD NEIGHBORS

There's nothing new about companion planting—wise gardeners have been using it for centuries to keep their gardens healthy and free of pests. Here are a few of the companion planting methods I use in my own gardens.

Chives (*Allium schoenoprasum*)

Chiara Chandoha Lee (photographer Walter Chandoha's daughter and assistant) had a tip for me about chives: After each blooming, cut them back and allow them to rest and regain strength to bloom again. She and I agree that planting a chive border is a good way to discourage lots of pests in the garden. It's easy to do, too, because once you have one good clump of chives growing, that clump can be divided into several additional clumps.

You can continue dividing until you have all the chives you need to make a border around your garden.

Mints (*Mentha* spp.)

If you've ever heard me talk about (or read about) my experiences with mint, it may surprise you to know I'm still planting it in and around my gardens. I've called it the worst bully on the block, and it is, but it has so many good qualities I can't give it up. In order to grow my gardens organically, I need the help of some plants, and mint is a cheap way to keep pests from the garden. I do spend some time pulling out mint when it threatens to take over a bed. An advantage of lasagna gardening is that it's easy to remove roots and stems from my rich, friable soil.

In the meantime, mint helps to deter aphids, flea beetles, and various sorts of pests that invade your garden. I have been particularly fond of 'Ginger' mint and its golden variegated leaves. When I hear of someone who has mice to contend with, I take them lots of mint to strew around the area where the mice were spotted. The mice will be gone in a short time.

Mustards (*Brassica* spp.) and Cleome (*Cleome hasslerana*)

What to do about flea beetles? You know you have them when you find tiny holes in all your mustard leaves. If you don't care for eating mustard greens, you can plant some to attract flea beetles away from other crops.

If (like me) you plant mustard because it is one of your favorite leafy vegetables, you don't want flea beetles making all those little holes. Plant cleome, also known as spider flower, and the flea beetles will desert the mustard.

Parsley (*Petroselinum crispum*)

Once thought to be just a pretty bit of green on a dinner plate, parsley has come about and is respected as an herb with a lot to offer. Filled with vitamin C and possessed of the ability to freshen your breath, it is also the principal food source for the caterpillars (sometimes called parsley-worms) of the swallowtail butterfly. No doubt about it, parsley is a good herb to have around. Once I read about its ability to repel asparagus beetles, I began planting a border of it around the asparagus patch each year. It seems to be working.

Southernwood (*Artemisia abrotanum*)

I intend to always plant lots of southernwood. Once I found out it was a great way to keep from being eaten alive by biting insects, I passed the information along to all the fishermen I knew. They stand in the stream, ready to cast for the big one, and expose themselves to intense insect assaults.

One day at the farm, a fisherman's wife saw me standing in a large southernwood plant. She watched as I rubbed myself with sprigs broken off the southernwood plant and then tucked them into my hatband. When she asked, I explained it was to release the oil onto my exposed skin. It keeps insects, even blackflies, away.

Once the word got out in the fishing community about what would later be dubbed "the fisherman's friend," I couldn't keep enough southernwood plants in stock. Plants can be buddies to people, too!

In addition to being the fisherman's best friend, southernwood is also a friend to the homemaker. Dried southernwood repels moths and can be used in linen closets and storage areas. In my gardens, the plants that have shared space with southernwood have never had problems with insect infestation.

Tansy (*Tanacetum vulgare*)

One of the best friends to other garden plants, tansy has so many good uses you can forgive its invasive nature. It's the perfect companion to roses, blackberries, and raspberries. It is invasive, but I find it easy to keep in its place by pulling hard on the stems and bringing up root runners.

Tansy has been a friend to the homeowner for a very long time and is still used to deter ants. Plantings of tansy around the foundation, by low windows, and by the back door will keep even black ants from getting in.

My grandmother use to use her pie safe not only for pies but also for dinner (or lunch) leftovers. These foods were what we would eat for supper and stayed safe from flies and ants in the pie safe. She laid sprigs of tansy on each shelf to keep ants out. She also placed little dishes filled with water under each leg of the pie safe. I think she figured if they could swim or jump across the water, the tansy would be a last resort.

Thyme (*Thymus vulgaris*)

Want a plant buddy for your vegetable garden? Plant thyme near the nightshade family: tomatoes, eggplant, and potatoes. Want to grow cabbage without worms and lupines without whiteflies? An underplanting of thyme will take care of those pesky problems.

Thyme has some problems of its own, but nothing common sense can't deal with. If your thyme plants develop root rot, chances are the area needs better drainage. Try adding sand to the surrounding soil to remedy that. If your thyme plant gets spider mites, use a strong spray of cold water from the hose to knock the pests off the plants, or spray with a mixture of dish detergent and water or insecticidal soap.

Yarrow (*Achillea millefolium*)

One of my favorite wild herbs is yarrow. I like the small, tight, celadon green flowers for use in my dried arrangements, and I have used the leaves many times to stop a cut or insect bite from bleeding. When I lived on the farm, I picked huge baskets of wild yarrow from my own fields.

During those years on the farm, I found out yarrow was important in many other ways: It attracts beneficial insects like predatory wasps and lady beetles. These beneficial insects feed on the harmful insects that attack other plants, keeping them safe and clean. Herbal researchers have claimed that yarrow increases the essential oils of other herbs planted nearby. It's a real plant buddy.

Now, in my smaller garden spaces, I grow hybrid yarrows such as 'Coronation Gold', 'Moonshine', and 'Paprika'. These yarrows are part of a list of dependable plants that give substance to my gardens. The colors of these herbs are brilliant, their flowers are huge, and I get several cuttings of flowers from each plant. I still pick a leaf and use it to stop the flow of blood on my arms and legs from minor injuries I get in the garden.

Yarrow has almost no real problems but may develop stem rot (check to see if the ground is too wet) or powdery mildew (plants need to be thinned for better air circulation). When the plant grows too big and the overtall blooms fall over other plants, it may indicate that the soil is richer than yarrow needs or wants. Divide the plant and provide support to keep the stems from falling forward and the blooms off the ground.

Epilogue

I used to worry about being able to support myself, but now I worry about keeping up with the demand for my time. It's been more than 12 years since I sold the inn and retired to my Catskill Mountain farm for a life of gardening and writing for my local paper.

The gardens at the farm created a stir with local folks who followed my garden exploits in my weekly newspaper column. I started writing articles for national magazines, which led me to Rodale Books and an 8-year association that has resulted in three lasagna gardening books.

It wasn't long before I was being asked to give talks to groups about my success in the garden. And then came the requests by tour groups wanting to visit my gardens (and wanting to arrive by the busload). Before the first bus arrived at the farm, I created a greenhouse, a gift shop, a plant house, and a tea room, in addition to the display gardens I already had underway. This was all so successful that I talked my daughter Mickey into becoming my partner and buying a property in the village of Wurtsboro, New York, where the weather was kinder and the location easier to get to.

We created our business, "The Potager," in a former church. Our 1890 building was complete with shiplap and fish-scale siding, stained-glass windows, pressed tin ceilings, pine floors, and a steeple bell. We painted the Potager bright yellow, and it stood out as the happiest building in town.

The Potager became a second home and operation central for all that Mickey and I did: We researched ideas for new books in the display gardens surrounding the building and discovered that those gardens lured thousands of garden lovers who came for lunch and shopping in the gift shop and garden center. We catered small groups who wanted to keep up with the lasagna gardener and see for themselves what was inside the yellow building.

There is still a huge audience of would-be gardeners who are looking for the perfect garden method that allows them to have it all and be a friend to the earth at the same time. With my Web site, www.lasagnagardening.com, and a monthly E-newsletter, I am able to reach those who just need a little encouragement to get out in the garden and those who have already become advocates of lasagna gardening. I welcome your e-mail at patlasagna@aol.com and would love to share your success stories with other lasagna gardeners. I have projects on the horizon that I'm anxious to get started on, including a book about lasagna gardening for kids and a booklet called *Career Diversity: Surviving in Today's Economy.*

And now I have another interest—the Antrim Lodge. The town of Roscoe, New York, is in the heart of trout-fishing country and is home to a legendary home-away-from-home for countless fly fishermen, hunters, and legendary sports writers since 1890. The Antrim Lodge was a grand old place but it stood alone and neglected when I saw it in 2001.

Suffering from a moment of madness, I bought the property, saving it from condemnation and possible demolition. It was a last minute decision, and it emptied my bank account. The lodge was old, tired, abused, and worth every cent. What I got for my money is almost unimaginable—a five-story, 22-room, 115-year-old eatery and watering hole with peeling paint, a leaky roof, basement mold, and a property full of overgrown trees. It also came with a fully equipped commercial kitchen, in-house laundry, and room after room of furniture, bedding, table service, and linens.

Life is still good and still getting better every day.

Your friend in and out of the garden,
Patricia (Pat) Lanza
P.O. Box 729
Wurtsboro, NY 12790

Acknowledgments

My thanks to the readers of all the lasagna gardening books

- who had given up gardening because they thought they were too old and couldn't do the traditional work they thought it took to garden;
- who had never gardened because they were intimidated by all the misinformation that told them that traditional hard work was necessary to have a garden; or
- who were intrigued by the title, found they liked the way I write, and then put into practice the techniques I wrote about and had wonderful results.

Also thanks to the many parents and teachers who took my books and inspired children to make gardens and especially thanks to the Master Gardeners who used information in my books to teach the lasagna gardening method to new gardeners across the country.

Thanks to the Rodale family of publishers who have taken my small talent and helped me spread the word about the importance of renewing and preserving the earth for all future generations of gardeners through a simple method called lasagna; and thanks to the editors at Rodale who have used their talents to shape my work into another terrific book.

Last, but far from least, heartfelt thanks to my family and friends who have continued to love and support me even though I am committed to a neurotic, obsessive, compulsive way of life where work gets in the way of everything else.

Resources for
Lasagna Gardeners

Seeds and Plants

Bluestone Perennials
7211 Middle Ridge Road
Madison, OH 44057-3096
Phone: (800) 852-5243
Fax: (440) 428-7198
E-mail: bluestone@
　　bluestoneperennials.com
Web site:
　　www.bluestoneperennials.com

Bountiful Gardens
18001 Shafer Ranch Road
Willits, CA 95490-9626
Phone: (707) 459-6410
Fax: (707) 459-1925
E-mail: bountiful@sonic.net
Web site:
　　www.bountifulgardens.org

Brent and Becky's Bulbs
7900 Daffodil Lane
Gloucester, VA 23061
Phone: (804) 693-3966
Fax: (804) 693-9436
Web site:
　　www.brentandbeckysbulbs.com

W. Atlee Burpee & Co.
300 Park Avenue
Warminster, PA 18991-0001
Phone: (800) 888-1447
Fax: (800) 487-5530
Web site: www.burpee.com

The Cook's Garden
P.O. Box 535
Londonderry, VT 05148
Phone: (800) 457-9703
Fax: (800) 457-9705
E-mail: info@cooksgarden.com
Web site:
    www.cooksgarden.com

Goodwin Creek Gardens
P.O. Box 83
Williams, OR 97544
Phone: (800) 846-7359
Fax: (541) 846-7357
E-mail:
    info@goodwincreekgardens.com
Web site:
    www.goodwincreekgardens.com

Gurney's Seed & Nursery Co.
Order Processing Center
Greendale, IN 47025-4178
Phone: (513) 354-1491
Fax: (513) 354-1493
Web site: www.gurneys.com

Harris Seeds
355 Paul Road
P.O. Box 24966
Rochester, NY 14624-0966
Phone: (800) 514-4441
Fax: (877) 892-9197
Web site: www.harrisseeds.com

Indiana Berry and Plant Co.
5218 West 500 South
Huntingburg, IN 47542

Phone: (812) 683-3055 or
    (800) 295-2226
Fax: (812) 683-2004
E-mail: berryinfo@inberry.com
Web site: www.inberry.com

Irish Eyes—Garden City Seeds
P.O. Box 307
Thorp, WA 98946
Phone: (509) 964-7000 or
    (800) 964-9210
E-mail: potatoes@irish-eyes.com
Web site: www.irish-eyes.com

Ison's Nursery & Vineyards
P.O. Box 190
Brooks, GA 30205
Phone: (770) 599-6970
Fax: (770) 599-1727
Web site: www.isons.com

Johnny's Selected Seeds
955 Benton Avenue
Winslow, ME 04901
Phone: (207) 861-3900
Fax: (800) 738-6314
E-mail:
    homegarden@johnnyseeds.com
Web site: www.johnnyseeds.com

J. W. Jung Seed Co.
335 South High Street
Randolph, WI 53957-0001
Phone: (800) 247-5864
Fax: (800) 692-5864
E-mail: Info@jungseed.com
Web site: www.jungseed.com

Park Seed Co.
1 Parkton Avenue
Greenwood, SC 29647
Phone: (800) 213-0076
E-mail: info@parkseed.com
Web site: www.parkseed.com

Pinetree Garden Seeds
P.O. Box 300
New Gloucester, ME 04260
Phone: (207) 926-3400
Fax: (888) 527-3337
E-mail: superseeds@superseeds.com
Web site: www.superseeds.com

Raintree Nursery
391 Butts Road
Morton, WA 98356
Phone: (360) 496-6400
Fax: (888) 770-8358
E-mail: info@raintreenursery.com
Web site: www.raintreenursery.com

Renee's Garden
7389 West Zayante Road
Felton, CA 95018
Phone: (888) 880-7228
Fax: (831) 335-7227
Web site: www.reneesgarden.com

Richters Herb Catalogue
#357 Highway 47
Goodwood, Ontario
L0C 1A0 Canada
Phone: (905) 640-6677
Fax: (905) 640-6641
Web site: www.richters.com

Sandy Mush Herb Nursery
316 Surrett Cove Road
Leicester, NC 28748-5517
Phone: (828) 683-2014
E-mail: sandymushherbs@main.nc.us
Web site: www.brwm.org/
   sandymushherbs

Seeds of Change
P.O. Box 15700
Santa Fe NM 87592-1500
Phone: (888) 762-7333
Web site: www.seedsofchange.com

Stark Bro's Nurseries & Orchards Co.
20947 Highway 54
Louisiana, MO 63353
Phone: (573) 754-5111
Fax: (573) 754-3701
E-mail: info@starkbros.com
Web site: www.starkbros.com

Stokes Seeds, Inc.
P.O. Box 548
Buffalo, NY 14240-0548
Phone: (716) 695-6980 or
   (800) 396-9238
Fax: (888) 834-3334
E-mail: stokes@stokeseeds.com
Web site: www.stokeseeds.com

Territorial Seed Company
P.O. Box 158
Cottage Grove, OR 97424-0061
Phone: (541) 942-9547
Fax: (888) 657-3131
E-mail: tertrl@territorial-seed.com
Web site: www.territorial-seed.com

Thompson & Morgan Inc.
P.O. Box 1308
Jackson, NJ 08527-0308
Phone: (800) 274-7333
Fax: (888) 466-4769
E-mail: tminc@thompson-morgan.com
Web site: www.thompson-morgan.com

Totally Tomatoes
P.O. Box 1626
Augusta, GA 30903
Phone: (803) 663-0016
Fax: (888) 477-7333
Web site: www.totallytomato.com

Van Bourgondien Bros.
P.O. Box 1000
Babylon, NY 11702-9004
Phone: (800) 622-9997
Fax: (516) 669-1228

Vermont Bean Seed Co.
334 West Stroud Street
Randolph, WI 53956-1274
Phone: (800) 349-1071
Fax: (888) 500-7333
E-mail: info@vermontbean.com
Web site: www.vermontbean.com

Well-Sweep Herb Farm
205 Mount Bethel Road
Port Murray, NJ 07865
Phone: (908) 852-5390
E-mail: herbs@goes.com
Web site: www.wellsweep.com

Gardening Equipment and Supplies

Bricko Farms, Inc.
824 Sand Bar Ferry Road
Augusta, GA 30901
Phone: (706) 722-0661
Fax: (706) 724-6901
Web site: www.bricko.com

Gardener's Supply Co.
128 Intervale Road
Burlington, VT 05401
Phone: (888) 833-1412
Fax: (800) 551-6712
E-mail for products and orders:
    info@gardeners.com

E-mail for general gardening
    questions: ga@gardeners.com
Web site: www.gardeners.com

Gardens Alive!
5100 Schenley Place
Lawrenceburg, IN 47025
Phone: (812) 537-8650
Fax: (812) 537-5108
E-mail:
    gardenhelp@gardensalive.com
Web site: www.gardensalive.com

Harmony Farm Supply and Nursery
3244 Highway 116 North
Sebastopol, CA 95472
Phone: (707) 823-9125
Fax: (707) 823-1734
E-mail: info@harmonyfarm.com
Web site: www.harmonyfarm.com

A.M. Leonard, Inc.
241 Fox Drive
Piqua, OH 45356-0816
Phone: (800) 543-8955
Fax: (800) 433-0633
E-mail: info@amleo.com
Web site: www.amleo.com

Peaceful Valley Farm Supply
P.O. Box 2209
Grass Valley, CA 95945
Phone: (530) 272-4769 or
    (888) 784-1722
Fax: (530) 272-4794
E-mail: contact@groworganic.com
Web site: www.groworganic.com

Plow and Hearth
P.O. Box 5000
Madison, VA 22727-1500
Phone: (800) 494-7544
Fax: (800) 843-2509
Web site: www.plowhearth.com

Smith & Hawken
P.O. Box 8690
Pueblo, CO 81008-9998
Phone: (800) 940-1170
E-mail: smithandhawken
    customerservice@innotrac.com
Web site: www.smith-hawken.com

Soil Testing Laboratories

For a state-by-state and province-by-province listing of soil test labs, visit:
www.organicgardening.com/library/soil_test_labs.html

Timberleaf Soil Testing
39648 Old Spring Road
Marrieta, CA 92563
Phone/fax: (909) 677-7510

Pat's Picks

Books

Allen, Oliver E. *Gardening with the New Small Plants*. Boston: Houghton Mifflin Co., 1987.

Armitage, Allan M. *Armitage's Garden Perennials: A Color Encyclopedia*. Portland, OR: Timber Press, 2000.

Barash, Cathy Wilkinson. *Edible Flowers: From Garden to Palate*. Golden, CO: Fulcrum Publishing, 1993.

Bartholomew, Mel. *Square Foot Gardening*. Emmaus, PA: Rodale Inc. 1981.

Benjamin, Joan, ed. *Great Garden Shortcuts*. Emmaus, PA: Rodale Inc., 1996.

Better Homes and Gardens. *Step-by-Step Successful Gardening*. Des Moines, IA: Meredith Corporation, 1987.

Brickell, Christopher, and David Joyce. *The American Horticultural Society Pruning and Training*. New York: DK Publishing Inc., 1996.

Brookes, John. *The Country Garden*. New York: Crown Publishing Group, 1987.

Carr, Anna et al. *Rodale's Chemical-Free Yard and Garden*. Edited by Fern Marshall Bradley. Emmaus, PA: Rodale Inc., 1991.

Cebenko, Jill Jesiolowski, and Deborah L. Martin, editors. *Insect, Disease & Weed I.D. Guide*. Emmaus, PA: Rodale Inc., 2001.

Chandoha, Walter. *The Literary Gardener*. Minocqua, WI: Willow Creek Press, 1997.

Clifton, Joan. *Making a White Garden*. New York:

Cole, Rebecca. *Potted Garden*. New York: Clarkson Potter, 1997.

Fell, Derek. *Bulb Gardening with Derek Fell*. New York: Friedman/Fairfax Publishers, 1997.

Gilkeson, Linda, Pam Peirce, and Miranda Smith. *Rodale's Pest and Disease Problem Solver*. Emmaus, PA: Rodale, 1996.

Greenwood, Pippa. *The New Gardener*. New York: Dorling Kindersley Publishing, 1998.

Grounds, Roger. *Small Garden*. New York: Canopy Books, 1994.

Hillier, Malcolm. *Container Gardening Through the Year*. New York: Dorling Kindersley, 1995.

Hodgson, Larry. *Annuals for Every Purpose*. Emmaus, PA: Rodale, 2002.

Hodgson, Larry. *Perennials for Every Purpose*. Emmaus, PA: Rodale. 2000.

Lanza, Patricia. *Lasagna Gardening*. Emmaus, PA: Rodale, 1998.

Lloyd, Christopher, and Richard Bird. *The Cottage Garden*. New York: Dorling Kindersley Publishing, 1999.

Pavord, Anna. *The Border Book*. New York: Dorling Kindersley Publishing, 2000.

Search, Gay. *Gardening without a Garden*. New York: Random House, 1995.

Magazines and Newsletters

Country Living Gardener, 224 W. 57th Street, New York, NY 10019.

Hortideas, 750 Black Lick Road, Gravel Switch, KY 40328.

Organic Gardening, Rodale, 33 E. Minor Street, Emmaus, PA 18098; www.organicgardening.com.

Index

Boldface page references indicate illustrations. Underscored references indicate tables.

USDA Plant Hardiness Zone Map

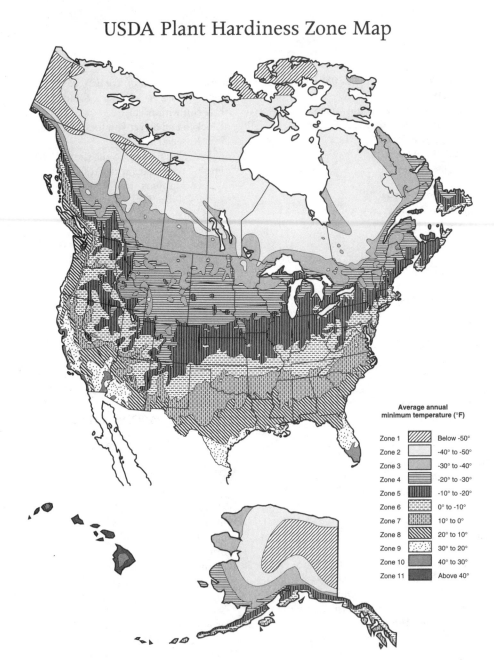

		Average annual minimum temperature (°F)
Zone 1		Below -50°
Zone 2		-40° to -50°
Zone 3		-30° to -40°
Zone 4		-20° to -30°
Zone 5		-10° to -20°
Zone 6		0° to -10°
Zone 7		10° to 0°
Zone 8		20° to 10°
Zone 9		30° to 20°
Zone 10		40° to 30°
Zone 11		Above 40°

This map is recognized as the best indicator of minimum temperatures available. Look at the map to find your geographical area, then match its shading to the key. When you've found your shading, the key will tell you what hardiness zone you live in. Remember that the map is only a general guide; your particular conditions may vary.